NEW HOLLAND

EUROPEAN BIRD GUIDE

Peter H. Barthel • Paschalis Dougalis

NH
NEW HOLLAND

Published in 2008 by New Holland Publishers
London • Cape Town • Sydney • Auckland
www.newhollandpublishers.com

Garfield House, 86-88 Edgware Road, London W2 2EA, United Kingdom
80 McKenzie Street, Cape Town 8001, South Africa
Unit 1, 66 Gibbes Street, Chatswood, NSW 2067, Australia
218 Lake Road, Northcote, Auckland, New Zealand

10 9 8 7 6 5 4 3 2 1

ISBN 978 1 84773 110 4

Publishing Director: Rosemary Wilkinson
Commissioning Editor: Simon Papps
Translation: Mathilde Stuart
Editors: Simon Papps, Marianne Taylor
Identification consultant: Keith Vinicombe

With 1,752 illustrations by Paschalis Dougalis and 445 distribution maps by Christine Barthel
Cover illustration: Bullfinches by Paschalis Dougalis
Illustration on pages 2-3: Avocets by Paschalis Dougalis

Reproduction by Blackbit Viani GmbH, Göttingen
Printed and bound in Italy. Printed on chlorine-free bleached paper
Originally published as *Was fliegt denn da?* in 2006 by Franckh-Kosmos
Verlags GmbH & Co KG, Stuttgart, Germany

Peter H. Barthel would like to dedicate this book to the memory of people who have inspired, influenced and shaped his ornithological work: "For some it is also the keeping of a promise. My grandfather Karl Barthel (1887-1966) tried to explain to me the differences between a Nuthatch and a Treecreeper when I still lay in my pram, my father Karl H. Barthel (1916-1980) supported my studies patiently, my teacher Paul Feindt (1905-1983) was a great ornithological educator, Peter J. Grant (1943-1990) left a legacy as founder of modern taxonomy and promoter of European co-operation, Dietmar G. W. Königstedt (1947-1999), with his extensive knowledge, wanted to write a book like this, Erwin R. Scherner (1949-2002) shaped my critical use of ornithological literature, and Andreas J. Helbig (1957-2005) can be thanked for much more than the modern ornithological taxonomy which for the first time forms the basis of this book."

NEW HOLLAND EUROPEAN BIRD GUIDE

Illustration of Broad-billed Sandpiper *Limicola falcinellus* from the 1950 edition of this book

FOREWORD

Once a book has proved itself for 70 years and seen 30 editions it rightly deserves to be called a classic. This field guide was first published by Wilhelm Götz and Alois Kosch in Germany in 1936. With the title literally translated as 'What is flying there?' it was the first complete pocket guide with colour illustrations covering 327 bird species of central Europe. It went through several reprints and in 1950 Heinrich Frieling made a complete revision, which continued to prove successful over the next four decades. In effect it was the German equivalent to the Peterson, Mountfort and Hollom field guide that proved so popular in Britain during the same period.

Forty years ago, when I started to study birds seriously, 'What is flying there?' was of course my first identification guide. After years of extensive use it fell apart, I replaced it with more modern bird books and forgot about it. In 1996 when the publisher suggested a complete revision and asked me to take on this task, I took my torn copy from the shelf and was surprised at how well thought out it actually was. Therefore it was an easy decision to agree to rewrite the book and to have the illustrations redone, but to retain what was a proven format. Ten years on the regularly updated book remained a complete overview of the birds of central Europe, aimed particularly at the beginner.

Since then a lot has happened. The countries of Europe have grown closer together, and on top of a common currency there now also exists, for example, a European Bird Protection Guideline, and more and more boundaries – for people rather than for birds – have been opened. Additionally, taxonomic studies have led to massive changes in the systematic classification of birds, while identification techniques have also been refined. At the same time the users' demands of topicality, completeness, European point of view, printing quality and modern presentation have risen so much that even a classic could not evade them any longer. Four years ago, when we started to translate these justified wishes, we at first did not realize that a whole new book would develop which had only the title in common with its predecessors.

A number of factors have lead to the success of this guide: it is good value, small and easy to carry at all times, but it also includes all the information necessary for identification and covers all species that commonly occur in Europe, along with a number of the more regular vagrants. It is also ideal for the beginner who would be confused by the many additional bird species which are never seen in Europe that are included in larger field guides. The clear arrangement of similar-looking species on one colour plate facilitates straightforward comparison and identification. The concise text is easily understood and does not look to answer questions that the user is not even asking. We have tried to satisfy this existing demand. However, this is no longer just a book for beginners. Hopefully, the advanced birder will find much knowledge compressed in the text and the detail of the new plates that will serve as a memory aid and in addition familiarise people with the latest taxonomy. This is the first European field guide to give separate treatment to recently 'split' species pairs such as Balearic and Yelkouan Shearwaters, Tundra and Taiga Bean Geese, Yellow-legged and Caspian Gulls, European and Siberian Stonechats, Common and Iberian Chiffchaffs, Balearic and Marmora's Warblers and Eastern and Western Olivaceous Warblers.

I would also like to take the opportunity here to express my heartfelt thanks to Paschalis Dougalis, who managed the unbelievable and in just two years illustrated all the birds of Europe not only with wonderful accuracy but also in their full beauty.

I am grateful to my publishers, whose patience has been much tested, for their investment and the great trust they have shown in this project. Many thanks are due to the exceptional natural history editor Rainer Gerstle, who has cultivated this title over decades and now has led it into a new era with his typical almost youthful enthusiasm, just before retiring. He himself has become a classic, along with this book and many other field guides, and I owe him much.

The primary goal remains that this book may continue to help many users to become familiar with the world of birds. The more knowledge that each individual has, the greater becomes our shared responsibility to our feathered companions, whose survival is threatened more than ever.

Peter H. Barthel, 2008

INTRODUCTION

By using this book you have become part of the great community of birdwatchers. All over the world millions of people look for birds and observe them in their spare time. The beauty of this hobby is that you can practice it at any time and in almost any place, and that it barely requires any equipment. At the beginning one needs only patience, curiosity, a desire to learn, binoculars and a notebook, as well as this book of course. As knowledge increases it is often the case that the desire to study and obtain a greater understanding of birds grows further. For this purpose there is a wealth of additional equipment and books available that will be briefly mentioned here. Also, the fact that ornithology, as part of biology, is actually a serious science is not particularly important in the beginning. Initially the identification of species has to be learnt, and that is the primary goal of this book.

First of all it is wise to become familiar with a few of the basics in order to be able to use the book properly and not end up with too many misidentifications. The following introductory sections have been deliberately kept short and to the point so that they will actually be read, and also so that the reader will not have to carry too much weight when taking this book into the field, where it will be of greatest practical use. They are intended for use in conjunction with the species accounts.

AREA OF COVERAGE

This book deals with all bird species that occur regularly in Britain and the rest of Europe, whether breeding, wintering or migrating through, along with a selection of the more regularly occurring rare visitors. The eastern boundary of the area covered runs through Russia roughly following a line from the Kola Peninsula via Moscow to the Black Sea. Therefore the Urals, the Caucasus and the Asian part of Turkey are not covered, but the island of Cyprus, a member of the EU, is. We have also excluded the many species of North Africa and the Middle East which are very rarely or never seen in Europe but are often included in other bird books, as that would have increased the number of pages dramatically. These species would also have confused the European beginner, which is also the case with some of the very rare vagrants from other continents.

In the text, the emphasis in the distribution section in each species account is placed solely on Britain, although the ranges of migratory species outside the breeding season are generally described at the end of the habitat section in each account.

EQUIPMENT

The first and most important principle when searching or observing is not to endanger or disturb the birds themselves or their habitat. To be able to watch birds from a distance so that they do not feel threatened and to still make out the details of their appearance it is best to use binoculars. Binoculars with a seven- to ten-times magnification and 30-40 mm objective lenses are generally best and these are the most commonly used. When buying new binoculars make sure that they can also be focused at close range (for example for observations at a bird-feeder close to the window), have a wide field of view and are optically of sufficient good quality that even long use does not cause headaches. A general rule is that the more you pay, the better the quality. It is essential to test a model before buying as different binoculars suit different people and not everyone is suited to a particular model.

In certain parts of Europe various species of birds still fall prey to hunters and are therefore extremely shy around people. Often they only rest at great distances from humans, for example on the sea, mudflats or large inland water bodies such as reservoirs. On top of that many species can only be confidently identified when details of structure and coloration can be observed. Due to these factors there is often a limit beyond which identification is not possible with binoculars alone. Therefore many birdwatchers make additional use of a telescope with a 20- to 30-times magnification and a 60-80 mm objective lens.

The second piece of essential equipment is a simple notebook in which observations can be documented. As well as listing the names of the birds and the numbers seen, the date, time, locality and weather conditions should also be noted. Details of appearance, behaviour or call will also be memorized more easily once written down.

Often it is not possible to immediately identify a bird, and in such cases it helps to make detailed notes so that it can be checked later in a book at home. Making sketches is also useful as the process of drawing forces the observer to look at the bird in greater detail. A well-kept bird diary focusing, for example, on a local patch allows the observer over several years to determine the average arrival date of migratory birds in a particular area, or to supply important data about a certain species or site to the relevant nature conservation authority, therefore lending genuine conservation significance to the records.

TOPOGRAPHY OF A BIRD

To be able to describe and identify a bird it is necessary to learn the correct words defining its body parts. They are clearly illustrated here using different examples. Almost all are obvious and don't have to be explained in more detail.

In the plumage one differentiates between the larger feathers consisting of the primaries, secondaries (together these are called the flight feathers or remiges) and the tail feathers (or retrices), and the remaining smaller feathers. The inner secondaries are also called tertials; they are often shaped and coloured differently and lie almost protectively over the other flight feathers. How far the primaries protrude beyond the tips of the tertials is often an important identification feature when separating two similar species. Often the tips of the greater coverts and sometimes even those of the median coverts are paler and appear as wing-bars – these can also be formed by pale bases of the primaries or secondaries. In ducks, a different coloured patch within the secondaries is called a speculum.

Each of these different parts of the plumage can show its own characteristic colouring and pattern. Different stripes on the head, together

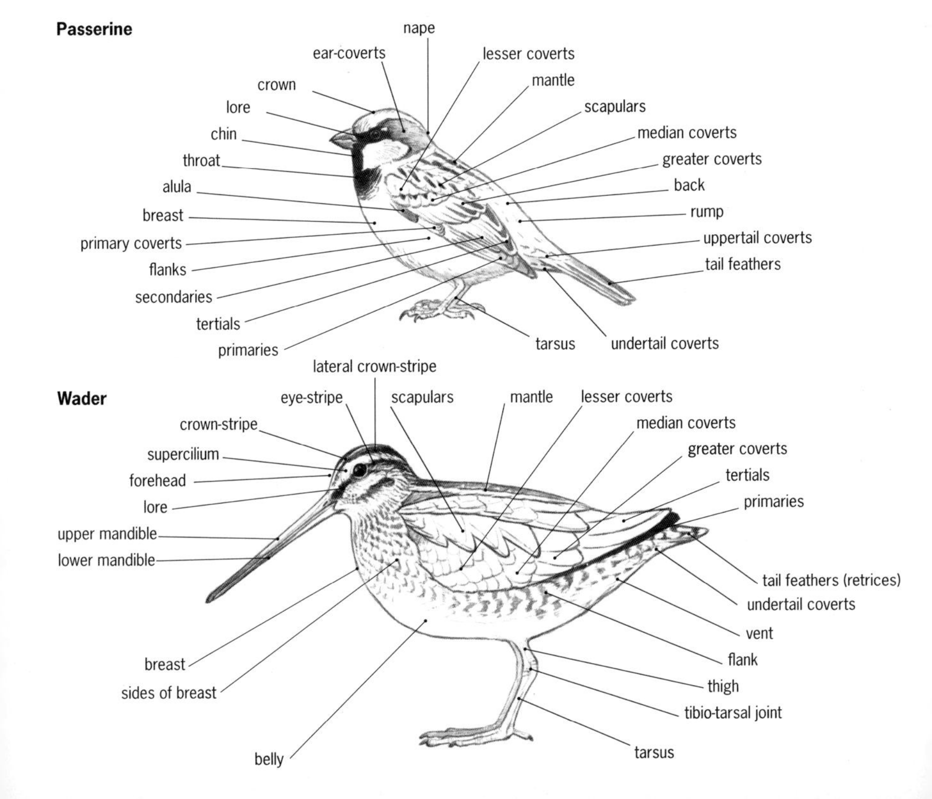

with the shape of head and beak, can lead to a typical 'facial expression' in many species, and one should try to memorize these as they can be very useful for identification. Around the eye some species have either a bare orbital ring (for example, Herring Gull) or a feathered eye-ring (for example, Song Thrush) of a different colour.

Of course it is also important to take note of the colour, length and shape of other body parts. The bill can be longer or shorter than the head or the tarsus; it can be straight or curved up- or downwards, thick or thin, and its sides convex or concave. Other body proportions, for example the distance between wing-tip and tail-tip, and the length of the primaries extending beyond the

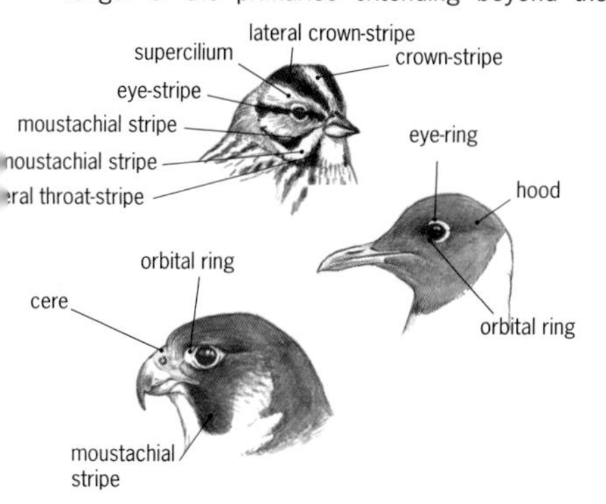

secondaries (the primary projection), often give clear identification hints in otherwise very similar species.

Finally, the shape of the tail (wedge-shaped, rounded, square, notched or forked) is an important identification feature. Also important is the shape of the wing and the wing-tip, for example the board-like wing with many separately visible finger-like primaries of an eagle, or the slender pointed wing of a falcon. Another identification pointer is flight pattern, straight or undulating, flapping or soaring, with raised or lowered wings.

PLUMAGE

In some bird species it is not possible to differentiate male (symbol: ♂), female (♀) and young in the wild, while others can confuse the beginner with a whole array of very different plumages. Knowledge of the terms for the different plumages is necessary in order to make an exact identification. Feathers wear out relatively quickly, and as the survival of the bird depends upon it maintaining its plumage, they must be renewed on a regular basis. This process is called moult. In each species it follows a certain pattern, mainly during or after the breeding season. Many of the species that occur in Europe change their larger feathers once a year but their smaller feathers twice. Therefore, it is frequently the case that the bird shows a brilliant plumage before the breeding season but a duller, less remarkable one at other times. Some species, for example many songbirds, shed their juvenile plumage and moult straight into adult plumage, while other species, for example gulls and eagles, take several years to acquire full adult plumage. In principle one can differentiate the following types of plumage:

The first feathers of a bird are the down feathers. In nidifugous species the chick hatches from the eggs with down feathers, while in nidicolous chicks the down feathers emerge in the first few days after hatching. Normally chicks of that size are not seen so down plumage is not described in the species accounts.

Upperwing of a passerine

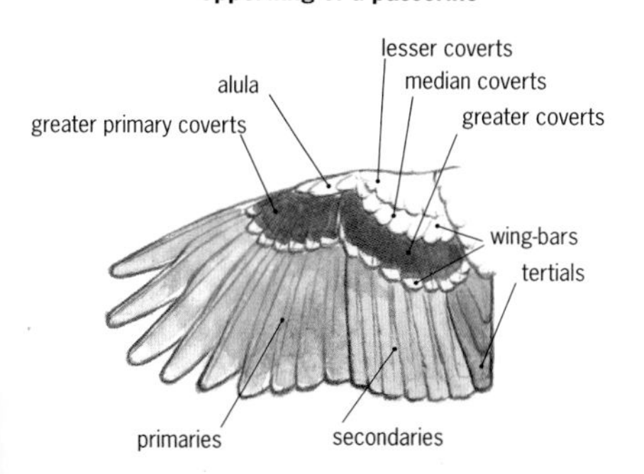

Upperwing of a duck

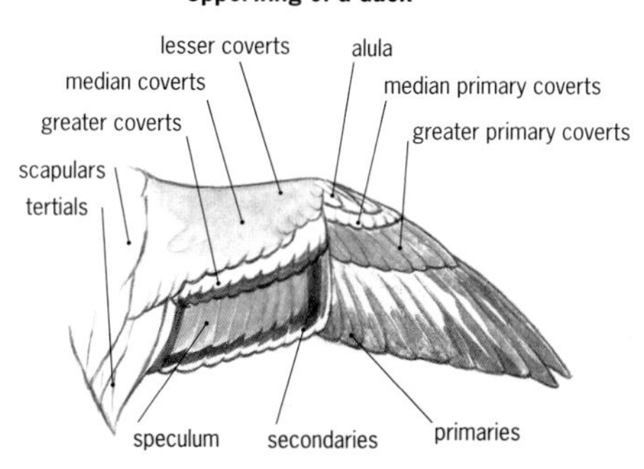

The first full plumage with which a bird is able to fly is called the juvenile stage (abbreviated to juv throughout the book). Although a good proportion of songbirds lose this plumage quite early, many larger species retain it for several months. Many waders, for example, maintain this during their first migration to their winter quarters.

In many species the next plumage stage cannot be separated from that of the adult plumage (ad). Birds with fully developed plumage are called adults. Some species retain the same adult plumage all year round. In many species, however, the plumage changes shortly before, or during, the breeding season to a characteristic and colourful breeding plumage. For the rest of the year the plumage reverts back to a more modest non-breeding plumage. Although normally less flamboyant, the females of some species may also moult into a breeding plumage.

In some species, for example gulls and eagles, it takes several years for the full adult stage to develop. Birds that no longer show the juvenile plumage but have not reached adult plumage are called immature (imm). Today more precise definitions are used as in-depth study of the characteristic patterns has enabled a more accurate age classification. The first-winter plumage (1w) follows the juvenile plumage in late summer or autumn of the first calendar year, the first-summer plumage (1s) appears in the summer of the second calendar year. In species with very slow development, consecutive plumage changes are called second-winter plumage (2w), second-summer plumage (2s, starting in spring of the third calendar year) and so on. The inner back cover shows some examples.

As an adaptation to different geographic regions some bird species have developed subspecies, which sometimes can be distinguished in the wild by their different plumage – these are described in the species accounts where relevant. Additionally, there are species whose colouration can vary greatly between individuals (for example, Common Buzzard and Ruff) and others that appear in lighter and darker forms or morphs in the same population (for example Snow Goose, Pomarine and Arctic Skuas, Eleonora's Falcon and Booted Eagle). These variations are also illustrated.

BIRD SOUNDS

As an observer becomes familiar with birds, it is soon apparent that knowledge of bird sounds is very important. Often you hear a bird long before you see it. With rails, owls and songbirds living in a forest canopy it is often the case that hearing songs and calls is the only way of ascertaining whether a species is present. Most bird songs and calls are specific and characteristic. Therefore, not only is a description included in the main text of the species accounts, but there is also a separate section from page 167 where eight identification tables clearly describe the calls and songs of a wide range of species in respect to season and habitat.

GENERAL HABITS AND REPRODUCTION

In a book concentrating on the identification of birds it is not possible or practical to include all details on behaviour, migration routes, winter quarters or reproductive biology for all species. Some data has been included in the overview of bird orders and families from page 11 onwards, as details are often similar in closely related species. In the back of the book there is a list of book titles which deal in greater detail with the many fascinating aspects of birdlife.

LIMITS OF THIS BOOK

Many bird species from outside Europe are increasingly kept in captivity – and sometimes they escape. With ducks, falcons, parrots or buntings one is probably able to recognize the family they belong to but with other species it may not even be possible to identify to that level. Of course, all these escapees are not listed in European bird books.

Within Europe some species groups lead even the experienced birdwatcher to despair: some of the larger falcons, female and immature harriers, some eagles, a few of the larger gulls and the *Acrocephalus*, *Hippolais* and *Phylloscopus* warblers. Other books seldom help and extensive specialist literature in scientific journals is often necessary. But this is no reason for dejection: with this book and a little effort you will immediately be able to identify almost every bird which is likely to be encountered in Europe down to species, and often to age and sex.

ORDERS AND FAMILIES OF EUROPEAN BIRDS

As birds are the only group of living creatures with feathers, they are grouped together in their own class. Worldwide this class comprises more than 10,000 species and just over 500 of these occur regularly in Europe. The science of taxonomy is meant to bring some system and order into this diversity, and this also helps the birdwatcher as the species are sorted naturally by their relationships and similarities. If you want to identify birds it is sensible to study the principles of taxonomy.

If we ask the question: "What is that bird?", we want the name of a bird species as the answer. In biology the **species** is the most important unit, comparable to the atom in chemistry. A species defines a group of populations which is so isolated from the populations of other species that they will not combine with each other into one species. There are reproductive barriers that lead to genetic separation between species; these barriers are caused by differences, for example, in coloration, voice or behaviour, and some of these we can recognize. These help the observer to differentiate between the species.

Very closely related bird species are grouped together in the same **genus**. This is often but not always reflected in the English names, but always in the scientific name, which is printed in italics throughout. The first part of this comprises a genus name which is identical for related species, for example, *Larus* for many of the gulls, and then the species name, for example, *ridibundus* for Black-headed Gull and *argentatus* for Herring Gull. Closely related genera belong to the same family, for example, the chats and flycatchers to the **family** Muscicapidae.

Closely related families are again grouped together into **orders**, for example, the kingfishers, bee-eaters and rollers into the order Coraciiformes. Of course the sequence of the orders in the whole system follows the degree of the relationship. The goal of taxonomy is to sketch a genealogical tree for birds which mirrors the evolution and relationship among them in the correct fashion, but this has not as yet been fulfilled, as new methods of genetic techniques are continuously leading to new insights and reclassifications.

Additionally, in some species of bird subspecies have developed and therefore a third designation has to be added after the scientific genus and species names, for example, *Luscinia svecica svecica* for the nominate Red-spotted Bluethroat subspecies of northern Europe and *Luscinia svecica cyanecula* for the White-spotted Bluethroat subspecies of southern and central Europe (see below). As long as these subspecies are recognizable in the field they have been included in this book. Also note that several of the species listed in this work were previously regarded as subspecies until it was proven that they differ genetically and were raised to full species status – the 'splitting' of Balearic and Yelkouan Shearwaters is a good example.

The sequence of orders and families in this book follows modern taxonomy and therefore differs notably from older books in some sections. There are occasionally deviations from this in the species account section in order to make comparison easier. The following overview of the 26 orders and 73 families, however, reflects modern taxonomic thinking. Here we have included details of similarities, special characteristics, general habits, reproduction and other notable features. These have not been repeated in the species accounts, and the two sections should be used together. The illustrations of some of the typical representatives of the different families will be helpful in making a preliminary identification to determine which family an observed bird belongs to. Each family account is cross-referenced with the page numbers where the relevant species accounts can be found. A summarized overview is also presented on the inner cover pages.

The systematic location of the Bluethroat

Class	Birds
Order	Passeriformes
Suborder	Passeri
Family	Muscicapidae
Genus	*Luscinia*
Species	*Luscinia svecica*, Bluethroat
Subspecies	*Luscinia svecica cyanecula*, White-spotted Bluethroat

All bird species of Europe are divided into two large and essentially different groups: firstly the Gallo-anserae (the closely-related orders of gamebirds (Galliformes) and waterfowl (Anseriformes)) and secondly the Neoaves (all other orders). Thus in modern taxonomy these two orders are put at the head of the sequence.

WILDFOWL

Wildfowl are more or less bound to water bodies and they possess webbing between their front toes. Chicks hatch with dense down feathers and are precocious (nidifugous). Most species are social outside the breeding season and sometimes occur in very large flocks of mixed or single species. Many wildfowl only visit Britain as passage migrants or winter visitors from as far away as Greenland and Siberia. Although all species here belong to one family (Anatidae – swans, geese and ducks) they are immediately distinguishable into several groups and genera through their appearance.

Swans are conspicuous by their large size and the all-white plumage which is shared by the adults of all European species. Their large nests are made up of plant stems and are found on inland water bodies. Swans lay 2-10 eggs per clutch. Both sexes are the same colour; immatures have brown-grey plumage and remain with their parents during their first winter. Pairs bond for life. Pages 32-33.

Mute Swan

Geese are medium-sized to large and outside the breeding season are often found in large flocks. On migration they form impressive flight formations with lines of birds arranged in V-shapes. Both sexes have similar plumage, pairs bond for life and 3-8 eggs are produced per clutch. Families stay together during the first winter, which makes it easier to identify juveniles which do not show adult plumage as yet. Although some species have orange or pink bills or legs, this difference is often not easily visible in the field and may be obscured by mud. To differentiate between the species of 'grey geese' (the *Anser* species) it is important to note the colour patterns on the head and bill. To differentiate between the 'black geese' (the *Branta* species) note the distribution of white on the black head and neck. Hunting in some countries can result in these birds being very shy. Pages 32-35.

Greylag Goose

Dabbling ducks feed on plant-matter, either on the surface of the water or brought up from the bottom of shallow water, typically by 'upending'. They take off from the water surface with a single wing-beat. In contrast to the colourful males, the females are drab brown and it is generally necessary to note the colour and shape of the bill, the colour of the speculum and the body shape for identification. Juveniles are the same colour as females, as are the adult males during summer in their dull eclipse plumage, although they often keep the colourful bill patterns

Mallard

(see illustration of Mallard on inner back cover). Pages 36-37, in flight page 42.

Diving ducks feed on plants and small invertebrates that they find by diving. Often their tail is held flat against the surface of the water. To take off they usually have to first take a run-up on the water surface. It is important to note the wing pattern and the head pattern when identifying juveniles and females. Pages 38-39, in flight page 42.

Tufted Duck

The best known **seaduck** are the eiders and scoters; this group also dives readily, especially looking for crustaceans and molluscs such as mussels. They breed almost exclusively in northern regions and nests are mostly built in vegetation on the banks of water bodies (many species breed on inland waters) and are lined with down feathers from the belly of the female. Only the Common Goldeneye nests in tree holes. Pages 38-41, in flight page 43.

Sawbills (or mergansers) possess serrated cutting edges to their slender bills – these help them to hold on to their prey, which mainly consists of fish. Females and immatures are known as 'red-heads'. Both the Smew and Goosander nest in hollows. Pages 40-41, in flight page 43.

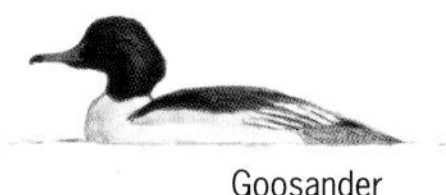

Goosander

Escapes are frequently seen as almost every species of wildfowl is kept and bred in Europe. These exotic forms are usually not included in a book on European birds, although a few of the most regular escapes are dealt with.

Hybrids of wildfowl species are not only common in captivity, but also in the wild. The features of the parent species are not always apparent in their offspring and sometimes it is not possible to identify them. Hybridization is particularly prevalent among geese and *Aythya* diving ducks but can involve almost any species.

GAMEBIRDS

Gamebirds live mainly on the ground, feeding on plant material, and with their plump bodies and rounded wings they are generally not very strong flyers. The chicks are precocious. With the exception of the **Quail**, which spends the winter in Africa, all other members of the group are sedentary. The female plumage of grouse in particular often lacks obvious features, so the body shape and colour of the tail may be the best clues to identification. They can be roughly divided into two groups, but they are no longer regarded as separate families.

Grouse have feathered legs and toes, lay 6-12 eggs in ground nests and perform extensive courtship displays. They inhabit undisturbed forests, moors or mountains and are generally quite thinly distributed. **Pheasants and partridges** are characterised by unfeathered smooth legs and toes and mainly live in open areas. They are often encountered in small groups or family parties. Clutches can contain 15 or more eggs. Pages 44-45.

Pheasant

Greater Flamingo

FLAMINGOS

Flamingos are the only family in this order. They are unmistakable with their pink plumage and deep, decurved bills with lamellae, with which they sieve shallow water with head held upside down to filter out the smallest living creatures. They breed in large colonies on cone-shaped mud nests. They are very distinctive in flight with their long outstretched necks, long legs and crimson-and-black wings. As well as the one native European species, exotic flamingos regularly escape from captivity.

Great Crested Grebe

GREBES

This order contains only one family. All species have the legs set far back on the body and with lobed toes they are perfectly adapted to live on and below the water surface. Floating nests are built from dead plant material, clutches contain 2-7 eggs. The chicks typically show black-and-white stripes on the head and neck and are often transported by the parents on their backs. The colour and pattern of the head, shape of the bill and ear tufts during breeding plumage are characteristic. The sexes have identical plumage. Grebes are now considered to be more closely related to flamingos than divers, although their appearance would suggest otherwise. Pages 46-47.

Black-throated Diver

DIVERS

This order contains only a few species within one family. These are rather archaic looking birds that breed on inland waters of the northern reaches of the Northern Hemisphere and spend the winter mainly at sea, but also appear on inland waters, particularly large reservoirs, during migration and winter. The legs have webbed feet and are situated far back on the streamlined body. When diving to catch fish they do so in a smooth motion. Divers are very clumsy on land; their nests are positioned at the edge of the water and usually contain 2 eggs. Sexes cannot be differentiated. For identification look at the colour and pattern of the head and neck, while the shape and posture of the bill are also especially important. Pages 46-47.

Leach's Storm-petrel

TUBENOSES

Tubenoses are exclusively oceanic seabirds and are characterized by the tube-shaped structure on top of the nostrils, which serves to secrete excess salt. They only come to coasts to breed in large colonies where each pair hatches a single egg. Neither sexes, nor juveniles and adults, can be differentiated in the field. The best-known family in the Southern Hemisphere is the albatrosses.

Storm-petrels are small and dark with a fluttering flight and breed in burrows. All regular European species are blackish with a white rump. Pages 48-49.

Shearwaters and **petrels** are larger and superficially can look rather similar to gulls, although they typically glide over wave crests and through troughs with stiff wings. Pages 48-49.

Fulmar

PELICANS

Pelicans scoop fish out of the water with their large bill pouches, with birds often hunting as a group in formation. All the toes are connected with webs; in flight the neck is folded back. The large nests are constructed in colonies in reedbeds of south-east Europe. The chicks are altricial. Pages 50-51.

White Pelican

CORMORANTS AND GANNET

In the species of this group all toes are connected with webs of skin, the chicks are altricial and the development of the adult plumage may take several years.

Gannets are marine birds and they dive head-first into the sea from heights of up to 20 metres when hunting their fish prey. They fly with slow wing-beats and also glide frequently. They breed in large colonies on, or on top of, steep cliffs in the north Atlantic. Pages 50-51.

Cormorants have a hook at the tip of the bill, they are often seen drying themselves with wings spread at the water's edge and they dive from the swimming position. Their flight is rather goose-like. Breeding colonies are located in trees or on cliffs, by inland waters and at the coast. Pages 50-51.

Gannet

Cormorant

IBISES AND SPOONBILL

Ibises breed in colonies and fly with their long necks outstretched. Both sexes have similar plumage and juveniles soon take on the appearance of adults. The **Spoonbill** has a bill with a broadened tip, which it uses to sieve through shallow water for small organisms by sweeping the head to and fro. The ibises probe vertically with their decurved bills. Pages 52-53.

Spoonbill

HERONS, EGRETS AND BITTERNS

Herons fly with their necks folded back against their bodies and with slow beats of their rounded and slightly down-curved wings. They hunt by waiting quietly and suddenly striking at fish, small mammals or birds, insects or amphibians with their dagger-like bills. Most species breed in colonies in trees or reedbeds and only the bitterns are solitary breeders. During the breeding season many species develop longer ornamental feathers and the colour of the bill and legs changes and becomes more intense. The sexes are identical in all species except Little Bittern; also juveniles look rather similar to adults except for Night Heron. Pages 52-55.

Grey Heron

White Stork

STORKS

Storks are unmistakable with their long legs, red bills and black-and-white plumage. Male, female and young are almost identical. They use updrafts extensively for thermalling and gliding, particularly during migration. The neck is always held stretched straight forward in flight. Their enormous nests are used regularly for many years. Pages 54-55.

BIRDS OF PREY (RAPTORS)

All birds of prey possess a hooked bill and sharp talons; they are carnivorous and kill their prey either on the ground or in the air. In most species the sexes are similar, although the females are larger. They lay 1-6 eggs in a nest on the ground, on a rock ledge or in a tree. Chicks are altricial. The population density as well as the number of eggs laid depends on the quantity of prey available – this prevents overpopulation. With one exception all species belong to one family.

Osprey

Osprey is in a family on its own. The species has a near worldwide distribution along coasts and on inland waters. It is a summer visitor to Britain and Europe and often hovers briefly over the water before diving down to catch a fish with outstretched talons. Pages 56-57.

Golden Eagle

The **Accipitridae** is a large and very diverse family containing a range of different species from the small Sparrowhawk, slender harriers and broad-winged buzzards, to the large eagles and mainly scavenging vultures. It is often more difficult to identify perched birds rather than individuals in flight. The silhouette with characteristic wing- and tail-shape, as well as the flight pattern, often give important hints as to which group the bird belongs. Eagles and vultures possess strongly fingered wings, harriers have long tails, kites forked tails, Short-toed Eagle and buzzards often hover in the air, harriers fly close to the ground with wings raised in a V-shape and Sparrowhawks appear lightning fast from cover in pursuit of their small bird prey. The plumages of juveniles and adults often differ and the larger species take several years to develop full adult plumage phases (see the illustration of plumage change with the example of Golden Eagle on the inner back cover). The identification of some raptors remains difficult, demanding experience and sometimes reference to more detailed literature. Pages 56-61, in flight pages 62-64.

Common Buzzard

Sparrowhawk

FALCONS

Falcons have similar habits to other raptors but they form a separate family within the order. They are small to medium-sized, feed on vertebrates or insects and are easily recognized by their pointed and slightly angled wings, with which they can achieve high speeds during flight. They do not build their own nests, but lay 3-7 eggs on a cliff ledge or in an old nest of another species. Females are clearly larger than males and have duller plumage in the smaller species. Pages 66-67, in flight page 65.

Kestrel

GRUIFORMES – CRANES, BUSTARDS AND RAILS

Three families in this order occur in Europe. They differ greatly in size, appearance and habitat requirements. All have relatively long legs and live mainly on the ground, where they also nest. The chicks are precocious. During moult many species are unable to fly as they lose the flight feathers at the same time.

Common Crane

Cranes are large with long legs and bills, but can be easily differentiated from herons and storks by their primarily grey colouring, bushy tertials, whooping calls and long stretched-out neck in flight. Pairs mate for life and in spring they perform courtship dances which include jumps high into the air. They lay 2 eggs in a large nest on the ground in a swampy area. They migrate in impressive flocks in V-formation, advertising their presence with trumpeting calls. In winter they form large gatherings at certain favoured sites in south and central Europe. Pages 68-69.

Great Bustard

Bustards inhabit rather drier steppe-like areas. The Great Bustard is the heaviest European bird capable of flight. The adult males are much larger than the females and young and have an imposing courtship display, spreading their feathers in such a way that makes them look like a white ball. There is no pair bonding. Pages 68-69.

Rails and **Crakes** are starling- to pigeon-sized wetland birds with quite different habits. Coots mostly dive and swim on open water like ducks, the Moorhen is equally at home on water, in reedbeds or in open fields and meadows, while the Water Rail and small crakes mainly hide in dense vegetation close to the water's edge and the Corncrake inhabits long grass. Many species are nocturnal and often their call is the only clue to their presence. Pages 68-71.

Water Rail

CHARADRIIFORMES – WADERS, AUKS, SKUAS, TERNS AND GULLS

This very large order comprises families and species that are bound to oceans, coasts, mudflats and inland waters and wetlands. The very varied bill shapes have developed as specific adaptations to feeding in their respective habitats. Various differences in reproduction have also developed. Common characteristics are certain anatomical features, small clutch size of between 1-4 eggs and often similar plumage in males and females, although juvenile and non-breeding plumages are clearly different in many cases. Many species migrate great distances with, for example, the Arctic Tern breeding in northernmost Europe and wintering off southern Africa.

Stone-curlew

Oystercatcher

Avocet

Northern Lapwing

Dunlin

The species in this order can be divided into two groups. The first five families can be grouped together as waders, which are also known as shorebirds. Apart from during the breeding period, which many of them spend in wetlands and tundra areas in the arctic, a large number of species require mudflats, where they can feed on worms, larvae and other small organisms. Great flocks can be observed in certain coastal areas, especially on estuaries such as The Wash and Morecambe Bay. Inland they rest on muddy riverbanks, lake shores and floods. Almost all species lay about 4 eggs in a scrape in the ground, some spend barely two months in their breeding area and spend the rest of the year elsewhere. With most species the adults start their southward migration several weeks ahead of the juveniles.

Buttonquails (or hemipodes) don't even look as if they belong to this group and were previously considered to be more closely allied to the Gruiformes. The remaining families are close relatives of the gulls and are more complicated and diverse. Skuas get much of their food by piracy, auks are like flying versions of the unrelated penguins and only terns and gulls seem to obviously belong to the suborder of gulls and their relatives.

In Europe the **stone-curlews** (or thick-knees) are represented by just one species, which differs from many other waders by preferring drier, steppe-like habitats. It is nocturnal and lays only 2 eggs. Pages 70-71.

Oystercatchers are about the size of a pigeon and in Europe are represented by just one species which lives mainly along coasts and has distinctive black-and-white plumage, pink legs and a long, straight orange bill. In contrast to other waders they lay only 3 eggs and feed the chicks until they are ready to fly. Pages 70-71.

Avocets and stilts (Recurvirostridae) occur mainly on salt water. There is one species of each in Europe, with only the Avocet occurring commonly in Britain. They are slender and elegant with long bills and legs and black-and-white plumage. Pages 70-71.

Plovers and allies (Charadriidae) have more rounded bodies, relatively short (not longer than the head), straight bills and only medium-long legs. While picking up food they run over the ground with a distinctive 'stop-start' action. Often the wing pattern gives a good indication of which species it is. Pages 72-75, flight illustrations pages 80-81.

Sandpipers and allies (Scolopacidae) constitute a large and diverse family, but some genera can be identified more easily than others. The *Calidris* sandpipers are sparrow- to thrush-sized with short to medium-long legs and bills often decurved and up to the same length as the head. The snipes are characterized by their cryptic plumage, short legs and extremely long, straight bills. The larger godwits (*Limosa*) and curlews (*Numenius*), however, have long legs and bills, the bills of the latter being strongly decurved. The medium-sized *Tringa* shanks and sandpipers typically have long and sometimes brightly coloured legs, long bills and often bob their bodies up and down. The phalaropes have reverse sexual dimorphism, with the females being bigger and more colourful than the males; they swim on open water and pick up insects from the surface with their slender bills. Within the Scolopacidae some species maintain normal pair bonding through the breeding season, for example Black-tailed Godwit, but in many others females mate with several males (many sandpipers), only males sit on the eggs (phalaropes), or males and females do not form a close bond (Ruff). The chicks have camouflaged down feathers, leave the nest early and look for food themselves with the adults only guarding them. The identification of waders is often confusing for the beginner as one has to differentiate breeding, non-breeding and juvenile plumages (see the illustration of the different plumages for the example of Dunlin on the inner back cover). Many species are very similar in appearance and the distance at which they are observed is often great. The most important pointers are the length and colour of the legs, the bill length and shape, the patterns on the wings and tail in flight and the calls. Pages 74-85, flight illustrations pages 80-81.

Common Snipe

Redshank

Buttonquails look totally different from other birds in this order but they are now considered to be relatives of the gulls. They inhabit drier areas with low and dense vegetation. In Europe there is only one species, **Small Buttonquail** (which is also known as Andalusian Hemipode), which breeds very rarely in Spain but is more common and widespread in Africa. The roles of the sexes are reversed and females undertake the courtship display. Page 70-71.

Small Buttonquail

Pratincoles and coursers (Glareolidae) live primarily in dry habitat such as steppe and the Cream-coloured Courser even occupies deserts. The pratincoles have short legs and bills and forked tails – they specialize in catching insects in an elegant and rather tern-like flight. All European species are restricted to the south and are rare vagrants to Britian. Pages 86-87.

Collared Pratincole

Skuas are relatives of the gulls. They breed in northern Europe and specialize in harassing other seabirds until they drop or regurgitate their prey. Their plumage is largely brown, but unless the birds are in breeding plumage, when three species have elongated central tail feathers, identification is often difficult for anyone other than the experienced observer. Two species have dark and light plumage morphs. In contrast to gulls, females are larger than males. Skuas breed in loose colonies and lay only two eggs. They are pelagic outside the breeding season with the three smaller species wintering primarily far to the south of Europe. Pages 86-87.

Arctic Skua

Common Guillemot

Auks are birds of the open sea for most of the year; they come ashore only when breeding. With their black-and-white plumage and distinctive posture they look a bit like penguins. With the exception of Black Guillemot (2 eggs, usually breeding in single pairs), they live mostly in huge colonies on steep rocky coasts and cliffs ('stacks') in northern Europe and lay only one egg on a narrow rock ledge (or a burrow for the Puffin). Bill shapes and the patterns in the black-and-white plumage are the best ways to identify them in non-breeding plumage. Pages 88-89.

Black-headed Gull

Gulls are elegant in flight, they are mainly white or grey in colour and are familiar to most people. As they are strongly associated with coasts and wetlands they have webbing between their toes. Most species breed in large colonies near the sea, although many also nest inland. They lay two or three eggs in a nest on the ground (although the Kittiwake breeds on a cliff ledge); the chicks hatch with down feathers, but remain on the nest for a long time and are fed by the adults. Males are usually markedly larger than females. Most gulls are highly opportunistic and as a result of additional food sources (refuse dumps, waste from fisheries) some species have increased in numbers and widened their distribution. To reach adult plumage takes two years in smaller species and up to five years in larger ones (see the illustration of plumage changes in Herring Gull on the inner back cover as an example). In many cases the identification of immatures is very difficult even for experts, and additional specialized literature is required. This is especially the case for Herring, Yellow-legged, Caspian, Lesser Black-backed and Heuglin's Gulls. Pages 90-97.

Common Tern

Terns generally differ from gulls by their more slender wings, smaller bodies, pointed bills and usually clearly forked tails. The mainly grey-and-white 'sea terns' occur mainly along coasts (Common Tern is an exception in Britain), usually breed in colonies, lay 1-3 eggs in a scrape in the ground, and feed on fish and other small water creatures which they hunt by diving from the air. The three species with blackish breeding plumage are known as 'marsh terns' (Page 100) and breed on inland water bodies where they construct their nests on floating vegetation (they occur on coasts during migration). Flying low they dip down to the water surface to pick off their food. The identification of terns in breeding plumage is easier if the colour of the bill can be determined. Pages 98-101.

Pin-tailed Sandgrouse

SANDGROUSE

Sandgrouse are approximately partridge-sized inhabitants of arid areas and deserts. They have long, pointed wings and fly great distances to water sources to drink each morning and evening. They drink by sucking up the water like pigeons. Males can carry water to the precocious chicks in their specially evolved belly feathers. Pages 100-101.

PIGEONS AND DOVES

Pigeons and doves are familiar and easily recognizable by their small heads, fairly short bills and legs and heavy bodies, and also by their soft cooing calls. They lay two eggs in an untidy free-standing nest and the chicks are altricial. Only the Stock Dove breeds in tree holes. The species can be easily differentiated by their wing-patterns and collars (not present in juveniles), and also by the base colour of the plumage. A special feature of the doves and pigeons is their ability to suck up water when drinking (rather than having to tilt their heads back) and to feed the chicks with their own 'crop milk'. Pages 102-103.

Woodpigeon

PARROTS

Parrots are primarily birds of the tropical regions and Southern Hemisphere. There are no native European species but escapees of several species have started colonies in a number of European cities in various countries and many of these are expanding. Their preferred habitat is parkland and gardens, where they lay three to six eggs in tree hollows. The three species covered here are the most common and widespread in Europe, but isolated colonies of other species also occur. Pages 110-111.

Ring-necked Parakeet

CUCKOOS

A large family with a worldwide distribution and two species breeding in Europe. In flight cuckoos can resemble small falcons. They lay their eggs in the nests of many other bird species (the Great Spotted Cuckoo almost exclusively in Magpie nests). Further characteristics are the feet with two toes pointing forwards and two backwards, and the large quantity of hairy caterpillars in their diet – these are normally avoided by other birds. Pages 108-109.

Cuckoo

OWLS

Mainly nocturnal hunters, owls mostly remain hidden in a secluded roosting spot during hours of daylight. When seen they are easily recognizable by their large round heads, which can be turned 270°, and large forward-pointing eyes. While the Pygmy Owl is only Starling-sized, the Eagle Owl is even larger than a Common Buzzard. Correspondingly the prey size varies as well, from insects and earthworms to mice and birds and even up to mammals the size of a young fox. Prey is located mainly by their excellent hearing, with the facial disc of stiffer feathers acting as a sound reflector. Owls do not build nests and most species lay their almost round, pure white eggs in natural hollows, some in old crows' nests (like the Long-eared Owl) or even on the ground (Short-eared Owl). The number of eggs depends largely on the availability of prey.

Eagle Owl

Barn Owl

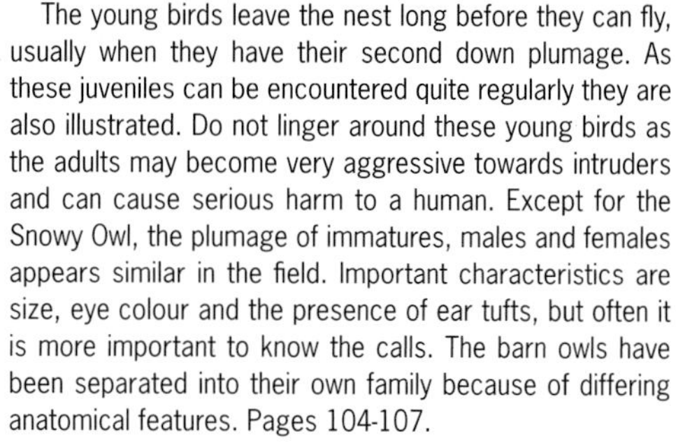

The young birds leave the nest long before they can fly, usually when they have their second down plumage. As these juveniles can be encountered quite regularly they are also illustrated. Do not linger around these young birds as the adults may become very aggressive towards intruders and can cause serious harm to a human. Except for the Snowy Owl, the plumage of immatures, males and females appears similar in the field. Important characteristics are size, eye colour and the presence of ear tufts, but often it is more important to know the calls. The barn owls have been separated into their own family because of differing anatomical features. Pages 104-107.

NIGHTJARS

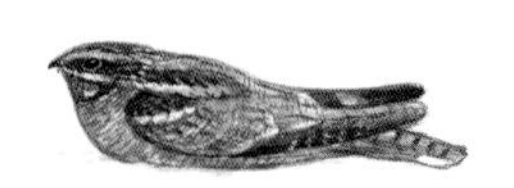
European Nightjar

Nightjars (Caprimulgidae) are the only family in this order that occurs in Europe. They have elongated bodies, cryptic bark-coloured plumage and narrow wings like those of falcons. Their bills are small but broad, and when fully opened gape widely to facilitate the capture of insects in flight at night over open ground. Two brown speckled eggs are laid on the bare ground. Pages 108-109.

SWIFTS

Common Swift

Swifts are very fast fliers with sickle-shaped wings. They are not closely related to hirundines but are considered to be closer to hummingbirds. The nest is in a hollow or crevice and 2-3 eggs are laid per clutch, the juveniles are altricial and both sexes have similar plumage. Swifts spend almost all their life in the air, even sleeping and mating there. They can barely walk and with the four toes pointing forwards can only grip while hanging. Pages 108-109.

CORACIIFORMES – ROLLERS, KINGFISHERS AND BEE-EATERS

European Roller

The 'flying jewels' of the bird world belong to this colourful order, they are divided into three large families, each with many species, and the few European representatives mainly occur in the south. All lay 4-8 white eggs in a hollows which is often self-excavated. The chicks are altricial and males and females are fairly similar in colour. Except for the Kingfisher they are all migratory birds that winter in tropical zones.

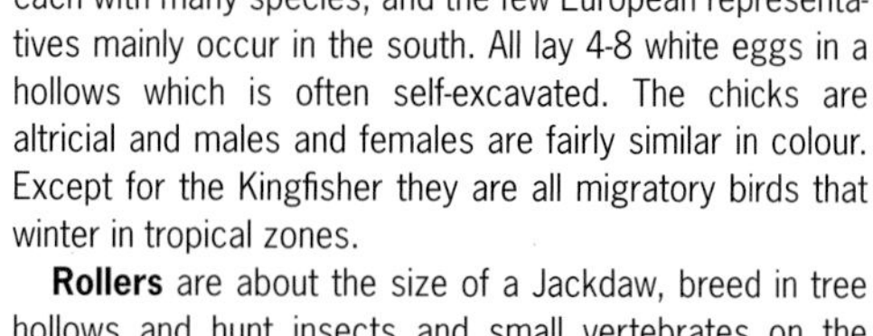

Rollers are about the size of a Jackdaw, breed in tree hollows and hunt insects and small vertebrates on the ground or from a perch. The iridescent blue wings are shown to their fullest in the male's 'rolling' display flight. Pages 110-111.

Kingfisher

Kingfishers dig nest burrows up to 1 m long in steep river banks. To make up for population losses during harsh winters they can rear up to three broods per summer. They feed on small fish and other aquatic creatures, which they hunt by plunge-diving and catching with their sharp bills. Pages 110-111.

In southern and central Europe bee-eaters (Meropidae) are represented by the colourful and widespread European Bee-eater, which has elongated central tail feathers. Like the kingfisher it builds a nest tunnel, but it mainly nests in colonies in sandy banks and catches insects in flight. Pages 110-111.

European Bee-eater

HOOPOES

Hoopoes share this order with the hornbill and woodhoopoe families. They breed in tree hollows, holes in the ground or wall cavities. During the breeding season they can excrete a foul-smelling substance to deter predators. With their decurved bills they dig for invertebrate prey such as cockchafer grubs. Pages 110-111.

Hoopoe

WOODPECKERS

Woodpeckers have strong chisel-like bills and long tongues to extract insects and grubs from rotten wood. Stiffened tail feathers serve as support and powerful feet with two toes pointing forwards and two backwards give them a good grip on vertical tree trunks. They excavate their own nest holes in trees and lay 4-8 white eggs, the chicks are altricial. During courtship they 'drum' by hitting the wood in a rapid rhythm. Their undulating flight is characteristic. The Wryneck is an exception within this group; it is the only woodpecker that migrates, it never drums and does not excavate its own nest. In identifying the woodpeckers it is important to note the extent and position of red patches on the head, the face pattern and white areas on the back in the black-and-white species. Juveniles and the sexes can be distinguished in most cases. Pages 112-115.

Great Spotted Woodpecker

PASSERINES

With more than 6,000 species the passerines make up more than half of all bird species in the world and are by far the largest order with the most families; 30 in Europe alone. Of the two suborders only one occurs in Europe, the Passeri (or 'songbirds'). Sometimes – incorrectly – the whole order is referred to as 'songbirds'. Within the Passeri there are two very different groups. The orioles, shrikes and crows and allies form their own superfamily which developed independently from all the other passerine families. Following new scientific insights they are listed at the beginning of this order.

Within the enormous diversity of the passerines a whole range of avian forms has developed: from the tiny Goldcrest weighing only four grams to the 1.7 kg Raven, from the solitary warblers to the social Long-tailed Tits, to the swarming Starlings, from the melodious song of the Nightingale to the screeching Rook, from the Common Chiffchaff hunting aphids to the Hawfinch cracking open cherry stones, from the Dipper running along the stream-bottom and the Nuthatch running down tree trunks head first to the House Martin hunting flying insects high in the sky.

Nevertheless they do have many features in common which enables their separation from all other orders. Three of the four toes point forwards and one backwards, forming a foot that can grasp. Almost all species build nests, the chicks hatch blind and naked, are altricial and are fed by the parents for a long time. Last but not least all songbirds have a well-developed larynx, with which they often produce melodic song that is usually species-specific although some species have evolved to imitate others. Almost all live on dry land and many are at home high in trees or bushes.

Within the songbird group different families show characteristic features which enable quick identification and the birdwatcher should be familiar with these. Some families are very small and only represented by one or two species in Europe (for example, wrens and accentors), while others are so large that it is even possible to define differences between the genera (for example, chats and flycatchers). For identification first look at the bill (seed-eaters have a deep bill, insect-eaters have a slender bill), body shape (squat or slender), movements (slow or quick) and tail shape (rounded, squared or notched), then at the distribution of colour or obvious markings, and again take note of any call.

Golden Oriole

Orioles weave a hanging nest in a horizontal tree fork. These thrush-sized birds feed on fruit and invertebrates, including many hairy caterpillars. Although brightly coloured they are not easy to observe as they usually hide in the canopy of trees. Pages 116-117.

Red-backed Shrike

Shrikes are vaguely reminiscent of small falcons when perched due to their hooked bills and long tails. They live in open areas where they hunt invertebrates and small vertebrates from perches and sometimes impale their prey on thorns to create a 'larder' (they are known as 'butcher birds'). They have an undulating flight and build their nests in dense bushes. Page 116-117.

Raven

Crows and allies are among the most highly developed and intelligent of birds. Although they are the largest songbirds they utter rather coarse calls. Many of the pigeon- to buzzard-sized species are black with little or no pattern, although the Jay is very colourful. The sexes have similar plumage. All have powerful feet and heavy bills and feed on almost anything. The nests are mainly built from twigs and contain 3-7 bluish-green and speckled eggs. The species in this highly successful bird family occur in almost all habitats, from high mountains to city centres, and some are often highly social. Pages 116-119.

Penduline tits live in trees along water bodies and build hanging nests that look like woollen socks. In contrast to the true tits, northern populations are migratory and spend the winter in southern and western Europe. Page 122.

Tits are primarily resident. They move with great agility through the branches while looking for seeds and insects and several species are frequent visitors to bird-feeders. These true tits (Paridae), in contrast to other families also called 'tits', nest in tree holes and also utilize nestboxes. They lay up to 16 white eggs with red speckles and line the nest with moss. Only the Crested Tit and Willow Tit excavate their own nest holes in old wood. In winter tits often come together in mixed species groups. Pages 120-121.

Larks live in open areas mainly on the ground and are generally fairly plain brown in colour. They feed on seeds, other plant material and invertebrates. The males sing in flight. Three to five brown-spotted eggs are laid in a ground nest. They can be differentiated from the superficially similar pipits by their more robust bodies, broader wings and heavier bills. Pages 124-125.

Hirundines (swallows and martins) are mainly observed while elegantly hawking for insects in the air. They have narrow wings and a forked tail (except for Crag Martin). Each species has its own nesting behaviour, sometimes forming colonies and building a mud nest or excavating a nest tunnel in the earth (Sand Martin). Before migration large groups gather on cables and vast flocks of swallows and martins can be seen above reedbed roosts. Pages 122-123.

In Europe the **Bearded Tit** is the sole member of its family and is present only in large reedbeds. It has a longish tail, is social and can compensate for heavy winter losses by producing three clutches per summer. Pages 122-123.

Long-tailed Tits are social and are resident in bushy scrub or forests with abundant undergrowth. They can be easily recognized by their tiny bodies and very long, narrow tails. They build spherical nests from moss and lichen, bound together with spiders' webs. Pages 122-123.

Bush-warblers are represented by just one species in Europe, Cetti's Warbler. It usually stays hidden in wet thickets, and in contrast to almost all other species has only 10 instead of 12 tail feathers. Pages 130-131.

Penduline Tit

Great Tit

Skylark

Swallow

Bearded Tit

Long-tailed Tit

Cetti's Warbler

Common Chiffchaff

Phylloscopus warblers (or leaf warblers) are small, very agile greenish birds. Several of the European species look very much alike and in many cases can be best differentiated by their songs. For identification take special note of the head pattern, wing-bars (if present), leg colour and primary projection. Often age and sex cannot be easily differentiated in the field. As they are insect-eaters most species (except some Common Chiffchaffs in south and west Europe) migrate south before the onset of winter. They build oven-shaped nests on or just above the ground. Pages 126-127.

Grasshopper Warbler

Locustella warblers differ from the superficially rather similar *Acrocephalus* warblers due to their broad, rounded tails with long undertail coverts and their mainly insect-like songs. In Europe they are represented by just three breeding species, all of which are rather inconspicuous and brownish and often remain hidden in dense vegetation for much of the time. Pages 128-129.

Reed Warbler

Acrocephalus warblers are a family that primarily frequents wetland habitats. They can be divided into species with streaked upperparts and ones with plain upperparts. They usually live in reedbeds and other vegetation bordering wetlands, build attractive cup-shaped nests strung between vertical reeds and their songs and calls are quite coarse (pages 128 -131).

Zitting Cisticola

Some **_Hippolais_ warblers** are known for their excellent imitations of other bird calls, which are incorporated into their songs. They live in bushes and trees and have a characteristic head shape with a long bill and they often raise their crown feathers. In contrast to the *Acrocephalus* warblers the base of the bill is broader and the undertail coverts are shorter; sometimes the outer tail feathers are paler (see page 132). In both genera it is necessary to carefully note details of plumage and structure in order to identify the species, and often identification can only be confirmed if the typical song or call is heard. Pages 132-133.

Blackcap

Cisticolas live mainly in Africa and the only species in Europe is the Zitting Cisticola. It inhabits open grassland and marshes in southern Europe. Pages 128-129.

Goldcrest

Sylvia warblers live in forests and scrub, where they construct their neat cup-shaped nests. They are mainly insectivorous, but also feed on berries, particularly just prior to autumn migration. In contrast to other warblers, in the more colourful *Sylvia* warblers the sexes can often be differentiated. Their beautiful songs are often rather melodious, although some are scratchy. Pages 134-137.

The **kinglets** (or 'crests') are Europe's smallest birds. They are very agile and construct spherical nests of moss and lichen high in coniferous trees. Their calls are of such high frequency that elderly people often cannot hear them. Pages 138-139.

Waxwings feed mainly on insects in summer but in winter switch to fermented berries. Their unique liver is enlarged and can rapidly break down the alcohol. Another feature is the small red wax-like appendages on the secondaries. Pages 140-141.

The **Wallcreeper** climbs among rocks in search of invertebrates, which they hunt with their decurved bills. This species is the sole member of its family but its range extends into east Asia. Pages 138-139.

Nuthatches appear stocky because of their short tails. They can run down tree trunks head first and their nest in a tree hollow (or rock crevice for Rock Nuthatch) is lined with pieces of bark and the entrance closed to their own size with plastered mud. In Europe there is one widespread species and three more that occur locally in the south. Pages 138-139.

Treecreepers are tit-like, streaked brown birds. They climb like small woodpeckers up and down tree trunks and search for invertebrates in crevices in the bark with their decurved bills. They construct their nests behind protruding pieces of bark. Pages 138-139.

Wrens are easy to recognize due to their small size and short, cocked tails. The only European species builds a spherical nest out of old leaves which is positioned close to the ground in dense scrub. Each clutch contains 4-8 rust-coloured, spotted eggs. The other 80 or so species in this family occur in the Americas. Pages 140-141.

Starlings can be immediately distinguished from thrushes by their shorter tails and the fact that they walk rather than hop on the ground. They have very versatile, chatty songs and calls full of whistles and mimicry. Each clutch of 4-6 white eggs is laid in a hollow and they feed on invertebrates, berries and fruits. Outside the breeding season they congregate in large flocks and often roost in reedbeds or trees. Pages 140-141.

The **Dipper** is the only European species in family of the same name. It lives along running streams and feeds mainly on aquatic invertebrates. They lay 4-6 white eggs in an oven-shaped moss nest by the water and are the only songbirds that can dive underwater. Pages 140-141.

Blackbird

Thrushes form a large family of medium-sized species, all with relatively long legs and large eyes. They hop along the ground looking for invertebrates but also feed on berries and fruits. The open, cup-shaped grass nests with 3-8 colourfully patterned eggs are located in trees or bushes. Juvenile plumage is clearly speckled. In most species sexes cannot be differentiated in the field. They typically have loud and melodious songs. Page 142.

Pied Flycatcher

Old World flycatchers are a large family restricted to the Old World that comprises genera with widely differing outward appearances, including Rufous Scrub Robin, flycatchers, rock thrushes, wheatears, chats and redstarts. Many of these were previously considered to be more closely allied to the thrushes than to the flycatchers. Most of them are rather small, stand very upright and specialize in hunting insects from a perch, in flight, or on the ground. This behaviour is especially well developed in the true flycatchers, which breed in hollows. Several species with melodious songs, including Nightingale, Bluethroat and Robin, spend most of the time in dense vegetation close to the ground and also breed there. The two species of redstarts stand out due to the coloration of their tail feathers; they also breed in hollows. Another distinctive group is the wheatears, with their white rumps and black-tipped tails; they show a preference for open areas. Pages 144-149.

Robin

Dunnock

Accentors are rather nondescript and often confused with sparrows, but their bills are more slender. Each clutch of 3-6 turquoise eggs is laid in a moss nest close to the ground. In contrast to almost all other bird families their distribution is limited to Eurasia. Most species live in mountains, but the Dunnock also inhabits lowlands.

House Sparrow

Sparrows possess heavy bills typical of seed-eaters, are generally rather plain in colour and have rather uninspiring songs and calls. They lay 3-7 spotted eggs in untidy nests in a recess and some species also make use of nestboxes. The Spanish Sparrow often builds free-standing nests in colonies, and sometimes may be 'lodgers' in large stork nests. Most of the time these birds gather in flocks, especially in open areas with abundant grass seed. Pages 150-151.

Meadow Pipit

Wagtails and pipits are slender, elongated, long-legged insect-eaters, often wagging their tails continuously up and down. They have a markedly undulating flight and often inhabit open ground. The streaky brown pipits are frequently difficult to identify and both sexes look similar. The wagtails are found mainly near water, they have long tails, are distinctly patterned and in most cases their plumage can be easily differentiated. Both genera build their nests, with four to seven eggs, on the ground although the Pied and Grey Wagtails will also nest higher up in hollows. The different 'yellow wagtails' (*Motacilla flava*) are listed here as subspecies, but are regarded by some authorities as separate species following the modern biological species definition. Pages 152-155.

White Wagtail

Finches show different variations of the cone-shaped bill typical of seed-eaters – it is very small in Serin, short and deep in Bullfinch, long in Goldfinch, massive in Hawfinch and with crossed mandible tips in crossbills, all are adaptations to each species' method of feeding. They occur everywhere where suitable seed stock is available, from wasteland to gardens and forests. In most species the sexes can be differentiated and the males often utter trilling songs in flight. The open grass nests with 3-6 spotted eggs are located in bushes or trees. For flight identification the patterns on the wings, rumps and tails are clear features (see inner front cover page). Most species are short-range migrants and some are irruptive. Many individuals leave Britain in winter but many others arrive here from the Continent, when a variety of species occur at garden bird-feeders. Pages 156-161.

Chaffinch

Buntings also feed on seeds and also have the typical bills of seed-eaters, but they live almost exclusively in open areas. They lay 3-6 eggs variably marked with swirling patterns in ground nests. Females are usually plainer and browner than males, and the latter can often be best identified by their head and breast patterns. Most show white outer tail feathers. They often sit on elevated perches calling monotonously or delivering a simple or melancholy song. Pages 162-165.

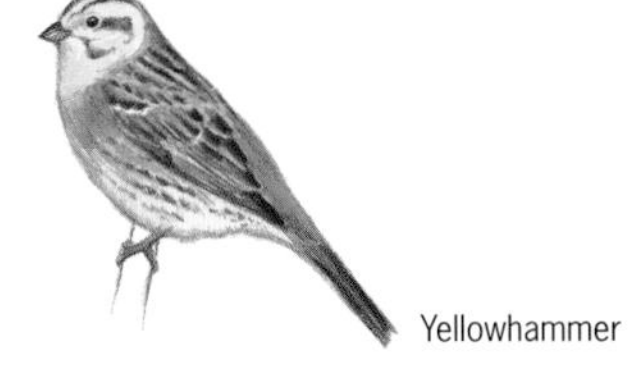

Yellowhammer

DIRECTIONS FOR USE OF SPECIES ACCOUNTS

COLOUR PLATES

Upon seeing an unknown species the initial reaction will usually be to check through the colour plates to find an illustration that resembles the bird most closely. If the person is a more experienced birdwatcher who is already familiar with the characteristics of the different orders and families (see pages 11-29) the search can be more specific. Then it should be possible to find the bird more rapidly by looking at the overview of bird families illustrated on the inner covers (non-passerines at the front, passerines at the back), which give reference to the specific colour bars indicating the relevant page numbers.

The species are dealt with in taxonomic order, but in some cases similar looking species or families have been put closer together to make comparison more easy even though they are not closely related to each other.

The plates show the birds in the most common plumages likely to be encountered in Britain and Europe. Where sexual and age differences are distinctive these have also been illustrated and marked using the following abbreviations:

♂	male
♀	female
br	breeding plumage
non-br	non-breeding plumage
ad	adult
juv	juvenile
1w	first-winter plumage
1s	first-summer plumage
2w	second-winter plumage

Detailed explanations of the various plumages can be found on pages 9-10. The same abbreviations have also been used in the text. If the illustration is not identified as a certain age, plumage or sex such differentiation is not possible in the field. The descriptions have also been omitted where they are obvious, for example 'adult' if the juvenile plumage is illustrated and marked as such next to it.

For easier identification of many species the typical habitat is depicted in the **background illustration**. **Lines** point to the most important identification features. For unmistakable species, or for clearly visible features, these lines have often been omitted so as to not distract from the beauty of the bird.

The **number** next to each illustration refers to the relevant species account on the opposite page.

TEXT

Next to the **number** of the illustration the **common English name** of the bird species is given. **L** indicates **length** of the bird, measured from the tip of the bill to the tip of the tail (extremely elongated central tail feathers in certain species have not been included in this measurement). For larger species, which are also often seen in flight, the **wingspan** (abbreviated **WS**) is also given. In principle one should deal very carefully with measurements when identifying birds because variations between individuals may exist and the sexes often differ in size. However, it is almost impossible to judge the true size of a bird without a direct comparison. Some comparative sizes for the more common birds are illustrated as silhouettes on the inner front cover.

For every species that breeds in Europe a **breeding distribution map** is also included. During the breeding season it allows an assessment of the likelihood of encountering a species in a certain area. Many of the species only breeding in the north appear, often commonly, in large areas of Europe south of the illustrated distribution during migration or as winter visitors. Additional information on the occurrence and distribution outside the breeding season are found in the last two sections of the species account.

The first line of the text block starts with the **scientific name** printed in italics. It gives an indication as to which genera the species belongs and to relationships between species and also aids international communication.

The letters **ID** start the section on the special **identification** features. Usually the general characteristics of shape, plumage colour and distribution are mentioned first. They are followed by details of different plumages should they be characteristic. Sometimes information on the flight pattern or typical behaviour is added at the end. Some of the pointer lines on the illustrations are explained here. Of course many more features exist but the ones mentioned in the text are certainly enough to enable identification and they should all be visible on the observed bird. Many more differentiating characteristics can be easily found by the reader when the detailed illustrations are studied and carefully compared.

The letter **V** starts the description of **voice**. For species whose song is heard in Europe, this is described first. After the semi-colon follow details of other calls that can often be heard all year round. For vagrants, or passage migrants, only the calls outside the breeding season are mentioned. Although some of the spellings of the voice descriptions seem incomprehensible they do give an imitation of the sound of a bird call when read out in a whispered tone. For the most common species of Britain and some special birds of continental Europe the calls are mentioned in more detail again in a **song and call identification key** at the end of the book (see pages 167-182).

The details of **habitat** follow the letter **H**. Should there be more than one listed, the first relates to the breeding location, the others to the migration and wintering sites. In principle many migrating birds can be found in almost all habitats during spring and autumn, at least for short periods. Additionally, for species which are not resident, the details of their range during the migration and winter periods are noted, whether it is in Europe or further afield.

The last section, marked **D**, deals with the **distribution**. The status is characterised by a letter code and relates almost exclusively to Britain, but in many cases this is also valid for Ireland and sometimes additional information is given for that country. The letters used stand for the following in terms of British status:

B fairly common to abundant breeding bird found in suitable habitat almost everywhere
b rare or locally restricted breeding bird only found in specific regions or habitats
M fairly common to abundant passage migrant
m uncommon to rare passage migrant in low numbers or restricted to specific regions
W fairly common to abundant winter visitor in suitable habitat
w uncommon to rare winter visitor, often only in specific regions
R resident, fairly common to abundant year-round in suitable habitat
r resident, restricted to certain regions or uncommon to rare
i introduced species
V vagrant, very rare and appears exceptionally and in small numbers in Britain originating from distant regions
- not recorded in Britain since 1950

For migratory birds the numbers **(1-12)** identify the **months** in which they are normally found in Britain, but there may be a difference of several weeks between the arrival and departure dates in the north of Scotland and the south of England. Also bear in mind that a few individuals may leave late, return early or even remain out of season.

For accurate bird identification it is always necessary to make sure that all features are correct. If many details do not fit with the observed bird it is likely that a mistake has been made and the observer should try to find a better matching description or illustration. However, it is frequently the case, for beginners and experts alike, that it is not possible to note all of the characteristics and make a positive identification before the bird disappears. Part of the appeal of birds is that they are agile, mobile and often very shy – they are not flowers, stars or shells that one can observe for as long as necessary. However, as it is better to give no name than an incorrect one, the answer to the question: "What is bird that?" will often be: "I don't know…."

SWANS, GEESE AND DUCKS

1 Mute Swan L 150 cm WS 220 cm

Cygnus olor **ID** Best known swan, found on many water bodies including park lakes and small streams. Large, white, bill dark orange with black lores and knob. When swimming wings often raised and neck S-shaped. From juv to 1s mainly grey-brown, bill paler and without knob. **V** Mainly quiet, sometimes soft snoring, in flight loud wing-throbbing. **H** All types of wetlands, also feeds in groups in meadows and fields. Resident in west of range, summer migrant in north-east. **D** BRMW, abundant.

2 Whooper Swan L 150 cm WS 230 cm

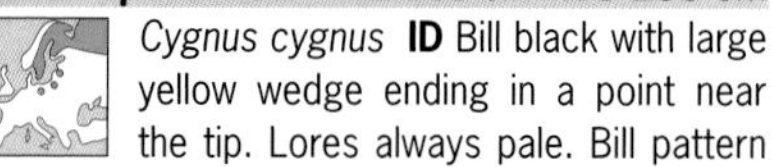

Cygnus cygnus **ID** Bill black with large yellow wedge ending in a point near the tip. Lores always pale. Bill pattern already visible in pale grey juv. Compared to 1, neck kept straight when swimming, tail shorter. **V** Nasal trumpeting *hoop-hoop-hoop* but wing-beats much quieter than 1. **H** Breeds on lakes in northern Europe, in winter meadows, fields and wetlands in central and western Europe and Black Sea. **D** mw 10-3, concentrates at favoured wintering grounds.

3 Bewick's Swan L 125 cm WS 195 cm

Cygnus bewickii **ID** Smallest swan, very similar to 2 but markedly smaller with smaller, rounded yellow bill spot, shorter neck, rounder head and goose-like body shape. In 1w dark parts of bill often reddish. **V** Calls higher-pitched than 2: *goog, hoo-hoo*. **H** Breeds on lakes on Russian arctic tundra, winters on wet meadows mainly in Britain and the Low Countries. **D** mw 10-3, more restricted in range than 2, scarce in Scotland.

4 Black Swan L 130 cm WS 180 cm

Cygnus atratus **ID** Large, black, bill red with pale band, in flight shows white primaries. **V** Musical trumpeting. **H** Ponds and lakes. An Australian species, introduced to various European countries. **D** ibr, scarce, escapes breed at several locations, apparently increasing.

5 Taiga Bean Goose L 75 cm WS 160 cm

Anser fabalis **ID** Legs orange, longer neck than 6, head profile wedge-shaped, bill heavier and more orange. **V** Deep *aahng*, high *ayayak*. **H** Breeds taiga, winters central Europe. **D** mw 11-3, very local.

6 Tundra Bean Goose L 75 cm WS 160 cm

Anser serrirostris **ID** Profile more like 7 than 5, rounded head, narrow orange band on bill. **V** Like 5. **H** Breeds on tundra east of Urals, winters coastal wetlands in north-west Europe. **D** mw 10-3, scarce, mainly on east coast.

7 Pink-footed Goose L 70 cm WS 150 cm

Anser brachyrhynchus **ID** Very similar to 6, but smaller, bill band and legs pink, silver-grey above (juv browner), greater coverts lighter than the dark rear flanks (in 6 both are dark). In flight more white on tail than 6, front of wings paler. **V** High-pitched *wink-wink*, vocal. **H** Breeds in Iceland and Spitsbergen, winters in coastal meadows in Britain and the Low Countries. **D** wm 10-4, predominantly in Norfolk, Lancashire and eastern Scotland.

8 Lesser White-fronted Goose L 60 cm

Anser erythropus **WS** 130 cm **ID** Similar to 9 but clearly smaller, in ad white reaches further up the forehead, yellow orbital ring (present in all ages), small pink bill and wing-tips reach beyond tip of tail. **V** Very high-pitched *keeyee*. **H** Very rare breeder in Lapland, in winter on meadows in south-east Europe. Birds from a Scandinavian reintroduction programme winter in The Netherlands. **D** V 11-3, rare but annual, often escapes from captivity.

9 White-fronted Goose L 70 cm WS 150 cm

Anser albifrons **ID** Medium-sized, compact goose, legs orange, bill pink without any black, ad with white forehead and black barring on belly. White forehead appears in 1w, nail on tip of bill still dark then. Darker and larger Greenland subspecies *flavirostris* which winters in Scotland and Ireland has orange bill. **V** Musical *kyoo-yoo*, also *kee-lik*. **H** Breeds in Greenland and on Siberian tundra westwards to the Kanin Peninsula, in winter on meadows and water bodies in north-west and south-east Europe. **D** MW 10-4.

10 Greylag Goose L 80 cm WS 165 cm

Anser anser **ID** Largest grey goose, pale grey, legs pink, bill orange with no black. In flight only goose with two-toned upper- and underwings, silvery grey at the front and blackish at the back. Bill pink in subspecies *rubrirostris* which occurs from Austria eastwards, and occasionally elsewhere as an introduction or escape. **V** Calls *gahng-ung-ung* like domestic goose, of which it is the ancestor. **H** Wetlands, meadows and fields. Migratory and feral populations in many places. Winters to south Europe. **D** MW 10-4, mainly in north and west; iBR, common and increasing.

1w
1
1w
1w
1w
3
2
4
5
6
1w
7
8
rubrirostris
flavirostris
1w
10
9

1 Bar-headed Goose **L** 75 cm **WS** 150 cm
Anser indicus **ID** Overall pale grey, white head with two black nape bands (absent in juv), back of neck has dark longitudinal stripe, legs and bill pale orange. **H** Breeds central Asia, winters northern India. Introductions and escapes frequent in Europe. **D** irb, escapee which occasionally breeds ferally and is often found with other geese.

2 Snow Goose **L** 70 cm **WS** 150 cm
Anser caerulescens **ID** White morph has all white plumage with black primaries, bill and legs pink; rarer blue morph dark with white head. **V** Harsh *kiah.* **H** North American species, occurs as vagrant or escape on wetlands and meadows. **D** V 10-3, rare but annual, mainly in north and west; ir, also a small feral population.

3 Red-breasted Goose **L** 55 cm **WS** 120 cm
Branta ruficollis **ID** Unmistakable small goose with rusty red on head, neck and breast, broad white stripe on flanks and small clearly patterned head on thick neck. **V** Harsh *kee-ak.* **H** Breeds on Arctic tundra along Taymyr, winters on farmland, marshes and meadows along west coast of Black Sea. **D** V 11-3, a few wild birds recorded each year, most often with Brent Geese. Also a frequent escapee.

4 Canada Goose **L** 95 cm **WS** 175 cm

Branta canadensis **ID** Large, brown, head and neck black with white chin-strap extending onto cheeks. **V** Shrill *ah-hong* and snoring *hrro.* **H** Introduced North American species. **D** BRi, abundant; V 11-3, some wild birds recorded each year.

5 Cackling Goose **L** 70 cm **WS** 125 cm
Branta hutchinsii (not illustrated) **ID** Miniature version of 4, head more rounded, body often darker. **H** Vagrant or escapee. **D** V 11-3.

6 Brent Goose **L** 60 cm **WS** 120 cm
Branta bernicla **ID** Grey body, black head and neck, white collar. Dark-bellied subspecies *(bernicla)* breeds Russia, Pale-bellied (*hrota*) breeds Greenland, Black Brant (*nigricans*) breeds east Siberia and America and has black belly and white neck- and flank-patches larger. **V** Subdued *rrott.* **H** Winters north-west Europe. **D** WM 9-5, coasts, *bernicla* in south and east, *hrota* in north and west; V, *nigricans*. a rare visitor to south and east coasts.

7 Barnacle Goose **L** 65 cm, **WS** 140 cm
Branta leucopsis **ID** Black neck with white face. Belly whitish, upperparts pale grey barred black. **V** Barking *kak.* **H** Wild birds breed in Greenland, Spitsbergen and Novaya Zemlya and winter on coasts in north-west Europe. Feral birds resident in many places. **D** MW 10-5, coasts in north and west; iR, increasing feral population in England.

8 Egyptian Goose **L** 70 cm **WS** 145 cm

Alopochen aegyptiaca **ID** Dirty grey- to cinnamon-brown, dark eye-patch in ad, bill and legs pink. **V** Hoarse hissing, also laughing *ankhaahaa.* **H** African species, introduced in north-west Europe where found on rivers, lakes and park ponds. **D** ibr, uncommon but increasing, England (mainly East Anglia).

9 Common Shelduck **L** 65 cm **WS** 120 cm

Tadorna tadorna **ID** Common on coasts. Bottle-green head, rufous breast band, red bill, ♂ with knob; juv plain whitish below, upperparts grey brown. **V** whistling mating calls and cackling *kack-ack-ah.* **H** Breeds mainly on coasts, often in rabbit burrows, occasionally also on rivers and lakes. **D** BRMW, especially common on intertidal mudflats, scarcer inland.

10 Ruddy Shelduck **L** 65 cm **WS** 120 cm

Tadorna ferruginea **ID** Whole body cinnamon-brown, head lighter, br ♂ with black ring around neck. **V** Honking *gag-ag* and dull *aauh.* **H** Scarce breeder on lakes and coasts of south-east Europe, increasing feral population in central Europe. **D** V 5-10, feral or wild; ir, escapes frequently seen.

11 White-headed Duck **L** 45 cm **WS** 65 cm
Oxyura leucocephala **ID** Body copper brown, tail raised steeply, in ♂ sides of head white and large blue bill, ♀ has dark bill with swelling at base and thick dark cheek-stripe. Dives frequently. **V** ♂ displays with grunting. **H** Fresh- and saltwater lakes in southern Europe, very rare. **D** V 9-4, extremely rare; ir, occasional escapes.

12 Ruddy Duck **L** 40 cm **WS** 58 cm

Oxyura jamaicensis **ID** Similar to 10, but smaller, bill more slender with concave upper mandible, white undertail coverts, ♂ has body red in summer, brown in winter, with black crown and nape, ♀ brown with narrower cheek-stripe on buff not white base. **V** ♂ produces drumming sound during display. **H** American species introduced to Europe, especially Britain. Considered by some to be a threat to 11 due to hybridization. **D** BR, fairly common in England.

juv
1
2
3
bernicla
1w
6
hrota
nigricans
4
8
7
♂
♀
9
juv
♀/non-br/juv
♂
10
12
♀
♂
11
♀
♂

1 Wood Duck **L** 47 cm **WS** 70 cm
Aix sponsa **ID** ♂ unmistakable, ♀ similar to 2, but darker grey-brown, white eye-patch larger, bill tip dark and underparts finely spotted. **H** North American species, breeds in tree hollows, introduced to various European countries. **D** ir, doubtful whether a self-sustaining population exists.

2 Mandarin Duck **L** 45 cm **WS** 70 cm
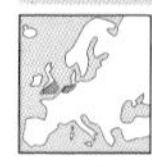
Aix galericulata **ID** ♂ very colourful with orange 'sails' formed by extended tertials and bushy orange 'beard', ♀ grey-brown, large spots on flanks, fine stripe behind white eye-ring. **H** Ponds and lakes with mature trees to provide nest-holes. East Asian species introduced into north-west Europe. **D** ibr, increasingly common in southern England.

3 Marbled Duck **L** 40 cm **WS** 66 cm

Marmaronetta angustirostris **ID** Small, plain, pale-brown feathers marbled with white, dark eye-mask, thin neck, rudimentary crest, secondaries paler, ♂ and ♀ identical; occasionally dives. **H** Densely vegetated ponds in southern Spain, very rare. **D** V, extremely rare; i, sometimes escapes from captivity.

4 Gadwall **L** 50 cm **WS** 90 cm
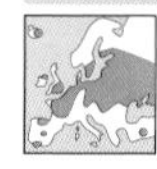
Anas strepera **ID** Speculum white, ♂ grey with blackish rump and bill, ♀ smaller than 7, white belly and parallel orange bill sides. **V** ♂ has wooden *errp*. **H** Lakes. Winters south and west Europe. **D** BRMW, common.

5 Eurasian Wigeon **L** 48 cm **WS** 80 cm

Anas penelope **ID** Medium-sized with round head and short neck, green-and-black speculum, blue-grey bill and white belly. ♂ has chestnut head, yellow forehead and large white patch on upperwing. Flocks often graze on land. **V** ♂ whistles *wee-oo*. **H** Breeds north Europe, winters coasts, lakes and floods from Britain south. **D** bMW, common, often in large flocks.

6 American Wigeon **L** 50 cm **WS** 82 cm
Anas americana **ID** Head of ♂ marbled grey with green mask and cream forehead, body pinkish, ♀ best distinguished from 5 through pure white instead of pale grey axillaries. **H** Vagrant from North America, sometimes found in flocks of 5. **D** V 10-5, very rare, also escapees.

7 Mallard **L** 56 cm **WS** 95 cm
Anas platyrhynchos **ID** Most common, best known and largest dabbling duck. Both sexes have blue speculum. Bottle-green head of ♂ separated from brown breast by white collar, body mainly silver-grey. ♀ brown with darker mottling, bill with irregular orange-coloured side spots, clear head pattern with dark crown, pale supercilium and dark eye-stripe and brownish belly. ♂ in eclipse is similar to ♀ but has yellow bill. Colour variants (for example, all white or plain brown body with white breast) occur due to artificially bred domestic forms. **V** ♂ displays *piu* and softly calls *rhaab*, ♀ calls declining *quack-quack-quack-ack*. **H** All types of wetlands. **D** BRMW, abundant.

8 Shoveler **L** 50 cm **WS** 78 cm

Anas clypeata **ID** Appears front-heavy due to short neck and long bill broadened at tip like a spoon. Speculum green, upperwing coverts blue-grey. ♂ unmistakable green head, white breast and rufous flanks, ♀ recognized by body and bill shape. **V** ♂ has nasal *wek-ek*. **H** Breeds on shallow waters rich in nutrients. During migration and winter also on deeper lakes. Summer migrant in east of range, winters south and west Europe. **D** BRMW, common.

9 Pintail **L** ♂ 70 cm, ♀ 55 cm **WS** 90 cm

Anas acuta **ID** Elegant with smallish head on long, slender neck plus long tail. Speculum dark brown-green with broad white trailing edge, bill blue-grey. ♂ has brown-and-white head pattern. ♀ more slender than 7, tail clearly pointed, head uniform. **V** ♂ has soft *kreeh*. **H** Breeds mainly on shallow waters in north-east Europe, winters on floodplains and lakes in the south and west. **D** bMW, scarce breeder, widespread and fairly common in winter, especially on coasts.

10 Garganey **L** 40 cm **WS** 62 cm

Anas querquedula **ID** Small, upperwing coverts grey. ♂ white supercilium, grey flanks, upper forewings chalky-grey. ♀ and juv from 11 by pale spot adjoining grey bill, dark centres to flank feathers, lack of pale line below tail. **V** ♂ has burping *krrrrk*. **H** Lakes, floods, meadows, winters Africa. **D** bm 3-9, uncommon.

11 Common Teal **L** 35 cm **WS** 60 cm

Anas crecca **ID** Very small, common duck with green speculum. ♂ has unmistakable head pattern and yellow patch with black border on each side of vent. ♀ and juv differ from 10 by plainer ear coverts, orange on bill and as outlined above. **V** ♂ has bright *krick* . **H** All types of wetlands. **D** BRMW, common, very common in winter.

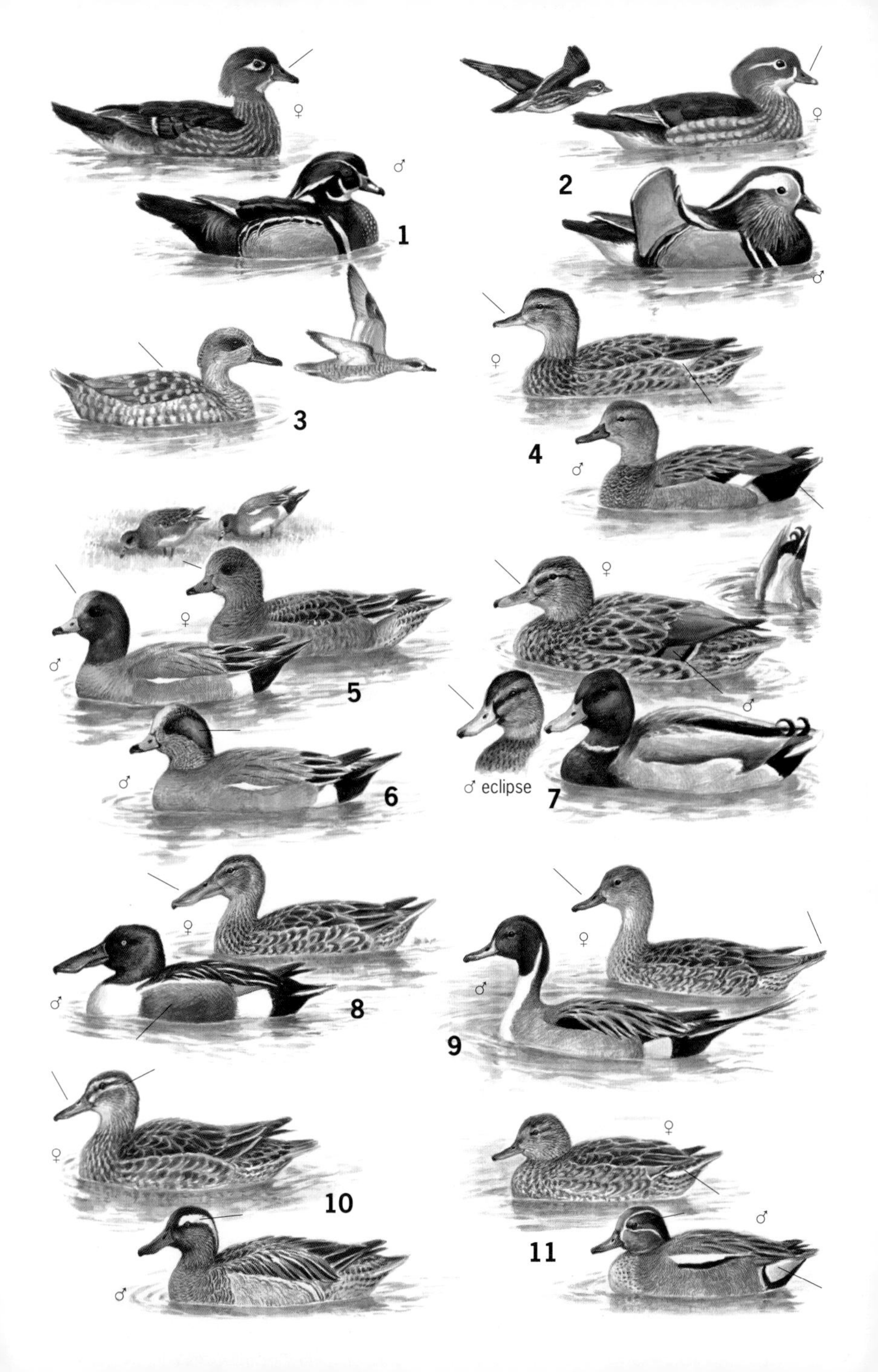
♀
♂
1
♀
2
♂
3
♀
4
♂
♀
5
♂
6
♂
♀
♂
♂ eclipse
7
♀
♂
8
♀
♂
9
♀
10
♂
♀
11
♂

1 Red-crested Pochard **L** 55 cm **WS** 85 cm

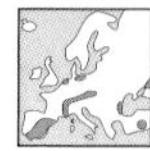

Netta rufina **ID** Large with round head and broad white wing-bars. ♂ has black breast and neck, steep forehead, orange head, red bill and white flanks. ♀ brown body with dark crown, pale cheeks and grey bill with pink edges and tip. Dives and dabbles to feed on vegetation. **V** ♂ calls rarely, sneezing *gheck*. **H** Well vegetated wetlands. **D** mw, rare; irb, increasing feral population in south England.

2 Pochard **L** 45 cm **WS** 78 cm

Aythya ferina **ID** Has distinctive head profile with long, concave grey bill blending into flat forehead, wing-bar pale grey. In ♂ head dark red, body mainly grey, ♀ more uniform grey-brown (browner in br). **V** Mostly quiet, ♂ whistles thinly *pee-pee*. **H** Breeds on ponds and lakes, in winter on water bodies of all types. Summer migrant in north and east Europe, winters in south and west. **D** BRMW, common.

3 Tufted Duck **L** 43 cm **WS** 70 cm

Aythya fuligula **ID** Most common diving duck, compact, tuft of plumes on back of head, white wing-bar. Black-and-white ♂ unmistakable, ♀ rather uniform dark brown with shorter tuft, sometimes with white undertail coverts (compare with 4) or much white at base of bill (compare with 5). **V** ♂ displays with trembling *piyibib* , ♀ warns with croaking *kurr*. **H** Wetlands of all types. Winters south to Mediterranean. **D** BRMW, very common.

4 Ferruginous Duck **L** 40 cm **WS** 65 cm

Aythya nyroca **ID** Overall mahogany-brown with white undertail coverts, white wing-bar very striking. ♂ has white iris while ♀ and juv's are dark. Duller chestnut-brown ♀ similar to some ♀ of 3, but no crest and dark eye. **H** Well vegetated ponds in southern and eastern Europe. **D** V 10-4, mainly in southern England. Escaped birds sometimes occur.

5 Scaup **L** 46 cm **WS** 78 cm

Aythya marila **ID** Medium-sized with rounded head without crest, wing-bar broad white. ♂ black and white with grey back, ♀ similar to 3, but a lot of white at base of bill, upperparts and flanks greyish in winter, brownish in summer. Juv brown with buff face. Hybrids between 2 and 3 often similar, but are smaller with a hint of a crest. **H** Breeds on coasts and lakes in northern Europe, winters mainly in large flocks on coasts south to France, Adriatic and Black Sea. **D** MW 10-4, mainly along coasts where locally common.

6 Ring-necked Duck **L** 41 cm **WS** 68 cm

Aythya collaris **ID** Like 3 but back of head pointed rather than tufted, bill has white band near tip and wing-bar grey. ♂ has white band at base of bill and white 'spur' in front of grey flanks. ♀ told by shape, diffuse white at bill base, white line around and behind eye and white band on bill. **H** American vagrant to west Europe in winter, often with other diving ducks. **D** V 10-4, rare but annual.

7 Common Eider **L** 60 cm **WS** 100 cm

Somateria mollissima **ID** The most common seaduck, very large with wedge-shaped head profile. ♂ unmistakable, immature ♂ and non-br ♂ can appear almost black or chequered black and white. ♀ has brown plumage strikingly barred and bill paler at tip. **V** ♂ displays *a-hooa*, ♀ calls stuttering *kokokok*. **H** Sea coasts. **D** BRMW, fairly common, breeds in north, winters around coasts, very rare inland.

8 King Eider **L** 58 cm **WS** 90 cm

Somateria spectabilis **ID** Smaller than 7, ♂ with orange and red bill. ♀ similar to 7, but plumage scaled rather than barred, feathers around bill stop well above nostril, gape line drawn up to give 'smiling' appearance, nail dark. **H** Breeds on arctic tundra, winters at sea. Mainly Norway and Iceland. **D** V, very rare, mostly Scotland.

9 Steller's Eider **L** 45 cm **WS** 75 cm

Polysticta stelleri **ID** ♂ has pale orange breast and flanks and white head with dark markings. ♀ small and dark with violet speculum bordered by white edges and long tertials. Has more rectangular head than other eiders with grey, unfeathered bill that appears to be glued on. **H** Breeds arctic tundra, winters off rocky coasts in the Baltic and north Norway. **D** V, extremely rare.

10 Long-tailed Duck **L** ♂ 58 cm, ♀ 40 cm

Clangula hyemalis **WS** 75 cm **ID** Small, round head and short bill, belly always white and breast dark, plumage otherwise very varied, complicated moulting and three different plumages during the year. ♂ with pink bill band (appears in 1w) and long tail streamers. ♀ recognizable by head pattern. **V** Very vocal, ♂ displays from winter with melancholy *a-ooh-lee*. **H** Breeds mainly on north European tundra, winters at sea south to Britain and Ireland. **D** mw 10-4, mainly coastal and more common in north.

♂ eclipse
♂
1
♀
♂
2
♀
♂
♂
hybrid 2 x 3
♂
4
3
♀
♀
♂
♂
5
6
♀
♀
♂
7 ♀
♀
8 ♀
8
♀
♂
♂ eclipse
7
♂
9
♀
♀ br
♂ non-br
♀ non-br
10
juv
♂ br

1 Common Scoter L 50 cm **WS** 80 cm

Melanitta nigra **ID** A dark seaduck with few markings and uniform dark wings. ♂ black except for yellow patch on top of bill. ♀ dark brown with paler grey-brown cheeks (compare with ♀ Red-crested Pochard). Imm has pale belly. **V** ♂ gives whistling *pheeuu* during display, also in flight. **H** Breeds north-east Europe, winters Baltic, North Sea and Atlantic. **D** bMW, rare breeder in Scotland but fairly common around coasts most of the year, rare inland.

2 Surf Scoter L 52 cm **WS** 85 cm

Melanitta perspicillata **ID** Similar to 1 with uniform dark wings, but larger and red (not black) legs. ♂ with unique pattern on bill, head and neck. Head pattern of ♀ similar to 3, but bill bigger and deeper, no white in wings and often has pale patch on nape. **H** Rare visitor to coasts of north-west Europe from North America, most often found in flocks with 1 or 3. **D** V, very rare, most often Scottish coasts.

3 Velvet Scoter L 55 cm **WS** 88 cm

Melanitta fusca **ID** Dark-bodied but larger than 1 and with white speculum on wings that is often visible when swimming. ♂ has yellow on sides of bill and white patch below eye. ♀ has two light patches on head (in front of and behind eye). **H** Breeds Scandinavia, winters close to coasts in the Baltic, North Sea and Atlantic. **D** mw 10-4, mainly along coasts, rare inland.

4 Harlequin Duck L 42 cm **WS** 65 cm

Histrionicus histrionicus **ID** Small with round head, short bill and wedge-shaped tail, wings dark, dives in strong surf. ♂ has unmistakable red, white and blue pattern which from a distance looks dark with white stripes. ♀ dusky brown with pale patches on head (compare with larger and longer-billed ♀ of 3). **H** In Europe only in Iceland where rather sedentary, otherwise in North America and north-east Asia along fast-flowing rocky rivers, in winter on rocky shores. **D** V, extremely rare.

5 Common Goldeneye L 45 cm **WS** 70 cm

Bucephala clangula **ID** Compact duck with triangular head on short neck, in flight much white on secondaries. Most often in small flocks, stays under water longer than other diving ducks. ♂ has breast and flanks white, head black with green sheen and circular white spot on lores. ♀ head brown, white collar, grey body. **V** In flight ♂ makes whistling noise with wings; ♂ displays in winter and spring by throwing head back and giving a sneezing *bee-berch*. **H** Breeds in tree hollows near water, winters lakes, rivers and sea west to Britain and south to Mediterranean. **D** bMW, breeds locally in Scotland, widespread and common in winter.

6 Barrow's Goldeneye L 47 cm **WS** 72 cm

Bucephala islandica **ID** Replaces 5 in Iceland; very similar but larger, head more elongated and forehead even steeper. ♂ has large white crescent in front of eye, purple-iridescence on black head and more black on upperparts (beware of imm ♂ of 5 which often share these characters). ♀ similar to 5 but different head shape. **V** ♂ displays with stuttering *wa-wa-wa*. **H** In Europe only on rivers and lakes in Iceland, where resident. Also in North America. **D** V, extremely rare.

7 Smew L 42 cm **WS** 60 cm

Mergellus albellus **ID** Smallest sawbill, bill rather short; in flight white secondary coverts on upperwing. ♂ white with black mask and grey flanks and tail. ♀ and imm grey with a red-brown cap and white throat and cheeks. **H** Breeds in tree hollows by lakes in taiga, winters on rivers, lakes and sea south to England and the Black Sea. **D** w 11-3, uncommon.

8 Hooded Merganser L 46 cm **WS** 68 cm

Lophodytes cucullatus **ID** Larger than 7 with slender bill and erectile crest. ♂ unmistakable, ♀ smaller than 9 with a browner body, shorter bill, longer crest, long tail and white lines on tertials. **H** North American species, but often escapes from collections in Europe. **D** V, extremely rare, escapes frequent.

9 Red-breasted Merganser L 55 cm **WS** 80 cm

Mergus serrator **ID** More slender and dark than 10. ♂ with rufous breast, shaggy crest, white collar, grey flanks. ♀ grey-brown, reddish head grades into body colour unlike 10, pale throat poorly defined. **H** Breeds lakes and coasts, winters south to Black Sea. **D** BRMW, widespread around coasts in winter.

10 Goosander L 62 cm **WS** 88 cm

Mergus merganser **ID** Largest sawbill, with a slender, red, hooked bill. ♂ mainly pinkish-white with green head. ♀ grey with brown head, bushy crest and clear-cut white throat. **V** ♂ displays with quacking *orr*. **H** Lakes, rivers, sea. **D** BRMW, resident in north, winter visitor in south. Much commoner inland than 9.

♂
♀
1
♂
♀
2
♂
♀
3
♂
♀
4
♂
♀
5
♂
♀
6
♂
♀
7
♂
♀
8
♂
♀
9
♂
♀
10

♂ illustrated above, ♀ below
Mallard
Gadwall
Pintail
Shoveler
Eurasian Wigeon
Garganey
Common Teal
Red-crested Pochard
Pochard
Ferruginous Duck
Tufted Duck
Ring-necked Duck
Scaup

♂ illustrated above, ♀ below
Common Goldeneye
Long-tailed Duck
King Eider
Common Eider
Harlequin Duck
Steller's Eider
Velvet Scoter
Common Scoter
Surf Scoter
Goosander
Red-breasted Merganser
Smew

GROUSE, PARTRIDGES AND PHEASANT

1 Red/Willow Grouse L 38 cm WS 60 cm

Lagopus lagopus **ID** In Britain and Ireland the Red Grouse (subspecies *scotica*) is uniform red-brown all year. From Norway east Willow Grouse (subspecies *lagopus*) has wings and belly white all year, body red brown in summer and all white in winter. **V** ♂ displays *kow-kow kekeke-kahog*, call *go-back go-back*. **H** Moors, taiga. **D** BR, heather moors.

2 Ptarmigan L 34 cm WS 56 cm

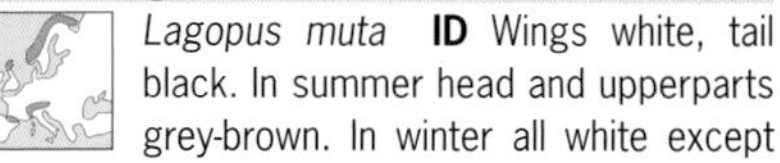

Lagopus muta **ID** Wings white, tail black. In summer head and upperparts grey-brown. In winter all white except for black tail tip, but ♂ has black lores (absent in 1, otherwise difficult to differentiate). **V** ♂ display call *arr ka-ka-kaka*; burping call *errr errrr*. **H** Rocky mountains above the tree line, although in north also on tundra. **D** br, only on high mountains in Scotland.

3 Black Grouse L ♂ 52 cm, ♀ 42 cm WS 75 cm

Tetrao tetrix **ID** ♂ all black with a lyre-shaped tail and white undertail coverts and wing-bar. ♀ barred brown and black all over with white wing-bar visible in flight. **V** ♂ leks with clucking and hissing sounds. **H** Moors, heaths, mountains at the edge of the tree line. **D** br, much declined in woodlands and moors in northern England and Scotland, now very rare in north Wales.

4 Capercaillie L ♂ 85 cm, ♀ 60 cm

Tetrao urogallus **WS** 90-120 cm **ID** Huge gamebird. ♂ dark with metallic blue-green sheen on the head and underparts and long, rounded tail which is fanned out during lek display; wings uniform brown. ♀ grey-brown with cryptic markings, but breast uniform rusty orange; no broad wing-bar, tail rounded. **V** ♂ displays with increasingly fast rattling sounds followed by a *plop* and hissing. **H** Old coniferous forests in mountains. **D** br, rare in pine forests in Scottish Highlands.

5 Hazel Grouse L 36 cm WS 50 cm

Tetrastes bonasia **ID** Small, grey-brown grouse with a short crest and grey tail with black terminal band. ♂ has black throat, both sexes have white border to throat. **V** Very high-pitched whistle *zuiiii-tiiti*, similar to Goldcrest; wings make a whirring sound in flight. **H** Conifer and mixed forests, often near water and in mountains. **D** -.

6 Rock Partridge L 35 cm WS 50 cm

Alectoris graeca **ID** Brown-grey with black and white barring on flanks, legs and bill red. Pure white throat distinguishes it from 7. **V** Harsh, rolling *tchertsivit-tchertsivit* and *gack-gack*, in flight *pitchii*. **H** Rocky slopes in Alps, Balkans and Italy. **D** -.

7 Chukar L 34 cm WS 50 cm

Alectoris chukar **ID** Like 6, but white supercilium does not reach forehead, no black at base of nostril, throat buff, brown behind eye. **V** Rhythmic *ga gaga-tchukar-tchukarr…* **H** Mountains in eastern Greece, locally introduced elsewhere, including Alps. **D** - (although was formerly released for hunting).

8 Red-legged Partridge L 34 cm WS 48 cm

Alectoris rufa **ID** Similar to 6 and 7, but white throat-patch smaller, black spotted collar and brown nape. Tail rufous in flight. **V** Displays with hoarse *kyu kii tcherr kutcherrt-sherr kyutcherrr…* . **H** Open regions, introduced to Britain. **D** iBR, common in lowlands.

9 Barbary Partridge L 34 cm WS 47 cm

Alectoris barbara **ID** Has red-brown crown, broad pale supercilium and pale-grey throat bordered by red-brown neck-band. **V** Long series of shrill sounds *kret kret kret kretchaw kret…* **H** In Europe only on Sardinia and Gibraltar. **D** -.

10 Grey Partridge L 30 cm WS 45 cm

Perdix perdix **ID** Orange face, grey breast, black belly patch and rusty barring on flanks; tail orange in flight. Juv browner overall. **V** ♂ display call *kirr-eck*. **H** Rough fields, meadows, farmland. **D** BR, much declined.

11 Quail L 18 cm WS 35 cm

Coturnix coturnix **ID** Smallest and only migrant gamebird, pale yellow-brown, whitish lines above, no rufous on tail; mainly in dense vegetation and only heard. **V** Characteristic *whip whip-whip*, especially at night. **H** Meadows, fields, fallow fields. **D** bm 5-10, scarce.

12 Pheasant L ♂ 85 cm, ♀ 60 cm

Phasianus colchicus **WS** 80 cm **ID** ♂ has chestnut body, green head, red face and often also a white collar. ♀ paler brown and heavily spotted with dark markings above and below and a long tail. **V** Croaking *koo-krock*, often followed by whirring wing-beat. **H** Fields and woods. Widely introduced Asian species. **D** iBR, abundant.

scotica
1
2
♀
♂
3
4
5
6
7
8
9
10
11
12
juv

GREBES

1 Little Grebe L 26 cm

Tachybaptus ruficollis **ID** Smallest grebe, rounded body, whitish vent and short bill with a pale gape. In br blackish with neck and rear flanks chestnut-brown and gape yellow; in non-br brownish above and warm buff below. **V** Pairs display in duet with trembling thrill; call *bii-biib*. **H** Densely vegetated wetlands, in winter also rivers. **D** BR, common.

2 Great Crested Grebe L 50 cm

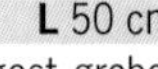

Podiceps cristatus **ID** Largest grebe, elegant with white neck and pink bill, in flight appears very slender with a lot of white on narrow wings. In br has crest, in non-br only a black crown with border above eye. Juv has dark stripes on head. Pairs perform remarkable courtship display. **V** Rough *korrr* and cackling *ak-ak-ak*, given day or night. **H** Wetlands of all types, in winter also at sea. **D** BRMW, common.

3 Red-necked Grebe L 45 cm

Podiceps grisegena **ID** Smaller, more compact than 2 with shorter neck and black bill with yellow base. Br has rufous neck, white cheeks and black cap below eye. Similar in non-br but neck greyish. Neck also quite red in juv, which has black stripes on cheeks. **V** Displays with whinnying *uaah-ek*. **H** Breeds on reed-fringed inland lakes in north-east Europe, winters on coasts of North Sea, Black Sea and Adriatic. **D** mw, uncommon, mainly on coasts.

4 Slavonian Grebe L 35 cm

Podiceps auritus **ID** Br has black head, erect yellow ear tufts and red neck (which may appear dark from a distance). In non-br similar to 5, but with clear-cut divide running through eye between white patches on side of head and black crown, bill straight, crown flat, back of head square. **V** Displays with a long trill; calls *hyarr*. **H** Breeds on reed-fringed ponds in north-east Europe, winters in north-west and south-east Europe. **D** mw 10-4, uncommon, mainly coastal; b, locally in Scotland.

5 Black-necked Grebe L 32 cm

Podiceps nigricollis **ID** Br has yellow ear-tufts and black neck. In non-br black crown extends onto cheeks, thin bill tilted upwards, forehead steep. **V** Calls *ir-eed*. **H** Breeds in colonies on shallow lakes, winters on lakes and coasts south to Mediterranean. **D** bmw, scarce breeder, uncommon in winter.

DIVERS

6 Red-throated Diver L 60 cm

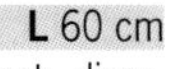

Gavia stellata **ID** Smallest diver, slender bill upturned and when swimming head mostly tilted upwards, appears generally pale. In br head and neck grey, throat brick-red. In non-br white on face extends above eye, grey-brown upperparts finely spotted with white. Juv and 1w similar to non-br but throat variably dusky, upperparts spotted buff. **V** Display calls *orr-ooh, arrooh*; in flight calls goose-like *ak ak*. **H** Breeds on lakes in northern Europe, winters on coasts and large inland lakes. **D** B, Scotland; MW 9-5, common and widespread around coasts in winter.

7 Black-throated Diver L 70 cm

Gavia arctica **ID** Very elegant, medium-sized diver, keeps head and straight bill horizontal when swimming. In br chin and throat black, hind-neck velvet grey and mantle black with white bars and spots. In non-br upperparts grey-black, white patch at rear of flanks characteristic, eye completely within dark crown, sharp line between white front and black back of neck. Juv and 1w similar, but browner and upperparts show clear bands of pale feather fringes. **V** Displays with loud moaning *clow-ooy clow clowy*. **H** Breeds on lakes in north Europe, winters at sea, sometimes on lakes and reservoirs. **D** b, north Scotland; mw 10-4, uncommon, mainly coastal.

8 Great Northern Diver L 80 cm

Gavia immer **ID** Larger than 7, stouter bill held horizontally, forehead steeper. In br black with white neck-bands and chequering on mantle. Non-br has pale eye-ring, grey bill black on top and at tip, dark half collar. Juv browner with scaled upperparts. **V** Displays with wailing call. **H** In Europe breeds Iceland (also in North America); winters north Atlantic and North Sea, rarely inland. **D** mw 10-5, uncommon, coasts and reservoirs, some summer in far north.

9 White-billed Diver L 85 cm

Gavia adamsii **ID** Similar to 8, but heavy and completely ivory bill upturned, head tilted upwards and pronounced swelling on forehead. Non-br paler than 8, juv very pale brown with larger white patches on sides of head and often a brown cheek-spot. **H** Breeds Siberia, winters Norway and Baltic. **D** m 3-5, tiny spring passage on Western Isles; V, very rare elsewhere.

non-br
br
1
juv
non-br
br
3
non-br
br
juv
2
non-br
br
4
non-br
br
5
1w
non-br
br
6
1w
non-br
br
7
1w
non-br
br
8
1w
non-br
br
9

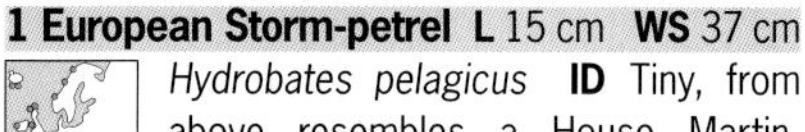

STORM-PETRELS

1 European Storm-petrel L 15 cm **WS** 37 cm

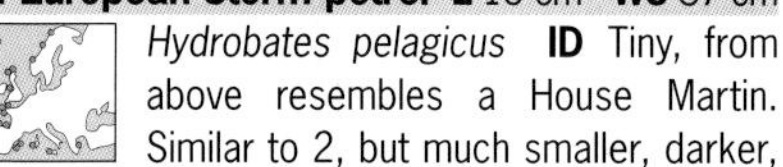

Hydrobates pelagicus **ID** Tiny, from above resembles a House Martin. Similar to 2, but much smaller, darker, rounder wings, noticeable white bar on underwing, white rump not divided, tail square and flapping flight without gliding. **V** Purring and grunting calls at night at nest sites. **H** Nests in burrow, otherwise at sea. **D** bm, breeds islands off north and west coasts, otherwise pelagic.

2 Leach's Storm-petrel L 21 cm **WS** 47 cm

Oceanodroma leucorhoa **ID** Has pale band on upperwing, white rump sometimes divided by black line, forked tail; pointed wings, flight jerky with gliding phases. Slower wing-beats than 1. **H** Breeds north-west Europe, otherwise pelagic. **D** bm, islands off north Scotland, passes western coasts mainly 10-11.

3 Madeiran Storm-petrel L 20 cm **WS** 45 cm

Oceanodroma castro **ID** Similar to 2, but white rump more extensive on sides, no clear band on upper- or underwings, tail slightly forked, bill thicker. Flight like 2 with periods of gliding. **H** In Europe breeds only off Portugal. **D** V, extremely rare.

FULMAR AND SHEARWATERS

4 Fulmar L 45 cm **WS** 105 cm

Fulmarus glacialis **ID** Resembles gull due to size and colour, but grey tail and wings lack black tips and with pale 'window', neck thick-set and bill short and heavy. Glides on stiff wings through wave troughs. **V** Cackles at breeding site. **H** Breeds on coastal cliffs in north-west Europe, otherwise at sea. **D** BRMW, common.

5 Great Shearwater L 48 cm **WS** 110 cm

Puffinus gravis **ID** Large, brown-grey, neat black cap, narrow white rump, underparts whitish with faint darker belly patch, obvious diagonal band on underwing. **H** Breeds in austral summer on south Atlantic islands, migrants pass through north Atlantic in late summer. **D** m 7-9, rare, most frequent off south-west headlands.

6 Sooty Shearwater L 45 cm **WS** 100 cm

Puffinus griseus **ID** Uniform dark-brown above and below, broken only by paler whitish panels on underwing. Glides through wave troughs on slender pointed wings. Could be confused with dark-morph skua. **H** Breeds in southern hemisphere during austral summer, passes through north Atlantic in late summer. **D** m 8-11, uncommon, gales bring birds closer to land.

7 Cory's Shearwater L 50 cm **WS** 115 cm

Calonectris diomedea **ID** Large, pale sepia-brown above, underparts whitish and lack markings, yellow bill with dark tip. Slow wing-beats alternate with gliding phases; only shearwater to circle at height. **H** Breeds on islands in the Mediterranean, otherwise at sea. **D** m 7-9, rare, most frequent off south-west headlands.

8 Manx Shearwater L 32 cm **WS** 80 cm

Puffinus puffinus **ID** Contrasting white below and black above. In flight tilts from one wing-tip to the other above wave-crests, alternating periods of rapid wing-beats with gliding. Formerly 'lumped' with 9 and 10 as one species. **V** Howling calls when visiting colonies at night. **H** Breeds north-west Europe, mainly on islands off Britain. Nests in ground burrows, otherwise pelagic; commonest north Atlantic shearwater. **D** BM 3-10, strictly coastal, common in west, uncommon in east.

9 Balearic Shearwater L 36 cm **WS** 85 cm

Puffinus mauretanicus **ID** Similar to 8, but larger, with slight 'pot belly', toes protrude beyond tail tip. Little contrast between brown upperparts and dirty brownish-white underparts with darker undertail coverts and axillaries. Compare also with 7 and 10. **H** Breeds on Balearic Islands, winters Atlantic and west Mediterranean. **D** m 6-9, uncommon, coastal headlands, particularly in south-west.

10 Yelkouan Shearwater L 32 cm **WS** 80 cm

Puffinus yelkouan **ID** Size and colour like 8, but upperparts somewhat browner, undertail coverts and axillaries dark, therefore less contrast between upperparts and underparts; toes protrude slightly beyond tail tip. **H** Breeds on islands and rocky coasts in eastern Mediterranean, outside breeding season also on Black Sea. **D** -.

11 Macaronesian Shearwater L 28 cm

Puffinus baroli **WS** 60 cm **ID** Recent 'split' from Little Shearwater of south Atlantic. Similar to 8 but clearly smaller, wings shorter and less pointed and head rounder with shorter bill. White cheeks extend above dark eye, whitish tips to greater coverts. **H** Breeds on Canaries, Madeira and Azores, wanders north to Biscay. **D** V, very rare.

1
2
3
4
5
6
7
8
9
10
11

FLAMINGOS

1 Greater Flamingo L 135 cm **WS** 155 cm

Phoenicopterus roseus **ID** Large, elegant, neck and legs very long and sag during flight when black flight feathers obvious. Ad pale pink with reddish legs and deep, decurved pink bill with black tip. Juv grey-brown. **V** Call goose-like *gaang-ang*. **H** Breeds on lagoons in south-west Europe and Turkey, winters Mediterranean. **D** (V), doubtful that wild birds have reached Britain; i, occasional escapes seen.

2 Chilean Flamingo L 105 cm **WS** 135 cm

Phoenicopterus chilensis **ID** Smaller than 1, more black on bill-tip, legs greyish with red joints and toes. **H** South American species, often escapes from zoos and occasional feral breeders in central Europe. **D** i, escapes occasionally recorded.

3 Lesser Flamingo L 85 cm **WS** 100 cm

Phoenicopterus minor **ID** Much smaller than 1, brighter pink, legs red and bill uniform dark pink, looks almost black from distance. **H** An African species. Recent breeders in Spain may be wild. Escapes recorded elsewhere in Europe. **D** -.

PELICANS

4 White Pelican L 160 cm **WS** 300 cm

Pelecanus onocrotalus **ID** Swan-sized, mainly white with short legs and large bill with throat sac. Often swimming and fishing in flocks on lakes or the sea. Ad has white wing coverts contrasting with black primaries and secondaries, pinkish sheen on body feathers, pink legs, yellow throat sac, drooping crest and large pink patch of bare skin around dark eye. Juv has dark-brown upperparts and yellow throat sac. **H** Rare summer visitor to lakes and coasts in south-east Europe. Winters in Africa. **D** (V), doubtful if wild birds ever recorded; i, occasional escapes noted.

5 Dalmatian Pelican L 170 cm

Pelecanus crispus **WS** 320 cm **ID** Similar to 4, but overall more greyish without pink tinge, legs grey, eye pale, throat sac red-orange, crest feathers curly, underwings uniform pale grey with no contrast. Juv has upperparts lighter sandy brown than 4 and with minimal bare skin around eye. **H** Breeds on inland lakes and coasts of south-east Europe, rarer than 4. **D** -.

6 Pink-backed Pelican L 130 cm **WS** 240 cm

Pelecanus rufescens **ID** Similar to 5 but much smaller and with greyish straggly feathers tinged pinkish in places, legs flesh-coloured, dark spot between eye and bill, throat sac pale orange and grooved crossways rather than lengthways. **H** African species kept in captivity across Europe. All records are escapes. **D** -.

GANNET

7 Gannet L 95 cm **WS** 175 cm

Morus bassanus **ID** Large cigar-shaped body, dagger-shaped bill, wedge-shaped tail and long, pointed wings, hunts by diving steeply. Ad white with black primaries and primary coverts; juv brown, birds attain more white over a period of 5 years. **H** Breeding colonies on rocky coasts in north Atlantic, otherwise at sea. **D** BRMW, breeds in north and west, widespread around coasts in migration and winter.

CORMORANTS

8 Cormorant L 90 cm **WS** 145 cm

Phalacrocorax carbo **ID** Large, dark diving bird with long hooked bill blending into flat forehead, swims with raised head, often stands with wings spread wide open. Br black with white patches on throat and thighs. Juv brown with paler whitish underparts. Subspecies *carbo* breeds on rocky coasts, subspecies *sinensis* breeds inland. *Sinensis* has straighter rear edge to bare face patch. **V** Strange growling and gutteral clucking sounds. **H** Coasts and inland waters. **D** BRMW, common.

9 Shag L 75 cm **WS** 100 cm

Phalacrocorax aristotelis **ID** Smaller than 8, bill evenly slender and thick yellow gape reaches beyond eye, forehead steeper. In br emerald sheen and curl of feathers on forehead. Imm brown but wing feathers tipped paler and pale throat stands out from darker underparts (although Mediterranean subspecies *desmarestii* has underparts whitish). **H** Rocky coasts, rare inland. **D** BRMW, common on coasts, breeds north and west, more widespread in winter.

10 Pygmy Cormorant L 50 cm **WS** 85 cm

Phalacrocorax pygmeus **ID** Much smaller than 8 with relatively long tail, small head and short 'snub-nosed' bill. Brownish-black with white speckles and brown head in br, white throat in non-br. Juv paler. **H** Vegetated lakes in south-east Europe, rare. **D** -.

juv
1
2
3
4
juv
br
br
juv
5
7
juv
6
br
br
br
sinensis
1s
carbo
non-br
8
non-br
8 non-br
9 non-br
10 non-br
non-br
non-br
br
1w
1w
desmarestii
9
10
br
juv

IBISES AND SPOONBILL

1 Glossy Ibis L 60 cm WS 90 cm

Plegadis falcinellus **ID** A rather dark, long-legged bird with a Mallard-sized body and a long decurved bill. Br mahogany with metallic green sheen on wings and white markings at base of bill. Non-br and juv duller dark brown with head and neck speckled white. Like all ibises flies with neck outstretched, flocks often keep in line formation. **V** In breeding colony calls growling, croaking *kraw*. **H** Wetlands in south Europe, especially in the south-east. **D** V, rare but with occasional long-stayers.

2 Spoonbill L 85 cm WS 125 cm

Platalea leucorodia **ID** Large and white with long, flat bill broadened at tip. Br has buff breast-band and throat and black bill tipped yellow. In juv bill pinkish-grey and wing-tips black (these remain black in imm). Feeds by sieving water with side-to-side head movement. **H** Breeds in large reedbeds around shallow wetlands in south Europe and The Netherlands. Winters west Europe and Africa. **D** mw, small numbers on south and east coasts, mostly in summer but some in winter.

3 Northern Bald Ibis (Waldrapp) L 75 cm

Geronticus eremita **WS** 130 cm **ID** As dark as 1, but larger and legs shorter and red. Red decurved bill the same colour as naked facial skin. Ad has shaggy ruff and metallic sheen to body plumage. **H** Breeds in colonies on cliffs in Morocco and Syria, almost extinct. Once bred central and south Europe, where birds from reintroduction projects in Spain and Austria may again be seen. **D** -.

4 Sacred Ibis L 70 cm WS 120 cm

Threskiornis aethiopicus **ID** Large, unmistakable black-and-white bird. The thick, decurved bill is black, as are head and hanging tertials. Narrow black trailing edge to underwings (compare to black wing-tips in imm Spoonbill). **H** African species that frequents fields and wetlands, often escapes from aviaries and has a large feral population in the south and west of France. **D** i, occasional escapes.

HERONS, EGRETS AND BITTERNS

5 Bittern L 75 cm WS 130 cm

Botaurus stellaris **ID** Large and rather plump, brown plumage marbled and striped with black and buff to offer perfect camouflage against dead reeds. Can be confused with juv of 7, which lacks blackish crown and moustache and has upperparts spotted white. Frequents large reedbeds, freezes in upright position when alarmed. Sometimes seen in owl-like flight over reeds. **V** In spring ♂ gives far-carrying dull, booming *woomb* or *oo-hoo-oomb* mainly at night; call in flight rough barking *cow* rather like a large gull. **H** Breeds in large reedbeds, in winter also in smaller patches of vegetation bordering ice-free wetlands. **D** bmw, rare breeder, mainly in East Anglia, more widespread in winter.

6 Little Bittern L 35 cm WS 55 cm

Ixobrychus minutus **ID** The smallest heron, much smaller than 5. In flight typically shows pale panel on upperwing, mantle always darker than rest of plumage, in ♂ iridescent black, in ♀ streaked brown. Only juv is similar in colour to 5, but much smaller and pale wing-panel present but spotted with brown. Also assumes erect camouflage posture when alarmed. During the day often flies low over reedbed with periods of wing-beats alternated with gliding phases. **V** Displaying ♂ gives long series of dull, rhythmic, *wro wro wro* notes; calls nasally *gack-eck-eck* and in flight *querr*. **H** Breeds in large and small wetlands with dense reeds or other vegetation, winters in Africa. **D** V 4-9, rare.

7 Night Heron L 62 cm WS 110 cm

Nycticorax nycticorax **ID** A rather small and compact heron with a short neck. Ad grey with black crown and mantle, legs yellow. Juv plumage cryptic brown but differs from 5 in more uniform head and neck and large white drop-like spots on mantle and coverts. In 1s similar to ad, but less contrast and breast still striped. Usually roosts in dense vegetation during the day, flying out at night to search for food and often calling. **V** Frog-like *waack*, given especially in flight. **H** Riparian forests and well-vegetated wetlands, especially in southern Europe. **D** V 4-10, rare but annual.

8 Squacco Heron L 45 cm WS 85 cm

Ardeola ralloides **ID** Small heron, appears rather plain light-brown when standing, but in flight the pure-white wings and tail are immediately obvious. In juv neck striped lengthways. Often stays hidden in vegetation during the day but becomes more active looking for food at dusk. **V** Call a duck-like *craw*. **H** Densely vegetated wetlands in southern Europe. **D** V 4-9, very rare.

non-br
br
1
juv
1s
br
2
3
4
5
♂
♀
♂
juv
6
ad
juv
1s
juv
7
br
non-br
8

1 Cattle Egret **L** 50 cm **WS** 92 cm

Bubulcus ibis **ID** Small, white heron with short, heavy, yellow bill. In br crown, breast and mantle tinged pale orange-buff, legs reddish; non-br and juv all white with greyish legs. Differs from Squacco Heron also in bill length and colour. Social and often seen feeding among grazing livestock, often in drier areas than other herons. **V** Call is a croaking *ark*, given rarely. **H** Breeds in colonies in trees beside wetlands, also visits dry regions. Found mainly in south-west Europe, range spreading north and east. Largely resident. **D** V, rare, more regular since the 1990s with occasional influxes.

2 Great White Egret **L** 95 cm **WS** 155 cm

Ardea alba **ID** Large, the size of a Grey Heron, and always completely white, very elegant with long neck and greenish lores. In br elongated mantle feathers hang down beyond tip of tail, bill mostly black and yellow tibia becomes reddish for a short period. In non-br and juv bill yellow and legs black. In flight legs protrude far beyond tail. **V** Rarely heard, wooden *krr-rrah*. **H** Forms mainly large colonies in extensive reedbeds, otherwise seen year-round on wetlands, also hunts prey such as rodents in meadows and fields. **D** V, rare, records have increased in recent years due to wandering birds from newly established colonies in France and The Netherlands.

3 Little Egret **L** 60 cm **WS** 90 cm

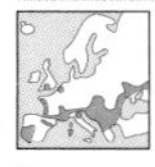

Egretta garzetta **ID** Very graceful, medium-sized heron, always white. Bill and legs always black with yellow toes (greener in juv). In br has long white plumes on nape and back. Also told from 2 by smaller size. **V** In flight a harsh *ktchar*. **H** Colonies in bushes by wetlands, outside breeding season on shallow water bodies and coasts. Mainly a summer visitor, winters Africa. **D** BR, colonized Britain and Ireland in 1990s and now a common resident in much of England and Wales, mainly on coasts.

4 Grey Heron **L** 95 cm **WS** 185 cm

Ardea cinerea **ID** Most common and best known heron, very large, mainly grey with black-and-white markings. Neck retracted in flight as in all herons, flight slow with wings bent slightly downwards. Hunts standing motionless on edge of water or in meadows, then catches prey (fish, amphibians, small birds) with bill at lightning speed. Juv plainer with less contrast. **V** Flight call hoarse croaking *kraark* and *chraa*. **H** Breeding colonies mostly high in trees, but sometimes in reeds or near ground; resident lakes and marshes, also visits meadows and fields to hunt rodents. Summer migrant in eastern Europe. **D** BRMW, very common.

5 Purple Heron **L** 85 cm **WS** 135 cm

Ardea purpurea **ID** Somewhat smaller, more slender and clearly darker than 4. Ad has chestnut-brown neck and head with black crown and neck-stripes. Juv paler and much browner with streaks on fore-neck. In flight can be differentiated from 4 by rich brown underwing coverts, sometimes also by outline due to bulging neck and longer toes which are often spread apart. **V** Call *haarr*, higher pitched than 4. **H** Breeds mainly in southern Europe in reedbeds, especially in wetlands with dense vegetation and reeds. Winters Africa. **D** V 4-10, rare, annual and most frequent in East Anglia.

STORKS

6 White Stork **L** 110 cm **WS** 165 cm

Ciconia ciconia **ID** Easily recognizable. Large, white plumage with black wings and long red bill and legs. Juv has paler brownish legs and red bill tipped dark. Flies with neck outstretched and migrates in flocks that often circle in thermal updrafts. Breeds mostly on buildings, particularly chimneys, occasionally also nests in large trees. **V** Silent, but clatters bill loudly, especially on the nest. **H** Wetlands, meadows, fields, ponds. Winters in Africa. **D** V 4-9, rare, several records each summer, plus occasional escapes from captivity.

7 Black Stork **L** 100 cm **WS** 155 cm

Ciconia nigra **ID** Shape like 6 but head, neck and upperparts black, in flight the underwings are also dark, with only the belly and axillaries white and sharply contrasting. Ad has red bill and legs and metallic green and purple sheen on black upperparts. Juv has bill and legs grey-green changing to dull red with age, and upperparts dull brownish-black. Shyer than 6 and less social, builds nest in large tree in undisturbed forest. **V** Calls *hee-leeh* on nest, sometimes mews like Common Buzzard in flight, rarely clatters bill. **H** Forests and wetlands, more dependant on water than 6, feeds mainly on fish. Winters in Spain and Africa. **D** V 5-9, very rare.

br
non-br
1
br
non-br/juv
2
non-br/juv
br
3
juv
br
5
juv
br
4
6
juv
7

OSPREY

1 Osprey L 56 cm WS 160 cm

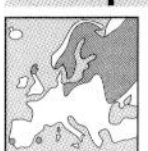

Pandion haliaetus **ID** Medium-sized raptor with long, narrow, angled wings. Often hovers high and plunges down to water to catch fish with outstretched talons. Head white with dark mask, underparts and underwing coverts white with dark carpal patch, upperparts brown, in juv scaled due to pale feather fringes. **V** Display call a moaning *yielp*; otherwise call a whistling *pyiep*. **H** Wetlands and coasts. Summer visitor, winters in Africa. **D** bm 3-10, breeds mostly Scotland, widespread but uncommon on passage.

HAWKS AND ALLIES

2 Short-toed Eagle L 65 cm WS 170 cm

Circaetus gallicus **ID** Quite large with long, broad wings, almost owl-like large head and square tail; frequently hovers. Underparts whitish, variably speckled brown, head and breast mostly dark, tail has three bands, no carpal patch, upperwings brown-grey, cere and legs grey-blue. Most likely to be confused with 1 or Honey Buzzard. **V** Display call a melodic whistling *piee-ou*. **H** Summer visitor to open areas rich in reptiles in southern and eastern Europe, winters Africa. **D** V, extremely rare.

3 Black-winged Kite L 33 cm WS 78 cm

Elanus caeruleus **ID** A small raptor, only about the size of a Kestrel, with large head, pointed wings and short slightly forked tail; often hovers. Plumage mainly grey and white and appears very pale with the only black being on the under-primaries and the secondary coverts above. In juv crown and breast tinged buff and upperparts scaled. **V** Displays with whistling *kiee-yip*; sharp alarm call *kreeyak*. **H** Open areas in south-west Europe, especially Portugal. **D -**.

4 Red Kite L 65 cm WS 155 cm

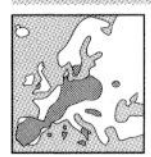

Milvus milvus **ID** Medium-sized with long wings with hanging primaries and long, deeply forked tail often manoeuvred in casual flight. Plumage rusty-brown with lighter head, underwing has whitish panel in primaries. Tail rusty-red; compare with 5. **V** Plaintive *heeyou-hiy-hiy-hiyou*. **H** Open forested hills. **D** br, Wales, with reintroduced birds in England and Scotland.

5 Black Kite L 55 cm WS 145 cm

Milvus migrans **ID** Medium-sized, elegant raptor, with shallow fork in tail (less deep than 4) which looks square or even rounded when spread. Often glides with hanging, slightly angled primaries. Plumage uniform dark brown, tail brown. Primaries barely paler underneath than rest of underparts, indistinct pale brown band on secondaries. In juv underparts somewhat brighter and streaked dark, narrow eye-mask and dark iris. **V** Calls vibrating *peeh-yirr*. **H** Summer visitor to partially open landscape, often in vicinity of water. Winters Africa. **D** V 4-9, rare, annual, mainly south England.

6 Egyptian Vulture L 60 cm WS 160 cm

Neophron percnopterus **ID** Smallest vulture with small head and long, wedge-shaped tail. Ad unmistakable with black flight feathers contrasting with otherwise whitish plumage, naked yellow facial skin. Juv almost completely brown, first white feathers appear in 2s. **H** Mainly in mountains but also other habitats in southern Europe. **D -**.

7 Griffon Vulture L 100 cm WS 250 cm

Gyps fulvus **ID** The most familiar European vulture, very large with huge, broad wings with deeply fingered primaries and short rounded tail. Body pale brownish, contrasting with darker wing and tail feathers and whitish head and long neck. Neck ruff white in ad, brown in juv, bill horn-coloured in ad, grey in juv. **H** Mountains, cliffs and gorges in southern Europe, mainly in flocks, breeds on rock ledges. **D -**.

8 Lammergeier L 115 cm WS 260 cm

Gypaetus barbatus **ID** Large vulture with very long, narrow wings and long, wedge-shaped tail. Ad plumage dark overall, with upperparts slate grey and only head and belly rust-coloured; black feathers above eye droop down to form 'moustache' or 'beard'. Juv upperparts dusky brown with odd pale feathers, belly grey. **H** Rare resident in rocky mountains of south Europe, mainly in Pyrenees; reintroduced in the Alps. **D -**.

9 Black Vulture L 108 cm WS 270 cm

Aegypius monachus **ID** A powerful raptor with long, broad, deeply fingered wings and short, rounded tail. Plumage always uniform dark blackish-brown. Ad has light-brown neck ruff as well as light patches of bare skin on crown and back of head, in juv these areas are blackish. **H** Breeds in forested mountain regions of south-west and south-east Europe. **D** V, extremely rare.

1
2
juv
3
4
5
juv
juv
juv
6
8
7
9

Eagles are very powerful, and in general rather rare, raptors with broad wings, the tips of which show at least six deeply fingered primaries, plus large bills and feathered legs. They often glide high on thermals without beating their wings for long periods. The development from juv to ad takes place in several stages over a period of up to five years, therefore identification and ageing is difficult even for experts. See also page 63.

1 Bonelli's Eagle **L** 60 cm **WS** 155 cm

Aquila fasciata **ID** Medium-sized, wings show little 'fingering', carpal joint often pushed forward, but trailing edge of wing straight, tail long and square. Underparts pale with broad dark diagonal band along length of underwing coverts and broad black band at the end of grey tail, often has a clear whitish patch on mantle. In juv underparts rufous with all large feathers finely barred. **H** Rather rare resident in mountains of southern Europe. **D** -.

2 Booted Eagle **L** 46 cm **WS** 120 cm

Aquila pennata **ID** Smallest eagle, only as large as Common Buzzard, but with six fingered primaries. Upperwing brown with pale band and white markings on shoulder. Flight feathers blackish above and below with inner three primaries lighter. Underparts whitish in pale morph, dark brown in dark morph. **V** At breeding site often calls *vee-vee-yik-yik*. **H** Old deciduous forests in open areas in south and east Europe. Winters mostly Africa. **D** V, extremely rare.

3 Golden Eagle **L** 85 cm **WS** 210 cm

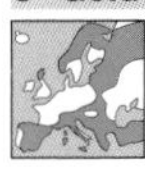

Aquila chrysaetos **ID** Large, rather narrow wings curved along trailing edge (soars with shallow V), long rounded tail and nape always golden-brown. In ad wing and tail feathers grey with black tips and 3-5 dark bands. In juv tail white with black band at tip and white patch at base of primaries on upper- and underwing. **V** Calls rarely, rough whistled *queue*. **H** Mainly in mountains, in north-east Europe also in forests and along coasts. **D** br, uncommon north and west Scotland, very rare north England and Ireland.

4 Greater Spotted Eagle **L** 65 cm **WS** 170 cm

Aquila clanga **ID** Like 5 but larger, more compact, darker tail faintly wedge-shaped, underwing coverts darker than flight feathers (opposite to 5), iris dark. In juv more white spots on wings than 5. **H** Breeds in forests, often near water, winters central and south-east Europe, often around wetlands. **D** -.

5 Lesser Spotted Eagle **L** 60 cm **WS** 150 cm

Aquila pomarina **ID** Slightly larger than Common Buzzard, uniform dark brown with head, neck and wing coverts a little lighter and whitish patch at the base of primaries. Underwing coverts mostly lighter than flight feathers. Juv has rusty patch on nape and white spots on wing coverts. **V** Loud *quuik* given at breeding site. **H** Breeds old forests with adjacent meadows. Winters Africa. **D** -.

6 Eastern Imperial Eagle **L** 76 cm **WS** 190 cm

Aquila heliaca **ID** Large and similar in shape to 3, but tail shorter and ad has white shoulder patches, grey tail base, paler nape and underwing coverts almost black. Juv plumage is pale buff overall with mantle and breast barred darker, and in flight shows characteristic paler inner primaries. **H** Breeds in open areas and steppe with groups of trees, but also mountain forests in south-east Europe. Mostly resident. **D** -.

7 Spanish Imperial Eagle **L** 78 cm **WS** 195 cm

Aquila adalberti **ID** Iberia only, where rare. Very similar to 6, but ad has larger white shoulder patch and white leading edge of upperwing. Juv very different to 6: pale fox-brown without stippling. **H** Resident in open landscapes with scattered trees. **D** -.

8 Steppe Eagle **L** 68 cm **WS** 180 cm

Aquila nipalensis **ID** Large with long and broad wings, flight and tail feathers always barred, thickened yellow gape reaches beyond lower back edge of eye. Ad uniform dark brown, nape often lighter, body darker than underwing coverts. Juv lighter brown, unmistakable with broad white band on underwing, when perched two white wing-bars are visible. **H** Breeds from Caspian Sea to central Asian steppes, rare on passage in south-east Europe. **D** -.

9 White-tailed Eagle **L** 85 cm **WS** 220 cm

Haliaetus albicilla **ID** Huge with board-like wings and deeply fingered primaries, massive bill and short wedge-shaped tail. Ad uniform brown with straggly feathers, head paler, bill yellow and clean white tail diagnostic. In juv plumage darker and more spotted, bill grey and tail mostly brown. Ad plumage develops over 5 years. **V** Calls laughing *kyi-kyi-kyi* at breeding site. **H** Old forests near larger wetlands. **D** bri, small reintroduced population in north-west Scotland, otherwise V.

juv
1
2
dark
light
juv
3
juv
4
juv
5
juv
6
juv
8
juv
7
juv
9

1 Common Buzzard **L** 52 cm **WS** 120 cm

Buteo buteo **ID** In almost all habitats the most common medium-sized bird of prey. Has broad wings with five notched primaries and a medium-long, slightly rounded tail. Feet and cere yellow. In flight holds wings flat or slightly raised; glides a lot, hovers occasionally, often perches on masts and poles. Plumage extremely variable from almost white to almost black or chequered, but mostly brown with typical lighter band on breast, tail has several bands. The wide blackish trailing edge to wing and dark band at tip of tail are typical in ad but not present in juv. North-east European subspecies *vulpinus* (known as 'Steppe Buzzard') reddish and similar to larger 4. **V** Calls mewing *hee-yoo.* **H** Forests, fields and wetlands. **D** BR, common and increasing.

2 Honey Buzzard **L** 54 cm **WS** 125 cm

Pernis apivorus **ID** Similar to 1 but flies mostly with wings flat or bent slightly downwards. Small head on long neck that protrudes far forward, long tail with rounded end and three bands, does not hover. Plumage extremely variable, underparts often barred, ♂ with grey head, ♀ browner. **V** Whistling *peeh-yoo.* **H** Forest edges bordering open areas, where digs out wasp nests (main food). Winters Africa. **D** bm 5-9, scarce.

3 Rough-legged Buzzard **L** 54 cm **WS** 130 cm

Buteo lagopus **ID** Larger and more elegant than 1, hovers frequently, legs feathered, base of tail always white with black band near tip, forehead pale and underparts whitish with contrasting dark carpal and belly patches (missing in ad ♂). **V** Similar to 1. **H** Breeds mountains, winters in open areas south to Britain and Black Sea. **D** mw 10-4, scarce, mainly east coast.

4 Long-legged Buzzard **L** 56 cm **WS** 140 cm

Buteo rufinus **ID** Larger and longer-winged than 1, often hovers. Plumage pale cinnamon-brown, with brown belly patch always darker than head, breast and vent; underwing pale with large dark carpal patch. In ad tail plain reddish, in juv beige and marked. **H** Summer visitor to steppe and mountains of south-east Europe. Resident Turkey. **D** -.

5 Goshawk **L** 55 cm **WS** 100 cm

Accipiter gentilis **ID** Large, in comparison to 1 wings short and broad, tail long and wide supercilium. Ad grey-brown above, underparts barred and white vent extends around sides of tail. Juv brown above, buff below with brown streaks. **V** Cackling *kyow-kyow-kyow* and drawn-out *peeeyee.* **H** Forests. **D** br, rare resident.

6 Sparrowhawk **L** 35 cm **WS** 70 cm

Accipiter nisus **ID** Smaller and paler than 5. ♂ upperparts blue-grey, underparts barred reddish. ♀ brown above, barred brown below, much larger, almost as ♂ Goshawk, but tail narrower with square not rounded tip. Young also brownish. **V** Warning *kyikyikyik.* **H** Forests, hedgerows, parks and gardens. **D** BR, common.

7 Levant Sparrowhawk **L** 36 cm **WS** 72 cm

Accipiter brevipes **ID** Very similar to 6, but underwings lighter with contrasting dark wing-tips, central tail feathers have no bands above, iris dark. ♂ with grey ear-coverts, ♀ and juv with dark stripe down centre of throat. **V** Typical call *kee-vick.* **H** Summer visitor to open deciduous forests in south-east Europe, main prey lizards. **D** -.

8 Marsh Harrier **L** 50 cm **WS** 120 cm

Circus aeruginosus **ID** Slender, long tail, low swaying flight with wings raised in V-shape. ♂ streaked brown with grey tail and flight feathers, ♀ dark brown with buff face and crown, juv darker with yellow head. **V** ♂ display call *kee-vee.* **H** Reedbeds, marshes, farmland. **D** bmr 4-9, mainly east coast.

9 Hen Harrier **L** 45 cm **WS** 110 cm

Circus cyaneus **ID** Slender with long tail, white rump and narrow wings raised in V-shape during low hunting flight. ♂ pale grey with extensive black on wing-tips. ♀ and juv brown above with paler underparts streaked with brown. ♀ and juv of 9, 10 and 11 very similar and can only be identified with experience. **V** ♂ display call *tchik-ikikikik.* **H** Moorland, farmland, marshes. **D** brmw, breeds moors, more widespread in winter, often on coast. Scarce.

10 Montagu's Harrier **L** 45 cm **WS** 105 cm

Circus pygargus **ID** Slighter than 9, wings more pointed. ♂ grey with black wing-tips and bars on secondaries, belly streaked brown. ♀ brown and lacks collar, juv underparts rusty. **V** Higher than 9. **H** Summer visitor to crops and marshes. **D** bm 5-9, rare.

11 Pallid Harrier **L** 45 cm **WS** 110 cm

Circus macrourus **ID** Slimmer than 9. ♂ paler with black wedge at wing-tip. ♀ has clear collar, juv like 10, but pale collar, dark nape and often has dark secondaries. **H** Breeds steppe, winters Africa. **D** V, very rare.

light
dark
1
juv
♂
2
4
3
juv
♂
5
juv ♀
juv
7
♀
♂
♂
6
♀
juv ♀
juv
8
♂
♀
juv
♀
♂
10
juv
9
♂
♀
juv
11
♂
♀

Egyptian Vulture
juv
Lammergeier
juv
Griffon Vulture
Black Vulture
♀
juv
♂
Marsh Harrier
♀
juv
♂
Hen Harrier
♀
juv
♂
Montagu's Harrier
♀
juv
♂
Pallid Harrier

Osprey
Short-toed Eagle
juv
2s
White-tailed Eagle
juv
2s
Golden Eagle
juv
Greater Spotted Eagle
juv
Eastern Imperial Eagle
light
dark
Booted Eagle
juv
Lesser Spotted Eagle
juv
Spanish Imperial Eagle
juv
Bonelli's Eagle

dark
light juv
typical
light ♂
dark ♀
Common Buzzard
vulpinus
Honey Buzzard
light juv
juv
Rough-legged Buzzard
Long-legged Buzzard
juv ♂
♀
Goshawk
juv
♀
♂
Black-winged Kite
Levant Sparrowhawk
♂
♀
Sparrowhawk
juv
Red Kite
Black Kite

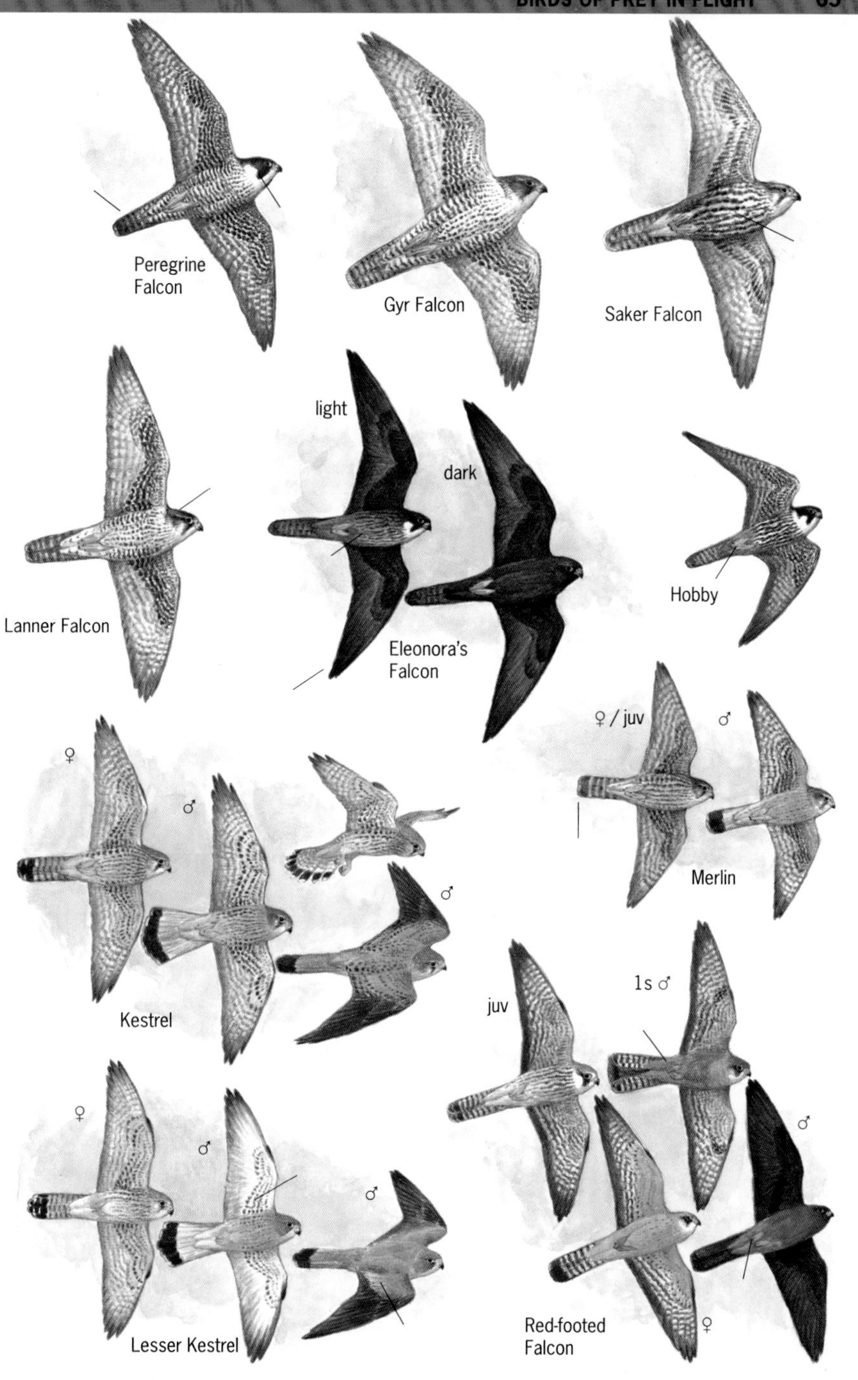
Peregrine Falcon
Gyr Falcon
Saker Falcon
light
dark
Lanner Falcon
Eleonora's Falcon
Hobby
♀ / juv
♂
Merlin
♀
♂
♂
Kestrel
juv
1s ♂
♂
♀
♂
♂
Lesser Kestrel
Red-footed Falcon
♀

FALCONS

1 Peregrine Falcon **L** 45 cm **WS** 105 cm

Falco peregrinus **ID** Most common and best known of the larger falcons, large, compact, with heavy build, ♀ larger than ♂ as in all falcons. In ad upperparts blue-grey, underparts white with black barring, black crown and moustachial stripe. Juv brownish and streaked below. **V** Calls rough *kre-kre-kre* at breeding site. **H** Mountains, cliffs, forests, towns, open areas across Europe, breeds on cliffs and high buildings. **D** br, uncommon but increasing.

2 Gyr Falcon **L** 58 cm **WS** 120 cm

Falco rusticolus **ID** Largest falcon, powerful, wings broad and relatively blunt, weak moustachial stripe, cheeks mostly dusky. Overall colour varies from dark brown-grey to grey (Scandinavia) to whitish (Greenland). Underparts pale with dark spots or patches, in juv dusky streaks. **H** Mountains and cliffs in far north Europe. **D** V 11-3, rare, most often north Scotland.

3 Saker Falcon **L** 51 cm **WS** 120 cm

Falco cherrug **ID** Powerful, relatively broad wings, warm-brown above, buff below with brown streaks, crown pale, weak moustachial stripe and dark 'trousers'. **H** Steppe and open areas in south-east Europe. **D -** (although escapes occasionally noted).

4 Lanner Falcon **L** 46 cm **WS** 100 cm

Falco biarmicus **ID** Smaller version of 3, but upperparts grey-brown, nape rufous, underparts paler with fine dark streaks turning to barring lower down. Juv darker above than 3, 'trousers' light and wing-tips reach tail-tip when standing. **D** Rare in mountains of south Italy and Balkans (subspecies *feldeggii*). **D -** (although escapes occasionally noted).

5 Eleonora's Falcon **L** 40 cm **WS** 95 cm

Falco eleonorae **ID** Medium-sized with long, slender wings and tail. Uniform dark morph unmistakable, light morph similar to 6, but belly buffish-brown and underwing coverts dark. Juv told from juv of 6 by size, flight silhouette and darkish underwing coverts. **V** Call hoarse and nasal *kyie-kyie*. **H** Colonial breeder on cliffs and rocky islands in Mediterranean, winters Madagascar. **D** V, extremely rare.

6 Hobby **L** 32 cm **WS** 76 cm

Falco subbuteo **ID** Small, streamlined, elegant falcon with a relatively short tail. Grey above and boldly streaked below, white cheeks bordered by black crown and moustachial stripe. Juv browner, lacks red patch on vent and 'trousers'. Hunts dragonflies and birds in flight. **V** Not as sharp as 7: *kyee-kyee-kyee*. **H** Summer visitor to open woodland, lakes and marshes. **D** bm 4-10, uncommon, south Britain only.

7 Kestrel **L** 34 cm **WS** 74 cm

Falco tinnunculus **ID** Commonest falcon in Europe, long pointed wings and long tail, often hovers. ♂ has grey head, rufous-brown mantle with black spots, dark flight feathers, buff underparts with dark streaks and grey tail with broad dark band near tip, ♀ and juv barred above with red-brown head and tail. **V** High-pitched *kikikikiki*. **H** Many habitats, even towns; breeds on cliffs, buildings and trees. **D** BR, common.

8 Lesser Kestrel **L** 30 cm **WS** 68 cm

Falco naumanni **ID** Like 7 but smaller, brighter, ♂ with plain mantle and grey rear wing coverts, ♀ almost identical to 7, but claws white, wings closer to tip of tail when perched. **V** Hoarser than 7. **H** Breeds colonially on buildings in open areas and towns. Summer visitor, much declined. **D** V, extremely rare.

9 Merlin **L** 29 cm **WS** 62 cm

Falco columbarius **ID** Small, compact falcon with short, pointed wings. Hunts in fast flight close to ground. ♂ blue-grey above, buff with dark spots below. Indistinct moustachial stripe. ♀ and juv darkish grey-brown above with tail-bands. **H** Breeds moors and heaths in north Europe, in winter also fields and marshes. **D** brmw, uncommon, breeds in north, more widespread in winter when often coastal.

10 Red-footed Falcon **L** 31 cm **WS** 70 cm

Falco vespertinus **ID** Small but with longer wings and shorter tail than 7 and more horizontal body when hovering. Catches insects in flight like 6 and is social. ♂ unmistakable, mostly blue-grey with red 'trousers'. ♀ barred slate-grey above, underparts (including underwing coverts) and head pale orange-buff and black eye-mask. Legs orange-red, flight feathers barred. Juv similar to 6, but smaller, tail clearly barred and forehead and ear coverts whitish. 1s ♂ has variable amount of grey and rusty-red feathers and barred flight- and tail feathers still from juv stage. **V** Calls drawn-out *tchree-tree*. **H** Breeds in colonies, mostly in old crow nests in open areas of south-east and east Europe. Summer visitor. **D** V 5-8, annual, mainly in south.

juv ♀
♂
1
Greenland
juv
2
juv
3
juv
4
dark
juv
light
5
juv
6
♀
♂
7
♀
9
♂
1s ♂
♀
♂
8
juv
10
♀
♂

BUSTARDS

1 Great Bustard L ♂ 100 cm, ♀ 80 cm

Otis tarda **WS** 180-240 cm **ID** Large and heavy with long legs. Belly and flanks white and upperparts barred rufous and black. Rufous-and-grey neck stretched in goose-like flight when extensive white wing-panels clearly visible. ♂ can weigh more than 15 kg and is much larger than ♀. Outside breeding season social but very shy, although reintroduced birds can be tame. ♂ turns into a white 'ball of feathers' during striking group courtship display. **V** Silent. **H** Meadows, steppes and fields. **D** V, extremely rare, formerly bred; i, reintroduction in progress in Wiltshire.

2 Little Bustard L 43 cm WS 110 cm

Tetrax tetrax **ID** Much smaller than 1, chicken-sized, wings mostly white. Br ♂ has black-and-white neck markings, in non-br neck and breast streaked brown like ♀ or juv. During display ♂ rhythmically throws head back and jumps up with flapping wings. **V** During display a rasping *prrrt* that can be heard from far away. **H** Open, dry landscapes in south Europe. Summer visitor. **D** V, extremely rare.

3 Macqueen's Bustard L 60 cm WS 140 cm

Chlamydotis macquinii **ID** (not illustrated) In size between 1 and 2, clay-brown above with grey-brown spots on back and conspicuous black vertical stripes on sides of neck and back of head. All flight feathers are dark, a white panel is present only at bases of primaries. **H** Central Asian steppes, very occasionally strays into Europe. **D** V, extremely rare.

CRANES

4 Common Crane L 110 cm WS 210 cm

Grus grus **ID** Very large with long neck outstretched in flight and long legs reaching far beyond the tail. Feathers grey, tertials bushy and stick out at back. Black, white and red head pattern of ad is only visible at close range (juv has brownish head). Very shy. Migrates by flying high in large V-shaped formations. **V** Calls loudly with a trumpeting *krooh*, performed by pairs in duet and groups on migration; young birds call a tweeting *meep* in autumn. **H** Breeds in damp forest clearings, wetlands, moors, fields and meadows; winters locally in central and south Europe. **D** br, tiny population in Norfolk, otherwise V.

5 Demoiselle Crane L 92 cm WS 170 cm

Grus virgo **ID** Smaller than 4, tertials longer and hang straight down rather than sticking out. Ad has front of neck black with feathers elongated over breast and white ear-tufts. In juv sides of head whitish and front of neck grey. **V** Calls more woody than 4. **H** Breeds on steppe from eastern Black Sea to central Asia, appears only on Cyprus as regular passage migrant, 4, 8-9. **D** -.

RAILS

6 Moorhen L 30 cm

Gallinula chloropus **ID** Ad has grey-black head and underparts, dark brown mantle, white undertail, red forehead 'shield', yellow bill-tip and white line bordering flanks. Juv paler brown. At home on land and on water, frequently bobs head and flicks tail. **V** Calls loud and sudden *curruc*, also *keck-eck-eck* during display. **H** Vegetated lakes, rivers and streams, often in towns. **D** BR, very common.

7 Coot L 39 cm

Fulica atra **ID** Larger than 6 with sooty-black plumage, on land rather round-backed in appearance, sits high in the water and nods head when swimming. Ad has white bill and forehead 'shield', juv has whitish fore-neck. Grazes in flocks on land, also dives. **V** Calls explosively *pix* and lower *pock*, in flight nasally *pneeu*. **H** All types of wetlands, common on park ponds. **D** BRMW, very common.

8 Red-knobbed Coot L 41 cm

Fulica cristata **ID** Requires good view to distinguish from 7: angle between bill and forehead shield rounded instead of acute, in flight lacks narrow white trailing edge to wing. Two small red knobs above the bill only develop in br and are not easily seen. **V** Calls, two syllable *kerrock*. **H** Very rare, in Europe restricted to well vegetated ponds in a few localities in southern Spain. **D** -.

9 Purple Swamp-hen L 48 cm

Porphyrio porphyrio **ID** Larger and bulkier than 7, about size of a chicken. Plumage iridescent blue, legs, bill and large forehead 'shield' red. Juv greyer overall. **V** Loud, piercing, nasal trumpeting. **H** Climbs around dense vegetation on inland waters; in Europe only locally in southern Spain, Mallorca and Sardinia. **D** - .

♂ courtship display
1
♂
♀
♀
♂
2
♂
♂ courtship
display
♀
4
juv
5
6
juv
8
juv
7
9
juv

1 Water Rail **L** 24 cm

Rallus aquaticus **ID** Laterally flattened, pear-shaped body, long red bill, flanks barred black and white, white undertail coverts and pointed tail usually held erect. Brown above with black feather centres, underparts blue-grey in ad, buff in juv. Mostly hidden in reeds, more often heard than seen. **V** Year-round pig-like grunting and squeaking and high-pitched *kip kip;* display calls *kurp kurp kurp* for ♂ and *tchik-tchik tchurr* for ♀. **H** Reedbeds and other vegetated wetlands. **D** BRMW, common but elusive.

2 Spotted Crake **L** 21 cm

Porzana porzana **ID** Smaller than 1 with short yellow-green bill which is red at base, green legs and buff undertail coverts. Head and underparts grey-brown with white barring, upperparts streaked brown and finely spotted white. Juv has head and breast warm brown instead of grey-brown. **V** Whip-like *quip, quip, quip* display call at night. Otherwise silent. **H** Marshes, flooded meadows. **D** bm 4-9, very scarce.

3 Little Crake **L** 18 cm

Porzana parva **ID** In contrast to 2 streaked light-brown above and not speckled with white, undertail barred black; primaries long, bill greenish with red spot at base. ♂ blue-grey on face, neck and breast, ♀ beige, juv whitish with slightly more obvious barring on flanks. **V** ♂ displays at night with descending croaking *queg queg-queck-kwaa-kwaakwekue*, unpaired ♀ displays barking *purck purck-purrr.* **H** Large reedbeds. Summer visitor. **D** V 4-9, very rare.

4 Baillon's Crake **L** 17 cm

Porzana pusilla **ID** Very small, similar to 3 but has shorter primaries, plain green bill (with no red), fine white streaking above and clearer barring on flanks. In juv breast barred brownish. **V** ♂ displays with frog-like *errrrrr* every 2-3 seconds, ♀ call is a soft *shrrr* similar to Reed Warbler's warning. **H** Sedge swamps, flooded meadows. **D** V 5-6, extremely rare.

5 Corncrake **L** 23 cm

Crex crex **ID** Rarely seen. Has short pink bill, rusty-brown wing coverts, greyish breast and flanks barred rufous. **V** Display call a continuous wooden rasping *rrrp-rrrp, rrrp-rrrp,* often given at night. **H** Wet meadows, also grain fields. Winters Africa. **D** bm 5-9, much declined and now very rare outside Western Isles.

BUTTONQUAIL

6 Small Buttonquail **L** 16 cm

Turnix sylvaticus **ID** Traditional name Andalusian Hemipode. Similar to Quail but smaller, tail and wings shorter, pale panel on secondary coverts, breast orange with black crescents on breast sides. Very secretive. Reversed sexual dimorphism with ♂ smaller and duller than ♀. **V** ♀ display call like distant mooing cow, *hoo hoo*, given at dusk. **H** Open, dry places with dense, low vegetation, often in fields. In Europe extremely rare, only in southern Spain, otherwise Africa and Asia. **D** -.

STONE-CURLEW (THICK-KNEE)

7 Stone-curlew **L** 42 cm **WS** 82 cm

Burhinus oedicnemus **ID** Cryptic brown plumage, black-and-white wings, large yellow eye; nocturnal. **V** Call whistling *crew-li* or *tree-iel* like Curlew. **H** Steppe, heath. Resident in Spain, otherwise summer visitor. **D** bm 3-10, local breeder in south England.

OYSTERCATCHER

8 Oystercatcher **L** 42 cm **WS** 78 cm

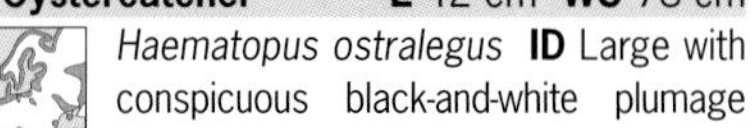

Haematopus ostralegus **ID** Large with conspicuous black-and-white plumage including broad white wing-bar, bill orange-red, legs pink; often in flocks. **V** Loud *kee-bik, bik, bik.* **H** Coasts, mudflats, wet meadows. **D** BRMW, common, breeds along coasts and also inland, particularly in the north.

STILT AND AVOCET

9 Black-winged Stilt **L** 35 cm **WS** 72 cm

Himantopus himantopus **ID** Graceful with extremely long red legs and thin straight black bill, wings completely black; juv to 1s with narrow white trailing edge. **V** Nasal *krit* and *kip.* **H** Shallow salt-water lagoons, especially along coasts of south Europe. **D** V 4-9, rare (has bred).

10 Avocet **L** 44 cm **WS** 72 cm

Recurvirostra avosetta **ID** Hard to mistake with long bluish legs, black bill curved upwards and black-and-white plumage with black cap and conspicuous wing pattern. **V** Full whistling *klooit* and *plutt.* **H** Mudflats, shallows. **D** brmw along coasts, occasionally inland. Less common and more local than 8, and rarer in north.

1
juv
2
♂
♀
3
juv
4
juv
5
6
7
non-br
8
9
10
juv

PLOVERS

1 Northern Lapwing L 30 cm WS 70 cm

Vanellus vanellus **ID** A conspicuous wader and often the most familiar species inland, frequently in flocks. Pigeon-sized with an unmistakable long crest (shorter in non-br and juv). Metallic green upperparts, white below with black collar (and throat in br), white tail with broad black band at tip. Wings broad and rounded, flies with slow, flappy wing-beats. **V** Calls *kee-vit* in different variations, during acrobatic flight display this is combined with loud throbbing sound produced by wings. **H** Wetlands, meadows, fields. Winters south and west Europe. **D** BRMW, common.

2 Spur-winged Lapwing L 27 cm

Vanellus spinosus **ID** Pale grey-brown above, cheeks white, crown, throat and belly black, legs dark. In flight tail white with broad black band, primaries and tips of secondaries black, separated from brown mantle and wing coverts by a sickle-shaped white area. Juv scaled above due to pale feather fringes. Named after a small, barely visible spur on the carpals. **V** Calls loudly *kip-kip-*... and *kri-kri*.... **H** In Europe summer visitor to coastal wetlands in eastern Greece, otherwise Middle East. **D** - (occasional records considered escapes).

3 Sociable Lapwing L 28 cm

Vanellus gregarius **ID** A little smaller than 1, pale grey-brown above, white supercilium, dark eye-stripe and crown, legs dark. Belly dark brown in br, breast streaked dark in juv. White triangle on trailing edge of wing in flight, wing-tips and tail-tip blackish. **V** Calls coarser than 1 *crashcrashcrash*. **H** Breeds on steppe in central Asia, winters from Turkey south, vagrant elsewhere. **D** V, very rare, most often in flocks of 1.

4 White-tailed Lapwing L 27 cm

Vanellus leucurus **ID** Legs yellow and much longer than 1, upperparts light grey-brown, head pale and unmarked. Juv scaled above. In flight has broad white diagonal band on wings, all-white tail and legs extending well beyond tip of tail. **V** Calls softly *khivit*. **H** Breeds on lakes from central Asian steppe west to Volga, occasionally Danube Delta. **D** V 5-9, extremely rare.

5 Grey Plover L 28 cm

Pluvialis squatarola **ID** Large, stocky, heavy-billed plover, silver-grey overall, paler than 6, in flight immediately distinguishable by black axillaries, broad white wing-bar, pale tail and white rump. In br black on belly reaches to the wings and white more extensive on breast sides; in juv breast streaked beige, but plumage sometimes yellowish and similar to 6. **V** Call is a sad whistle with three-syllable *plee-oo-ee*. **H** Breeds on tundra in High Arctic, winters along coasts of North Sea, Mediterranean and Atlantic, particularly on mudflats and estuaries. **D** MW, common on coast, present all year except mid-summer, rare inland.

6 European Golden Plover L 26 cm

Pluvialis apricaria **ID** Stocky plover with rolling gait, in flight has completely whitish underwings and axillaries (compare to 5, 7 and 8), only a weak wing-bar and a dark tail and rump. Upperparts always speckled golden-yellow, in br black underneath (less extensive in ♀ and in southern breeding populations) bordered by white lines on flanks. In non-br and juv belly whitish, yellowish breast with grey-brown stippling. During migration and winter often found with 1. **V** Call is a mournful, whistling monosyllabic *dew*, in butterfly-like display flight delivers a repetitive *doo-di-ew*, followed by a softer rhythmic trill. **H** Breeds on moorland and tundra in northern Europe, winters on fields and meadows in south and west Europe, less strictly coastal than 5. **D** BRMW, fairly common, breeds in north, more widespread in winter.

7 Pacific Golden Plover L 23 cm

Pluvialis fulva **ID** Rare vagrant. Similar to 6, but smaller and more elegant with longer legs, underwings including axillaries pale brown-grey (not white), toes protrude beyond tail in flight. In br flanks and undertail coverts black or mottled black, juv generally more yellowish. **V** Call a reliable identification feature: a disyllabic whistling *choo-it*, similar to Spotted Redshank. **H** Breeds on tundra in north Siberia, winters Indian Ocean and south Pacific. **D** V, very rare.

8 American Golden Plover L 25 cm

Pluvialis dominica **ID** Very similar to 7, also a vagrant. Smaller than 6 and like 7 with brown-grey underwings and axillaries, but wings protrude far beyond tail when at rest. In br ♂ underparts completely black. Juv greyer than in 6 and 7, dark crown edged by whitish supercilium. **V** Calls higher than 6: *kloo-ee*. **H** Estuaries, fields and wetlands. Breeds North America, winters South America. **D** V, rare but annual.

non-br
1
2
4
3
non-br
non-br
5
br
juv
br
non-br/juv
6
br
1w
8
7
br
1w

1 Little Ringed Plover **L** 16 cm

Charadrius dubius **ID** Most widespread small plover inland. Pale brown upperparts, white underparts, short dark bill, relatively short, pale fleshy legs, narrow yellow orbital ring, in flight no wing-bar. In br black breast-band and facial markings bold; juv has smaller brownish breast-band broken in middle and hooded effect due to indistinct supercilium. Runs with 'rolling' action over open areas and stops abruptly. **V** Calls whistling *tiu*, gives rough and rolling *chrechrechrechre* when displaying or in flight. **H** Breeds on inland marshes, lakes and gravel pits. Summer visitor. **D** bm 3-9, fairly common in south, absent in north.

2 Ringed Plover **L** 18 cm

Charadrius hiaticula **ID** Heavier than 1, orange legs and base of bill, no orbital ring, in flight shows a broad, white wing-bar. Juv told from 1 by conspicuous white supercilium and broader brownish breast-band often closed in the middle. **V** Call mellow *too-ip*, in display flight *too-videeh tu-videeh*. **H** Breeds mainly beaches and mudflats, in north also lake edges or tundra, sometimes inland, winters mainly coasts (rocky and muddy) in west Europe. **D** BRMW, common on coasts, inland on passage.

3 Kentish Plover **L** 16 cm

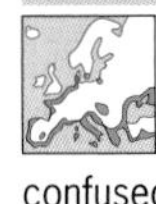

Charadrius alexandrinus **ID** Appears pale and dainty, but with large head, patches on breast sides (juv can be confused with 1) and legs and bill black. In flight shows broad white wing-bars. ♂ in br has rufous crown and small, neatly defined black patches on sides of breast, ♀ and juv paler than 1 and 2 and without black. **V** Calls *pip pit*, displays with *preerreerreerree*. **H** Sandy beaches, tidal meadows, locally inland on salt lakes. Summer visitor in north, winters around Mediterranean. **D** m 4-9, rare migrant to coasts in south Britain. Formerly bred.

4 Dotterel **L** 22 cm

Charadrius morinellus **ID** Medium-sized plover always with whitish supercilium connected at the nape, narrow white breast-band, yellowish legs, greyish underwings and uniform dark upperwings. Br has chestnut lower breast and flanks with blackish belly; belly whitish in non-br and juv, the latter scaly above ♀ brighter than ♂ and the latter is the lone carer for young. **V** Call a soft rolling *brrrut*, ♀ display call *butt, butt* while circling. **H** Summer visitor to tundra and mountain meadows during migration rests in flocks known as 'trips' on fields or high plateaus, winters Spain and north Africa. **D** bm 4-9, breeds Scottish Highlands, scarce on passage elsewhere.

SANDPIPERS AND ALLIES

5 Red-necked Phalarope **L** 18 cm

Phalaropus lobatus **ID** Graceful, often seen swimming, picks insect food from water surface with slender bill, often confiding, in flight shows narrow white wing-bar. In br brick-red neck markings, white throat and belly; br and juv have bold yellowish stripes above. Non-br and 1w have upperparts grey with whitish stripes, underparts white and black mask on face. ♀ is brighter in br than ♂, ♂ cares for the brood alone. **V** Call short *kepp*. **H** Breeds ponds and tundra pools in north Europe, stops on wetlands in central and east Europe en route to winter on the Arabian Sea. **D** bm 5-9, breeds locally on Shetland and Hebrides, rare migrant elsewhere.

6 Grey Phalarope **L** 21 cm

Phalaropus fulicarius **ID** Similar to 5, but slightly heavier and bill thicker with pale base, also swims in circles on water when feeding. In br underparts, including throat and belly, rusty-red, ♀ brighter than ♂. Juv buff on neck with narrow pale fringes to feathers on upperparts. Non-br has black mask and nape and plain grey upperparts (patchy grey-and-black in 1w). **V** Calls metallic *pick* and *kitt*, ♀ displays with *brrrrip* given in flight. **H** In Europe breeds only Iceland, winters south Atlantic, elsewhere scarce migrant to Atlantic and North Sea coasts, also occasionally on inland waters. **D** m, mainly 9-11, rare, almost always 1w and non-br.

7 Wilson's Phalarope **L** 23 cm

Phalaropus tricolor **ID** (not illustrated) Vagrant. Larger than 5 and 6 with longer needle-like bill and longer yellow legs (black in br), also swims but often on mud. Generally grey above, white below. In br with chestnut stripe on side of neck and orange breast. In non-br with yellow legs and grey eye-stripe and white supercilium both extending down neck; plain wings and square white rump. **V** Call *vitt*. **H** Breeds North American wetlands, winters South America, vagrant to Europe. **D** V 5-9, extremely rare.

juv
1
juv
2
juv
3
♀
♂
4
juv
juv
non-br
♀
juv / 1w
juv
5
non-br
♀
6
juv / 1w
non-br
♀

1 Curlew **L** 54 cm

Numenius arquata **ID** Large wader, strongly built with very long evenly downward-curved bill, long legs and brown streaked plumage; in flight with no conspicuous wing-bars, but white rump and white inverted V-shaped wedge up back. Bill longer in ♀ than in ♂ and juv. Often in flocks, with measured flight not unlike a gull. **V** Call a mournful whistling *coor-lee*, displays with long flute-like notes ending in rhythmic trills. **H** Breeds on moors and wet meadows, winters on mudflats and fields, often on coasts. **D** BRMW, resident, most common on coasts in winter.

2 Whimbrel **L** 42 cm

Numenius phaeopus **ID** Similar to 1 but smaller, bill shorter and decurved more sharply near tip, eye-stripe bolder and buff crown-stripe and black lateral crown-stripes; has faster wingbeats. **V** In flight seven-noted whistle is best feature, song similar to 1 but ends with even trill. **H** Breeds wetlands, moors, tundra, mostly coastal during passage, winters Africa. **D** bM 3-10, scarce breeder north Scotland, common migrant on coasts, occasionally winters.

3 Black-tailed Godwit **L** 40 cm

Limosa limosa **ID** Large, long legs and long straight bill always orange-pink at base. In flight shows broad white wing-bars, square white rump and broad black tail band. In br head, neck and breast rufous (deeper and more extensive in smaller Icelandic subspecies *islandica*), flanks and belly whitish with black barring. Non-br uniform brown-grey, juv like faded version of ad. **V** Calls *kevekue* and *vee-eeh*, during display flight *gritta gritta*. **H** Breeds wet meadows, winters coasts in south and west Europe. **D** bMW, scarce breeder East Anglia, widespread migrant and winter visitor, when mainly coastal.

4 Bar-tailed Godwit **L** 38 cm

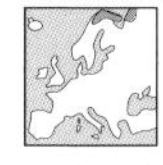

Limosa lapponica **ID** Similar to 3 but legs shorter, bill slightly upturned and no wing-bars, but tail finely barred and white rump extends up back in a V-shape. Upperparts patterned like 1. In br ♂ head and underparts deep rufous with no barring. **V** Calls nasally *kevue* and double *gheghe*. **H** Breeds tundra, winters on coastal mudflats from Britain southwards. **D** MW, common, present all year except mid-summer, rare inland.

5 Common Snipe **L** 25 cm

Gallinago gallinago **ID** The most familiar snipe, with very long, straight bill, short legs and cryptic plumage offering superb camouflage. Feeds by probing with bill in soft mud in wetland margins and damp meadows. When threatened first presses itself against the ground, then flies up in typical zigzag flight while calling. **V** Flight call a hoarse squelch, displays on the ground with a clock-like *ticka-ticka-ticka*, during 'drumming' display flight a mechanical throbbing and goat-like bleating are produced by tail-feathers. **H** Breeds moors and wet meadows, winters marshes and wetlands in south and west Europe. **D** BRMW, common (scarce breeder in south).

6 Great Snipe **L** 28 cm

Gallinago media **ID** Similar to 5 but much rarer. Body heavier, underwings and underparts heavily barred, no white trailing edge to wings, but two white wing-bars, a lot of white on outer tail feathers; flies up silently and straight with whirring wing sound. **V** During group 'lek' display on the ground chirping and clattering sounds. **H** Moors and wet meadows in north-east Europe, more often found on drier areas than 5. **D** V 5 and 9-10, very rare.

7 Jack Snipe **L** 19 cm

Lymnocryptes minimus **ID** Smaller and shorter-billed than 5, dark crown with no pale central stripe but 'double' supercilium, flanks streaked (not barred). Constantly bobs up and down while feeding, when threatened squats or flies up silently and straight often from right by observer, showing wedge-shaped tail lacking white. **V** Usually quiet, display call given in flight sounds like galloping horse. **H** Breeds moors and marshes, winters wet meadows in south and west Europe. **D** mw 10-4, uncommon, much more scarce and elusive than 5.

8 Woodcock **L** 35 cm

Scolopax rusticola **ID** Mainly crepuscular, heavy with very long bill, cryptic plumage, crown banded crossways rather than striped lengthways. **V** ♂ calls *org org pit* (first two notes deeply growled, third high-pitched) during evening 'roding' display flight above tree-tops, otherwise silent. **H** Secretive breeding bird in moist deciduous forests. Summer visitor in north-east Europe, winters south to Italy and Balkans. **D** BRMW, fairly common.

1
juv
2
3
br
juv
non-br
br
4
br
juv
br
non-br
5
6
7
8

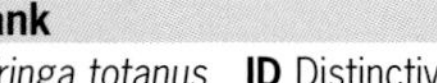

1 Redshank **L** 26 cm

Tringa totanus **ID** Distinctive medium-sized wader with long orange-red legs and medium-length bill with red base; in flight has unique broad white trailing edge to wing and white wedge on back. Head and body mottled grey-brown in br; in non-br uniform brown-grey above. Juv paler above with legs paler orange. **V** Calls whistling *tyoo-hoo(-hoo)*, warns *kip, kip;* displays in flight *tlooh-tlooh-tulit*. **H** Breeds saltmarsh and wet meadows, often by the coast but sometimes inland, winters coastal lagoons and mudflats from Britain southwards. **D** BRMW, common.

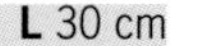

2 Spotted Redshank **L** 30 cm

Tringa erythropus **ID** Similar to 1 but longer legs and longer, finer bill; no white on wing, but oval white patch on back. In br otherwise almost all black, especially ♂, legs also dark, juv smoky brown with barred underparts, in non-br upperparts pale grey with white fore supercilium. **V** Whistles sharp *tchu-eet*; displays *trooh-eeh trooh-eeh*. **H** Breeds wetlands in taiga, during migration on mudflats, riverbanks. **D** Mw, locally fairly common on coasts during migration, present all year except mid-summer.

3 Greenshank **L** 32 cm

Tringa nebularia **ID** Large and pale with long greenish legs and greenish at base of slightly upturned bill; in flight with inverted white V up back, barred tail, wings plain. In br feathers on the upperparts have black centres, in juv brown with pale edges, in non-br plainer grey. **V** Call loud *tew tew tew*; during wavy display flight sings *kluvooh-kluvooh*. **H** Breeds north European wetlands and open forests, widespread during migration on marshes and mudflats. **D** bM 4-10, scarce breeder, common migrant.

4 Marsh Sandpiper **L** 23 cm

Tringa stagnatilis **ID** Much smaller, paler and more elegant than 3, with relatively longer legs, narrow straight bill and supercilium often conspicuously white; in flight toes protrude far beyond tail-tip. In br black spots on clay-brown mantle. In juv breast whiter, finely streaked only on sides (unlike 3). **V** Calls softly whistling *kyu* or *tyu-du*; displays *tyu-lyu tyu-lyu*. **H** Summer visitor, seen on passage in south-east Europe. **D** V 5-9, very rare.

5 Green Sandpiper **L** 22 cm

Tringa ochropus **ID** Medium-sized and rather robust sandpiper with strongly contrasting plumage. Upperparts are completely dark and barely mottled, underparts white with strongly separated dark breast; in flight upper- and underwings blackish, rump contrasting white (recalls giant House Martin). In juv upperparts somewhat paler and spotted. Dark breast can cause confusion with the smaller, paler Common Sandpiper. Often solitary or in small groups rather than in flocks. **V** Characteristic flight call *tluit-uit-uit*, warns sharply *tip tip*; sings *tloo-i tlui*. **H** Breeds in old thrush nests in damp forests, during migration found on water bodies of all types, winters south and west Europe. **D** M 3-10, common during passage, even inland; w, southern England.

6 Wood Sandpiper **L** 20 cm

Tringa glareola **ID** Rather small and elegant sandpiper with upperparts medium-brown with paler specks (markings more chequered in juv), whitish underparts with brown spots or streaks on breast and flanks, legs yellowish-green, bill dark. In flight upperparts uniform brown, rump white. Underwings pale in contrast to 5. Mostly single or in small flocks. **V** Call bright *chif-if-if;* displays *liltu-liltue*. **H** Breeds in north European wetlands, winters Africa, widespread on passage on mudflats and flooded meadows. **V** bm 4-9, uncommon.

7 Ruff **L** ♂ 30 cm, ♀ 23 cm

Philomachus pugnax **ID** Variable in colour and size and can be confused with several other species, ♂ larger than ♀, medium-sized slightly decurved bill, small head, slightly hunch-backed, in flight white wing-bar and with two white ovals on borders of rump; does not bob like *Tringa* waders. Ad with yellow to red legs, br ♂ with neck ruff, each patterned or uniform white, black or brown, ♀ smaller, in br with variable black spotting on belly and mantle, in non-br both sexes grey-brown above, whitish below. Juv buff-brown, upperparts neatly scaled, legs grey-green. **V** Silent; ♂ performs 'lek' display. **H** Breeds moors and wetlands, widespread on migration, especially on coasts, winters mainly Africa. **D** M 3-10, common; b, rare, East Anglia; w, scarce, south England.

juv
br
1
juv
non-br
br
3
juv
non-br
♂ br
2
juv
non-br
br
4
juv
br
5
br
juv
6
♀ non-br
juv ♂
♀ br
7
♂ br

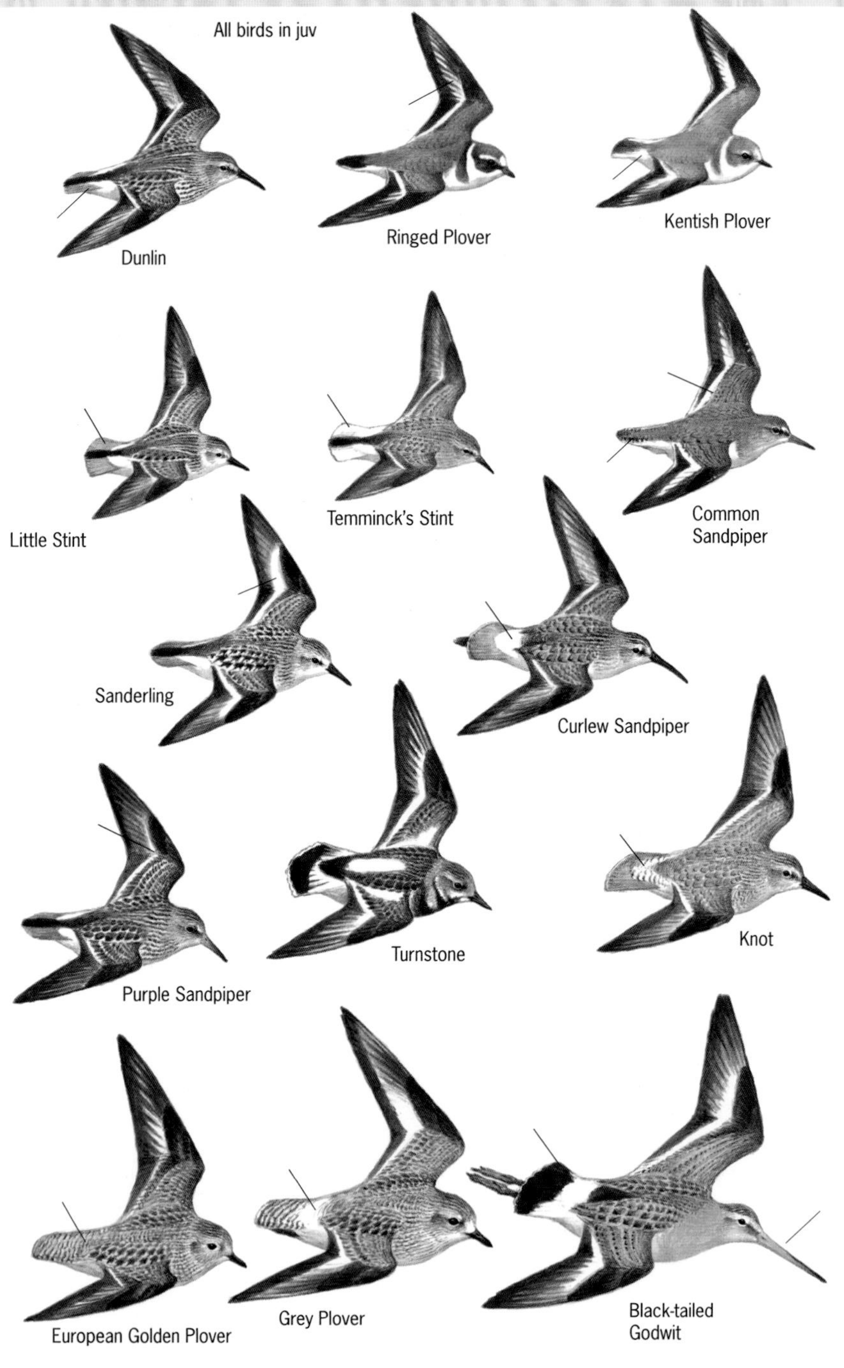
All birds in juv
Dunlin
Ringed Plover
Kentish Plover
Little Stint
Temminck's Stint
Common Sandpiper
Sanderling
Curlew Sandpiper
Purple Sandpiper
Turnstone
Knot
European Golden Plover
Grey Plover
Black-tailed Godwit

All birds in juv
Little Ringed Plover
Dotterel
Ruff
Wood Sandpiper
Green Sandpiper
Greenshank
Redshank
Spotted Redshank
Common Snipe
Bar-tailed Godwit
Curlew
Whimbrel

1 Common Sandpiper **L** 19 cm

Actitis hypoleucos **ID** Dumpy, very short-legged, longish tail. Warm-brown above (in br with blackish feather centres, in juv scaled), brownish breast clearly defined from white belly and flanks (in contrast to darker Green Sandpiper breast separated from carpals by white wedge). Bobs continuously; flies low with stiff wing-beats, clearly showing broad white wing-bar and dark rump. **V** Call high-pitched *hitititi*, warns shrill *heeeyt*; displays in flight *hidide-eh-didi hidideeh-didi*. **H** Breeds stony edges of rivers and lakes, seen on all types of wetland in migration, winters mainly Africa. **D** BM 4-9, breeds in north, widespread on passage; w, scarce in south.

2 Spotted Sandpiper **L** 19 cm

Actitis macularis **ID** (not illustrated) American counterpart of 1, tail protrudes just beyond wings at rest, wing-bar restricted on secondaries and does not reach body. In br boldly spotted black underneath, legs orange. Juv greyer than 1, tertial edges lack serrated pattern, bill pinkish at base, legs yellowish. **V** Call *kit*. **H** As 1. **D** V, rare.

3 Terek Sandpiper **L** 23 cm

Xenus cinereus **ID** Superficially similar to 1 in demeanour and behaviour, but larger, bill longer and curved upwards and legs yellow; in flight white trailing edge of wing similar to Redshank but narrower and less contrasting. Upperparts greyish rather than brown with black carpals in br and black V-shape on scapulars (distinct in ad, faint in juv). **V** Calls whistling *du-du-dyu*, display call a sad rolling *kla-klurrooh kla-klurrooh*. **H** Breeds on muddy shores in north-east European taiga, winters Africa and Asia. **D** V, very rare.

4 Buff-breasted Sandpiper **L** 19 cm

Tryngites subruficollis **ID** Mainly ochre-coloured American wader, neck often held outstretched, resembles juv ♀ Ruff but Dunlin-sized. Thin bill short and straight, legs bright yellow, upperparts scaled due to pale feather fringes, underneath completely ochre-buff with small black spots on sides of breast, dark eye surrounded by pale ring; in flight no white on rump, underwings white with dark crescent on greater primary coverts. Often confiding. **V** Calls seldom *prrrt*. **H** Breeds on tundra in North America and east Siberia, a few reach western Europe each year, often seen on muddy margins or short grass. **D** V, mainly 9-10, rare.

5 Knot **L** 25 cm

Calidris canutus **ID** Heavily built, bill almost straight, legs green-grey, rump barred grey. In br rusty-red and only possible confusion is with Curlew Sandpiper, in juv sandy-grey with upperparts scaled and underparts buff at first, in non-br upperparts grey. **V** Nasal, soft *knut* or *kwett*. **H** Breeds on tundra in High Arctic, widespread in flocks on mudflats on North Sea and Atlantic coasts during migration and winter. **D** MW, common except summer, mainly coastal.

6 Sanderling **L** 19 cm

Calidris alba **ID** Runs following waves 'like clockwork toy' on sandy beaches; belly and flanks always white, bill straight and short, legs black and broad white wing-bar. In br breast and face rusty-brown, upperparts spotted rufous, black and grey; juv upperparts blackish and spotted grey-buff; non-br very pale overall, grey above, white below, carpals blackish. **V** Calls short *plit*. **H** Breeds High Arctic tundra, on shores across Europe during migration and winter. **D** MW, common on coasts except summer.

7 Purple Sandpiper **L** 21 cm

Calidris maritima **ID** Dark, always dusky and rather squat with stout decurved bill, orange legs, tail extending beyond wing-tips at rest and narrow white wing-bar in flight. In br has rufous on crown, ear-coverts, mantle and breast-sides, with black-brown spots on flanks and breast. In non-br upperparts and breast uniform dusky slate-grey; juv and 1w similar but scaled wing-coverts and streaked below. Often in flocks with 8. **V** Calls softly *kutt, ke-vutt*; song similar to Dunlin. **H** Breeds stony tundra, winters south to Biscay along rocky coastlines and on jetties. **D** MW 8-5, only on coasts, commoner in north.

8 Turnstone **L** 23 cm

Arenaria interpes **ID** Very active, with short neck, short heavy bill, short orange-red legs and dark breast; in flight has distinctive pattern of dark-and-white markings. Head and upperparts striking in br, more uniform dusky black-brown in non-br and juv. Feeds by searching under stones and through seaweed with bill. **V** Calls hard *kitititit; kutt kutt* during display. **H** Breeds in stony tundra and along coasts, winters from Britain south to Mediterranean along rocky coasts and on breakwaters, seldom inland. **D** MW, common on coasts, present all year.

juv
br
1
3
br
juv
4
juv
non-br
5
br
non-br
non-br
6
br
juv
non-br
1w
8
br
7
br
br

1 Dunlin L 19 cm

Calidris alpina **ID** One of the commonest coastal waders during winter, about the size of a starling, bill slightly decurved and variable in length (longer in northern birds); in flight shows narrow white wing-bar, white sides to rump divided by black central band. In br has unmistakable black belly patch, crown and mantle rufous with black markings. Juv grey-brown above with pale to rusty-brown feather fringes, often pale V-shape on mantle feathers and scapulars, very dense (sometimes absent) black 'drops' on side of belly. Non-br plain grey above and white below, breast faded grey streaking. Also see illustration on inside back cover. Social, outside breeding season gathers in small to huge flocks. **V** Call nasal *chreep*, in display-flight whirring *rrewri-rrrrewree*, ending in a trill. **H** Breeds moors, tundra, during migration on intertidal mudflats, coast and sometimes inland, winters south to Mediterranean. **D** BMW, breeds moorland in north, otherwise widespread and common around coasts.

2 Curlew Sandpiper L 20 cm

Calidris ferruginea **ID** Elegant sandpiper, compared with 1 bill longer and more curved, neck and legs longer, wings protrude beyond tail at rest, in flight rump white and undivided (but in br can be barred). Head and underparts of br unmistakable deep rufous (but compare with stouter, paler, shorter-billed Knot). Juv has sandy-brown upperparts neatly scaled, flanks white, breast tinged buff at first and, like the white belly, without the dark streaking of 1. **V** Calls similar to 1 but disyllabic *chirrip*. **H** Breeds on tundra in Russian High Arctic, migrates to Africa via Europe, where widespread on coastal pools and mudflats in spring and autumn. **D** m 5, 8-10, uncommon.

3 Broad-billed Sandpiper L 17 cm

Limicola falcinellus **ID** Closely related to the *Calidris* sandpipers and in stature similar to 1, but legs shorter, movements slower and bill has wide base that appears square against forehead and is kinked sharply downwards at tip. Plumage blacker in br and juv with characteristic head pattern with dark lores and crown as well as double supercilium forking in front of the eye. In br dark spotting on breast and flanks, pale V-pattern on mantle. In juv flanks white, breast streaked and bold double V-pattern on mantle and scapulars. **V** Calls short *dret* and drier trilling *brrrit* which is more drawn out than that of 1, displays in flight with rhythmical buzzing. **H** Breeds on marshes in Scandinavia, seen on pools and mudflats in east Europe during migration. **D** V 5, 7-9, rare, mostly on east coast.

4 White-rumped Sandpiper L 17 cm

Calidris fuscicollis **ID** Vagrant, slightly smaller than 1, body longer, scissor-like wings protrude far beyond tail-tip at rest, bill shorter and slightly decurved with pale base to lower mandible, legs shorter and dark; in flight shows undivided white rump (compare with more extensive white rump of 2, see page 80). In br and juv crown and mantle rusty-brown, belly always white, breast and flanks streaked black (more intense in br), above white double V-marking (more marked in juv). Non-br like 1 but flanks finely streaked. **V** Call a high-pitched, mouse-like *jeet*. **H** Breeds High Arctic in North America and east Siberia. **D** V, rare.

5 Pectoral Sandpiper L 19-22 cm

Calidris melanotos **ID** Small to medium-sized (♂ larger than ♀) with long wings. Resembles a small ♀ Ruff when neck outstretched, legs and base of bill pale, densely streaked breast always sharply demarcated from white belly; narrow wing-bar in flight. Juv has rusty feather fringes on mantle divided by two sets of quite bold, pale V-markings. **V** Call a wooden *drrrk*. **H** Breeds on tundra in north-east Siberia and North America, rare migrant to marshes and mudflats in Europe. **D** V, rare but regular, mostly 5 and 8-10.

6 Little Stint L 15 cm

Calidris minuta **ID** Commonest very small wader; bill short, legs black, tail-sides grey. Variable. In br rufous on head and breast, becomes buff-brown by July. Juv less bright with paler forehead and double pale V-markings on back. In non-br like small version of 1. **V** Call high-pitched *pit*, display call thin *svi-svi-svirr*. **H** Breeds tundra, widespread on marshes and mudflats around European coasts during migration. **D** M 4-10, fairly common; w, uncommon.

7 Temminck's Stint L 14 cm

Calidris temminckii **ID** Body longer than 6, greyer overall, darker on breast, legs yellowish, tail protrudes beyond wings at rest, white tail-sides visible in flight. In br upperparts spotted black, in non-br uniform, in juv with pale feather fringes. **V** Calls soft *si-si-si-si-si*, display call chirping *titititi*. **H** Breeds wetlands, widespread on marshes and mudflats during migration. **D** m 5, 8-9, scarce; b very rare breeder north Scotland.

juv
non-br
br
1
juv
2
non-br
br
juv
br
3
4
juv
br
juv ♀
5
♂ br
non-br
juv
br
6
7
juv
non-br
br

COURSER AND PRATINCOLES

1 Cream-coloured Courser **L** 25 cm

Cursorius cursor **ID** Sandy-coloured wader, 'rolling' plover-like walk on long legs with sudden stops. Bill short and curved, primaries and underwing completely black. In juv head pattern faint, upperparts scaled. **V** Calls nasally *quitt* and rough *praaak*. **H** Breeds semi-desert in north Africa and the Middle East, in Europe only regular as vagrant to Spain. **D** V 4-11, extremely rare.

2 Collared Pratincole **L** 26 cm

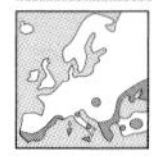

Glareola pratincola **ID** Tern-like wader with short legs, short bill and forked tail, brown upperparts and breast and white belly and vent. Underwing coverts reddish-brown (in flight often appear blackish), narrow white trailing edge to wing, in br the tip of tail is longer than tips of wings when perched. Yellow throat-patch edged with black in br, juv scaled above. Hunts insects in flight over open areas. Winters in Africa. **V** Calls nasally *kerrekek-kitik*. **H** Breeds in loose colonies on wet or dry mudflats. **D** V 4-9, rare.

3 Black-winged Pratincole **L** 26 cm

Glareola nordmanni **ID** In all plumages very similar to 2, but underwing coverts black and no white trailing edge to wing. In br tail tip shorter than wing tips, upperparts slightly darker brown, more black on lores and less red at base of bill. **V** Calls slightly lower-pitched than 2. **H** Moist steppes of south-east Europe and central Asia, occurs further east than 2. **D** V 4-9, very rare.

SKUAS

4 Long-tailed Skua **L** 38 cm **WS** 108 cm

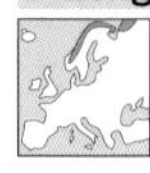

Stercorarius longicaudus **ID** Smallest skua, appears graceful, only a little larger than Black-headed Gull, flies almost tern-like on slender wings, often hovers. Ad only occurs as pale morph and is unmistakable in br due to extended central tail feathers which are 12-24 cm longer than the rest of the tail. Juv occurs as dark morph and pale morph. Dark morph juv difficult to distinguish from 5, variable in colour but smaller, mostly greyer and seldom with reddish tinge, only two outer primaries have white shafts, central tail feathers only slightly longer than tail and with rounded tips, undertail coverts evenly barred, bill shorter, appears deeper and is clearly bi-coloured with black tip. **V** Alarm call *krepp-krepp*, during display *keeyah*. **H** Breeds tundra, sometimes away from coast, otherwise oceans and coasts. Passes Atlantic and North Sea coasts to and from wintering grounds off Africa. **D** m 4-5 and 8-9, scarce.

5 Arctic Skua **L** 40 cm **WS** 113 cm

Stercorarius parasiticus **ID** The commonest skua, about the size of a Common Gull. Ad occurs as dark or pale morph, with underparts brown or whitish, as well as an intermediate variant which may or may not have breast band. In br pointed central tail feathers elongated by 5-8 cm. Juv uniformly barred variably light to dark brown, often with rusty tinge. In contrast to 4 in juv, larger, bill longer, more slender and uniform, slightly longer central tail feathers pointed, undertail coverts irregularly barred, shafts of outer 3-5 primaries white. **V** Calls meowing *aag-eeoo*. **H** Breeds coasts, widespread on coasts on passage, in winter open ocean. **D** B north Scotland; M 4-5 and 7-10, coasts, rarely inland.

6 Pomarine Skua **L** 46 cm **WS** 120 cm

Stercorarius pomarinus **ID** Size between Common and Herring Gulls, ad in dark or more often light morph (with or without breast band), in br central tail feathers elongated by 5-10 cm and twisted by 90°, shaped like spoons. Juv similar to 5 but larger, base of wing broader, light bases of the greater primary coverts create two whitish crescents on underwing, central tail feathers slightly elongated and rounded, undertail-coverts evenly barred, heavy bill is pale with black tip. **V** Alarm call low *geck*. **H** Breeds tundra, passes North Sea and Atlantic coasts on way to and from wintering grounds off Africa (often in flocks in spring). **D** m 4-5 and 8-10; occasional w.

7 Great Skua **L** 54 cm **WS** 132 cm

Stercorarius skua **ID** Large, heavy, thick-set skua, appears overall very dark. In flight always characterised by contrasting large white crescents on upper- and underwing, formed by the white bases of the primaries; has no protruding central tail feathers. In juv uniform dark brown, adults lighter or darker brown, many whitish feather edges make them appear shaggy. **V** Call a low *tok*. **H** Breeds in colonies on North Atlantic coasts, winters at sea. **D** B, north Scotland; M, 4-5 and 8-10, coasts; w, coasts.

1
juv
2
br
3
juv
4
juv
br
juv
juv dark
juv light
5
br dark
br light
br
juv
6
juv
br dark
br light
juv
7

AUKS

1 Puffin L 31 cm

Fratercula arctica **ID** Unmistakable in br with large, colourful, triangular bill, also pale triangular cheek patch, orange legs and somewhat 'pot-bellied' appearance. Horny appendages at base of laterally compressed bill are shed temporarily in late summer, bill therefore then smaller, but still deep, triangular and pale, also in non-br sides of head darker grey. Juv similar to non-br, bill even smaller and sides of head duskier, but characteristic features still present. Usually low-flying, underwing dusky, upperwing lacks white trailing edge, tail short, black collar always unbroken. **V** Calls in colony short *aohr*. **H** Breeds mainly in huge colonies around rocky coasts in north-west Europe, nests in a burrow or rocky crevice, winters far out on open sea. **D** B, grassy areas near cliffs in north and west; mw, mainly pelagic but occasionally seen from land.

2 Razorbill L 40 cm

Alca torda **ID** Typical black-and-white auk, characterised by deep black bill, flattened in vertical plane with white cross-bands that are often difficult to see. Can be confused with the more common 3, but upperparts deep black (not brown-black), flanks not striated, long tail pointed and like the bill held slightly upwards when swimming, throat thicker and shorter. Head and neck markings reduced in juv and non-br. In flight differentiated from 3 (and partially also 4) by pure white underwing coverts, plain flanks, more white at side of vent, feet not protruding beyond the tip of the tail, as well as head and tail raised higher and less hunch-backed appearance. **V** Call at breeding site a sadly growling *urrr*, flight display with extremely slow wing-beats. **H** Breeds in colonies on rocky coasts with cliffs, mostly together with 3, eggs laid below rocky promontories; in winter on open ocean. **D** B, cliffs in north and west; W, much more widespread around coasts.

3 Common Guillemot L 42 cm

Uria aalge **ID** Most common auk on European coasts, resembles a small penguin with its dark upperparts and white belly. Black bill is awl-shaped and quite long, upperparts brown-black to grey-black, underneath white with blackish flank hatching, some birds with narrow white eye-ring and white line stretching back from eye (known as 'Bridled Guillemot'). In non-br and 1w white sides of head divided by narrow black line. Appears slightly hunch-backed in flight, when feet protrude beyond tip of tail. **V** Calls in the colony rasping *aorr*. **H** Breeds in colonies consisting of many thousands of pairs on narrow ledges on steep coastal cliffs in north and west Europe; winters on North Sea and Atlantic. **D** B, cliffs in north and west; W, widespread and common around all coasts.

4 Brünnich's Guillemot L 42 cm

Uria lomvia **ID** Only occurs regularly in Iceland and northern Norway, breeds in mixed colonies with the very similar 3. Differentiated from 3 by blackish upperparts, thicker, shorter bill with white line along gape, lack of streaking on flanks and white underparts ending in an acute (not blunt) point on upper breast. Non-br separated from 2 and 3 by black reaching further back along the side of the head and in flight by white underwing coverts and more white on the side of the vent. **V** Calls more morose than 3. **H** Breeds and winters in far north Atlantic. **D** V 11-3, extremely rare.

5 Little Auk L 20 cm

Alle alle **ID** Very small auk, barely starling-sized, with short neck and small, black bill and white-edged scapulars. Swims with body high in the water, has whirring flight, often in flocks, very dark underwings. **V** Trills at breeding site. **H** Forms massive breeding colonies on scree slopes and weathered rock walls at the edge of the Arctic, winters in northern north Atlantic. **D** w 11-2, occurs along coasts, particularly east coast, in variable numbers, with large 'wrecks' sometimes brought about by autumn storms.

6 Black Guillemot L 35 cm

Cepphus grylle **ID** Medium-sized auk, less social than the other species, with awl-shaped black bill (and bright red gape), bright red legs and large white oval patch on wings shaped by the secondary coverts, this patch is especially conspicuous in otherwise all black br. In non-br and 1w mainly white and grey patterns above, in juv upperparts dusky, wing patch mottled up to 1s. **V** Displays with high-pitched cricket-like chirping *siirrrrp*. **H** Breeds in rock crevices, often at the edge of large seabird colonies, also in single pairs; winters close to coast. **D** BR, rocky north-west coasts from Cumbria to Aberdeenshire, often in harbours.

1
br
1w
non-br
br
2
br
non-br
non-br
br
3
br
non-br
non-br
br
4
br
non-br
br
5
br
non-br
non-br
br
6
br
1w
non-br
non-br
br

GULLS

1 Ivory Gull L 44 cm WS 106 cm

Pagophila eburnea **ID** Medium-sized gull from the High Arctic, which appears south of the pack ice only exceptionally. Looks rather pigeon-like when standing, with its round head, thick-set body, short black legs and horizontal body posture, but in flight very elegant. Ad with pure white feathers (beware albinos of other species), bill has bluish base and yellow tip. In 1w face darkened with 'dirty' appearance and plumage spotted blackish and dark brown to a variable extent. In contrast to other gulls it moults in 1s into white adult plumage. Often scavenges from carcasses and is not very shy. **V** Calls *frrrreeoh*. **H** Spends the whole year in the High Arctic and pack ice zone. **D** V 11-2, very rare, mostly northern coasts.

2 Sabine's Gull L 33 cm WS 84 cm

Larus sabini **ID** Small oceanic gull of the High Arctic, slender, elegant, with notched tail and distinctive wing pattern: a large white triangle and the trailing edge delimited by the black outer primaries and dark upperwing coverts. In br slate-grey hood, bill black with yellow tip, legs blackish, upperparts grey. Non-br ad has white head with dark smudges on nape and around eye. In juv, upperparts brownish grey with a scaled appearance caused by pale feather edges, black band at tip of tail, legs grey-pink. Instead of a hood the brown-grey colour of mantle extends over the nape to the back of crown and ear-coverts to form dark 'front end'; could be confused with 5 as juv. **V** Call a scratching *kye-kyerrr*. **H** Breeding bird of arctic coasts, winters in south Atlantic, appears on west European coasts after autumn storms. **D** m 8-10, rare, almost exclusively around coasts, particularly in south-west England.

3 Ross's Gull L 30 cm WS 77 cm

Rhodostethia roseus **ID** Small gull of the arctic tundra, can be confused with similar 4, but is slightly larger, has longer, more pointed wings and a wedge-shaped tail. In br no black on the wing (only thin line on outer leading edge of the primaries), characteristic narrow complete black collar, head white, underparts with pink tinge, underwings grey with broad white trailing edge (also on upperwings). Non-br identical, but no collar, instead nape washed-out grey and blackish spots in front of and behind eye. In 1w similar to 4, but wedge-shaped tail has only narrow black tip rather than a band, crown light, white triangle on wings larger, inner primaries white. **V** Calls at breeding grounds *kay-kay ki-kik*. **H** Breeds on arctic tundra of northern Siberia and northern North America, remains on pack ice in winter. Vagrant to Europe. **D** V 11-2, very rare, mainly occurs along northern coasts.

4 Little Gull L 26 cm WS 66 cm

Larus minutus **ID** Smallest gull, picks food from the surface of the water when swimming (like phalaropes) or in flight (like marsh terns). In ad wings have white tips without any black markings, but underwings characteristically blackish with broad white trailing edge, in br hood, including back of neck, black, in juv instead only small blackish patch on ear-coverts and dark hind crown. In 1w upperparts grey with blackish W-shaped band extending over the secondary coverts and primaries, pale underwings, black band at end of tail and dusky grey cap over hind crown and ear-coverts. Juv plumage retained only for short period and similar, but mantle, scapulars and nape dark brown, (confusion possible with much larger 5 in 1w). 1s similar, but W-shaped band pale brownish and sometimes a hint of a hood is present, in 2w like non-br, but with a variable number of black spots on wing-tip, underwings whitish to grey, in 2s like br, but still some black on wing tips, underwings grey to black. **V** Call nasal *kek*, during flight display gives *kyakikyakik*. **H** Breeds on inland water bodies mainly in north-east Europe, migrates along coasts and through continental Europe and winters on coasts from Britain south to the Mediterranean. **D** M 4-5 and 8-10, locally common; w, uncommon, mainly coasts.

5 Kittiwake L 40 cm WS 100 cm

Rissa tridactyla **ID** A true 'sea gull' being a bird of the open ocean. Ad similar to Common Gull, but 'dipped in ink' wing-tips completely black without white spots, short black legs, bill pure yellow. In non-br sickle-shaped dark patch on ear-coverts and paler grey collar below. From juv up to 1s has a blackish W-shaped band on the upperwings which fades to brown (like the much smaller 4), also has black nape band up to 1w. **V** In colonies vocal, calls loud meowing *kitti-way kitti-waik*. **H** In north-west Europe large colonies make nests of seaweed on cliffs, in winter mainly on open sea. **D** BRMW, locally common on coasts, breeding on cliffs and even buildings, more widespread in winter.

ad
1w
1
1w
ad
2
juv
br
non-br
1w
3
br
1w
1w
br
1w
5
non-br
1w
br
2w
br
4
non-br
1w
br

1 Black-headed Gull **L** 37 cm **WS** 92 cm

Larus ridibundus **ID** The commonest gull in many parts of Europe, especially inland, mostly seen in flocks. All ages share the following characteristics: relatively small size, white wedge on the long, slender, pointed wings (formed by the outer primaries) and with black border towards the wing-tip, and the more or less blood-red colour of the slender bill and legs. In br unmistakable, dark-brown hood does not reach the back of the neck, bill and legs dark red, in spring underparts often tinged slightly pink. In non-br head white with rather small dark spots on ear-coverts and above eye, legs red and bill red with black tip. In juv upperparts coloured dusky- to reddish-brown, legs and bill yellowish to pale red, in 1w becomes mainly grey above and has white head and body with head-markings as in non-br, but tail has black band at tip, secondaries are dark and there is a brown band on the secondary coverts. In 1s very similar but dark areas become paler, hood of br already faint or fully present. From 2w not distinguishable from ad. **V** Calls screeching *kraah* or *kriaarr* and a warning *kekek*. **H** Large breeding colonies on marshes, ponds and lakes with reeds, in winter on all types of water bodies, also parks, fields, farmland and rubbish tips. Winters south to the Mediterranean **D** BRMW, abundant (although can be uncommon inland in late spring and early summer).

2 Slender-billed Gull **L** 40 cm **WS** 96 cm

Larus genei **ID** Has very similar wing pattern to 1. In br head white, in non-br possibly with faint dark patch on ear-coverts, upperparts paler grey than 1. Slightly larger than 1 with longer legs and especially a longer neck with a typical head profile of a flat forehead gradually merging with long bill and feathers extending further onto upper mandible. In ad breast and belly often tinged with pink, in br legs and bill blackish-red, in non-br red to orange, iris yellow. From juv to 1s best told from 1 by structural features, from 1w also by light iris and mostly lighter colour of bill and legs. **V** Calls lower-pitched, more throaty and nasal than 1. **H** Breeds on coasts and lagoons, winters locally on coasts of the Mediterranean. **D** V 4-8, extremely rare.

3 Mediterranean Gull **L** 39 cm **WS** 98 cm

Larus melanocephalus **ID** Superficially similar to 1, but larger and chunkier, legs longer and bill heavier. Ad has pure-white wing-tips and underwings, in br black hood reaches far down nape, in non-br black wedge on ear-coverts. Juv similar to Common Gull but underwings white, 1w and 1s with clear grey panel on secondaries, narrow black band at tail-tip, blackish outer primaries, head pattern like non-br, bill and legs dusky green-grey. In 2w and 2s like ad, but black markings close to white wing-tip. **V** Lower and more nasal than 1: *gheeaah*. **H** Similar to 1; in winter mostly coasts. **D** bmw, uncommon except at certain sites in southern England.

4 Audouin's Gull **L** 48 cm **WS** 122 cm

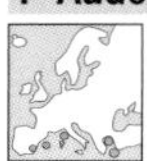

Larus audouinii **ID** Rare, medium-sized Mediterranean species. Slight possibility of confusion with Yellow-legged Gull, but smaller, more slender, bill shorter, forehead flatter and legs dark grey. In ad characteristic coral-red bill (with yellow at extreme tip bordered by narrow black band), dark eye, light-grey upperparts and barely any white in the extensively black wing-tips. Juv dark grey-brown above with pale scaling, breast, flanks and underwing markings brownish, tail completely black with narrow white band at tip and U-shaped white uppertail coverts, and bill grey with black tip. During 1w and 1s increasing amount of grey above, from 2w to 2s with narrow black band at end of tail, much black on primaries and secondaries and red bill. **V** Calls nasally *glee-ieh*, on breeding grounds also crow- and donkey-like sounds. **H** Breeds on small rocky islands in the Mediterranean, also winters there. **D** V, extremely rare.

5 Great Black-headed Gull **L** 63 cm

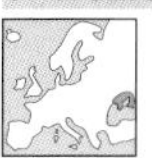

Larus ichthyaetus **WS** 155 cm **ID** Very large gull with black hood in br, in all forms iris dark, but upper and lower eye-ring white. Has small, long head, extending via flat forehead into massive bill. Ad has much white in primaries and narrow black band in front of white wing-tip, legs yellow, bill tri-coloured yellow, red and black; in non-br hood replaced by a striated mask from eye to back of head. In juv sharply defined black band at tail tip, sides of breast and scaled upperparts grey-brown, underwings light; from 1w head pattern like non-br, bill pink with black tip, upperparts increasingly grey. Continues to become more similar to non-br until 3w when there is still a lot of black on wing but little on tail. **V** Calls with low-pitched *ha-oo* and goose-like *ga-gaga*. **H** Breeds on steppe lakes from the Black Sea eastwards. Winters outside Europe. **D** -.

1
juv
1w
1w
br
non-br
br
2
1w
1w
non-br
br
3
2w
br
1w
non-br
1w
br
4
juv
juv
1s
br
br
5
1w
br
1s
non-br
br

1 Common Gull **L** 43 cm **WS** 104 cm

Larus canus **ID** Medium-sized gull found mainly in north Europe, where it occurs along coasts and is also widely found inland. Resembles a smaller version of 3, but is more delicate, head is rounder, bill more slender, wings narrower and eyes dark. In ad bill and legs greenish- to matt-yellow, head in br white, in non-br streaked dark including back of neck, bill often with black ring. Juv brownish with sharply demarcated black band at end of tail, from 1w to 1s legs still dirty grey-pink, bill with black tip is same colour or yellowish, mantle grey. In 2w and 2s has tail band only faint, wing coverts already grey, but primaries still extensively black. **V** Calls meowing *meeyoo* and *klee-you-klee-you*. **H** Breeding colonies on coasts, inland often in single pairs. Winters south to Biscay and Black Sea. **D** BRMW, found on coasts all year and more common during winter when also occurs inland.

2 Ring-billed Gull **L** 45 cm **WS** 115 cm

Larus delawarensis **ID** A North American species that is seen in Europe with increasing frequency. Rather similar to 1, but slightly larger, with heavier bill, the upper- and lower edges of which run almost parallel. In ad bill yellow with broad black band, iris pale, grey of upperparts paler than 1, legs brighter yellow, white tertial fringes narrower, less white in tips of two outer primaries; in non-br head streaked pale grey. In 1w mantle and greater coverts lighter grey than in 1, tail band dissolves upwards into several narrow shafts, flanks often have arrow-shaped spotting, bill is a clear bicoloured pink and black. In 1s wing-coverts are usually very worn, in 2w eye sometimes already light. **H** Breeds in North America but occurs every year in small numbers in western Europe, particularly along the Atlantic coasts. **D** V, rare, mainly western coasts, apparently increasing. Individuals often remain faithful to a site for many years.

3 Herring Gull **L** 60 cm **WS** 140 cm

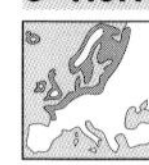

Larus argentatus **ID** Most common and best known of the larger gulls. Takes four years to reach adult plumage, during this time it can be confused with other species. Large, powerful, with thick bill, flesh-coloured legs and slow wing-beats. In ad upperparts light grey, bill bright yellow with red spot, legs flesh-coloured, eyes yellow, orbital ring yellow to orange, outer primaries black with white tips and spots (less white in western subspecies *argenteus*, more in northern *argentatus*). Eastern Baltic birds of the type '*omissus*' have yellowish legs – compare to 4 and 5. In non-br head and neck streaked dark; juv quite uniform grey-brown including underparts and underwings, pale 'window' on inner primaries, dark band at end of tail not clearly delineated above, turns paler during 1w and 1s, base of blackish bill then paler. In 2w and 2s more grey feathers on mantle, bill has flesh-coloured base, dark band and whitish tip, eye turns slowly lighter, in 3w and 3s similar to ad, but variable pale brown wing coverts, more black in primaries, tail band often faint, bill often yellowish-pink with black band, in 4w more black on primaries and primary coverts than in ad, mostly dark bill band. Compare sequence of feather changes on inner back cover. **V** Many different calls, for example *kyow-kyow, gegege, aa-ooh*. **H** Breeds in large colonies along north European coasts, often breeds inland, particularly on tall buildings in city centres, and in winter increasingly on lakes and refuse dumps. **D** BRMW, abundant on coasts, common inland in winter and also breeds increasingly inland.

4 Yellow-legged Gull **L** 55 cm **WS** 130 cm

Larus michahellis **ID** Large gull of southern and western Europe, in all forms very similar to 3, but appears heavier with longer wings; legs longer and bill heavier. Ad darker grey above than 3, with, more black on wing-tips, legs bright yellow, has faint dark streaking on head only in autumn. From juv to 1s head and underparts whiter than 3, inner primaries show less obvious 'window', tail whitish with sharply contrasting terminal band. **V** Calls deeper than 3, similar to Lesser Black-backed Gull. **H** Breeds coasts and inland lakes in southern Europe, spreading northwards, more widespread in late summer and autumn. **D** mw, uncommon in southern England; b, breeds very rarely on south coast.

5 Caspian Gull **L** 60 cm **WS** 140 cm

Larus cachinnans **ID** Longer body, legs and neck with slenderer, more pointed bill than 3 and 4. Ad like 4, but paler grey above, legs often paler, eyes darker, tips of outer primaries have less black more white. From juv to 2w white head and whitish underwings (in 4 brownish). **V** Laughing *aah-hehehehe-heh*. **H** Breeds from Black Sea eastwards on coasts and steppe lakes. **D** mw, scarce visitor to south England.

1w
1w
non-br
br
br
1
1w
1w
non-br
non-br
br
2
1w
2w
br
3
non-br
juv
1s
ad
4
juv
1w
non-br
br
br
5
1w
1w
non-br
br
br

1 Great Black-backed Gull L 70 cm

Larus marinus **WS** 160 cm **ID** Largest gull, very heavy and with a massive, deep bill, legs always flesh-coloured. Ad with almost black upperparts (possible confusion with the smaller 2, but recognizable by leg colour and in flight by more white on the wing-tips), head in non-br only faintly streaked dark. Imm is similar to Herring Gull and 2 but is superficially more like a large imm Yellow-legged Gull; it is best distinguished by size, coarser patterning on the paler feathers in comparison to Herring Gull, lighter colouration of head, underparts and tail, the broken banding of the tail and the lighter inner primaries compared with 2. Characteristic black feathers on the upperparts appear mostly only in 3w. **V** Calls very deep *kla-ou*. **H** Breeds singly or in small colonies on northern European coasts, also winters there and at sea. **D** BRMW, common on coasts all year and thinly distributed inland in winter, when most frequently seen on rubbish tips and large reservoirs.

2 Lesser Black-backed Gull L 55 cm

Larus fuscus **WS** 130 cm **ID** Elegant large gull, the same size as Herring Gull but more slender. Wings very long and protrude far beyond tail tip, head slightly rounded, bill relatively slender, ad always has yellow legs and barely any white on wing-tip. Occurs as three subspecies, in western Europe and Iceland *graellsii* has slate-grey upperparts, in the Baltic Sea region the upperparts of *fuscus* are black, and in south-west Scandinavia and along central European coasts *intermedius* black-grey to blackish above. Juv darker and more scaled above than Herring Gull, wings uniform dark, broad dark band at end of tail separated with more contrast. Moults faster than other large gulls, therefore slate-coloured mantle feathers and scapulars present from 1s. **V** Calls lower-pitched than Herring Gull. **H** Breeds mainly on north European coasts (but also inland), winters from Britain southwards, *fuscus* migrates to east Africa. **D** BRMW *graellsii* common inland and at coast all year, *intermedius* occurs on passage and during winter.

3 Heuglin's Gull L 60 cm **WS** 145 cm

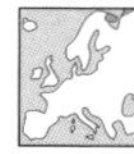

Larus heuglini **ID** Breeds on Siberian tundra from Kola Peninsula eastwards, more eastern in distribution than 2 and very difficult to distinguish from it. Ad upperparts similar colour to *graellsii* of 2. Slightly larger than 2 with fainter markings on head in non-br. Moults rapidly and already shows adult features in 1s. The eastern population *taimyrensis* is lighter above and has flesh-coloured legs, while southern subspecies *barabensis* from northern Kazakhstan is so light in colour that it is barely distinguishable from Yellow-legged Gull. The taxonomy of these gulls is still a source of great debate. **V** Calls *ga-agag*, possibly lower-pitched and stronger than 2. **H** Breeds in north-west Siberian tundra, winters mainly in Middle East and east Africa. **D** -.

4 Glaucous Gull L 65 cm **WS** 150 cm

Larus hyperboreus **ID** Body shape resembles a large, powerful, short-winged, light-coloured Herring Gull with long bill, but in all forms without any black on wing, legs always pink. Ad lighter grey above than Herring Gull, wing-tips pure white; in non-br head, neck and breast are strongly blotched with dark markings, emphasizing yellow eye. Juv and 1w variably whitish, light to dark 'biscuit-brown' with less pale brown bands across tail and brownish tips of the light primaries can be absent to obvious, bill characteristically pink with sharply delineated black tip, iris still dark; in 1s entire plumage fades to whitish. In 2w and 3w similar, but tip of bill light in front of dark band, eye increasingly light, amount of light grey feathers on upperparts increasing. Pale Herring Gulls with incomplete pigmentation are often similar, but with imm bill mainly dark, browner on wings and tail, while in albinos upperparts are white instead of pale grey. **V** Similar to Herring Gull. **H** Breeds in Iceland and along arctic coasts, winters in north Atlantic south to Britain and northern France. **D** mw 10-4, mainly coastal, more regular in north and west Britain.

5 Iceland Gull L 55 cm **WS** 135 cm

Larus glaucoides **ID** Arctic gull, in all forms coloration almost identical to 4 (vagrant Canadian *kumlieni* with pale grey in primaries), but smaller (never larger than Herring Gull), more slender, wings protrude further beyond tail tip. Rounder head, larger eye and shorter bill create a 'friendly' facial expression. In contrast to 4 in br red instead of orange-yellow orbital ring, in non-br fainter streaking on head, from juv to 1s blacker, bill lighter grey-pink at base. **V** Calls harsher than Herring Gull. **H** Breeds Greenland, winters in North Atlantic south to Britain. **D** mw 11-4, more regular in the north and west.

1
1w
2w
3w
1w
br
br
1s
juv
3
1s
br
br
juv
2
1w
2w
br
non-br
graellsii
fuscus
br
4
1w
1w
2w
non-br
non-br
br
1w
2w
5
1w
br
br
non-br

TERNS

1 Caspian Tern L 52 cm WS 135 cm

Hydroprogne caspia **ID** Largest tern, almost the size of Herring Gull, with heavy and conspicuous red bill with black tip, black legs and quite short tail. In non-br forehead streaked white, black cap in juv reaches lower on the sides of the head. Appears 'front-heavy' in quite gull-like flight. **V** Calls heron-like low and hoarse *kraaah*, juv continues to beg during migration, high-pitched *svee-vee*. **H** Breeds around Baltic and in south-east Europe, on passage in central and south Europe, winters Africa and Asia. **D** V 4-9, very rare.

2 Little Tern L 23 cm WS 52 cm

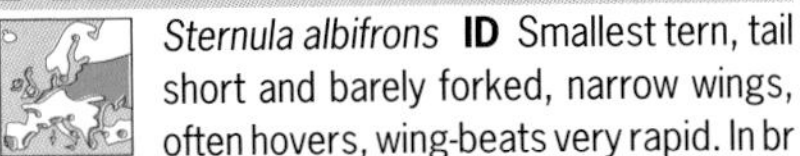

Sternula albifrons **ID** Smallest tern, tail short and barely forked, narrow wings, often hovers, wing-beats very rapid. In br forehead white, bill quite long and yellow with black tip, legs orange. In non-br bill dark and lores white, juv has scaly pattern above and only base of bill pale yellow. **V** Chattering calls. **H** Breeds on flat, sandy coastal beaches, also inland in continental Europe on stony lakes and rivers. Summer visitor. **D** BM 4-9, locally common, coastal.

3 Gull-billed Tern L 36 cm WS 105 cm

Gelochelidon nilotica **ID** Large, robust, a more gull-like species with heavy black bill, quite long black legs and short, only slightly forked tail, different from 4 with pale grey rump and tail, black trailing edge to primaries. Black cap of br is replaced by black 'bandit mask' in non-br. Juv paler, almost no dark pattern above and with more white on the forehead than the similar 4. Often hunts in flight over land for insects and small vertebrates. **V** Call is a laughing *keveck*. **H** Forms mainly small colonies in wet meadows and on dunes in southern Europe. Summer visitor. **D** V 4-9, very rare, a few records annually.

4 Sandwich Tern L 38 cm WS 100 cm

Sterna sandvicensis **ID** Large tern which is pale overall with rather short, black legs and long, slender black bill, in ad always with yellow tip. In br black cap with short shaggy crest, in non-br with white forehead, in juv strong scaly pattern above, dusky cap and completely dark bill. Long, slender wings often strongly angled in flight, tail relatively short. **V** Conspicuous through call, loud and rough *kirr-rik*. **H** Can form enormous colonies on sand banks along coast, winters Mediterranean and further south. **D** BM 3-10 common on coast, m inland, a few winter.

5 Common Tern L 34 cm WS 88 cm

Sterna hirundo **ID** On coasts often most common breeding tern, inland often the only one present. Slender, elegant, forked tail with elongated outer tail feathers (when standing almost reach wing-tips), light-grey above, white below, red legs are short, bill orange-red with black tip, in br entire cap black but in juv and non-br only crown and back of head. In juv upperparts brownish (fading to greyish) and faintly barred, clear dark leading edge to wing, bill base orange. Hunts fish in steep dive. To differentiate from 6 see next account. **V** Calls *kit, kirri* and *krrrri-ye*. **H** Often breeds in large colonies (but also as single pairs) along coasts and inland on rivers, lakes and gravel pits. Winters outside Europe. **D** BM 4-9, common.

6 Arctic Tern L 36 cm WS 86 cm

Sterna paradisaea **ID** The commonest tern along the coasts of northern Europe, in the north also on tundra. In all forms very similar to 5, but slightly smaller, more slender, tail longer, legs and bill shorter. In br bill uniform dark-red, underparts mostly tinged darker grey, tail protrudes clearly beyond wing-tips, primaries paler and seemingly transparent with only narrow, sharply demarcated black trailing edge (instead of dark outer and grey inner primaries often with dark wedge). In juv greyer above than 5, darker leading wing edge is narrower, secondaries appear white (instead of grey with white tips), bill mostly dark. Apart from plunge-diving also collects food in low flight from water surface like a marsh tern (see page 100). **V** Calls higher-pitched than 5. **H** Breeds in colonies along coasts, winters off Africa. **D** BM 4-9, coasts (most common in the north); m, inland.

7 Roseate Tern L 38 cm WS 80 cm

Sterna dougallii **ID** Similar to 5 and 6, but much rarer, plumage very white, tail, bill and legs longer. In br tail feathers protrude far beyond wing-tips at rest, underparts tinged pink, bill mostly black with red only at base (5 may show black bill), only outer three primaries darker. Colouration of juv varies only slightly from 4. **V** Call *choo-vik*. **H** Breeds very locally on coasts of Britain, Ireland and north-west France, winters west Africa. **D** bm 4-9, scarce, coastal.

1
juv
1w
br
br
2
juv
br
juv
br
3
juv
1w
non-br
br
br
4
1w
juv
br
non-br
br
5
juv
br
juv
non-br
br
6
juv
juv
1s
br
br
7
juv
br
juv
non-br
br

1 Black Tern **L** 23 cm **WS** 65 cm

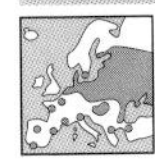

Chlidonias niger **ID** The most common of the three dark marsh terns, which occur mainly on inland water bodies where they also nest on floating vegetation. In contrast to the 'sea terns' they have broader wings, shorter and only slightly forked tails and pick their food, mainly insects and their larvae, from the water's surface instead of plunge-diving. In br unmistakable being dusky overall, head and belly black, dark grey above, underwings and tail light grey, only vent white. In non-br underparts white with characteristic dark patch on the sides of the breast, black cap extends like a 'droplet' onto the ear-coverts. Juv like non-br, but scaled on mantle due to pale feather fringes. **V** Call a nasal *kyeh*. **H** Standing inland water bodies, but also appears on coasts during migration when much more widespread, winters outside Europe. **D** m 4-9, uncommon, mainly southern England.

2 White-winged Black Tern **L** 22 cm

Chlidonias leucopterus **WS** 64 cm **ID** Often associated with 1, especially during spring migration, and is very similar to it in appearance and behaviour, but tail less notched, legs longer, bill shorter, wings broader. In br distinguished by black underwing coverts, also by whiter upperwings and white tail. Non-br similar to 1, but rump and uppertail coverts white, tail grey with white outer edges, dark cap only striated (not solid black) and no dark patch on sides of breast. Juv like non-br, but cap darker and similar to 1, brown mantle forms 'saddle' contrasting with rest of upperparts. **V** Calls roughly *kerek* and *kesh*. **H** Breeds mainly on eastern European inland water bodies, winters from southern Europe southwards. **D** V 5-9, rare, several records annually, most often in south and east, often joins flocks of 1.

3 Whiskered Tern **L** 24 cm **WS** 72 cm

Chlidonias hybrida **ID** Largest and palest of the three marsh terns, legs longer, bill thicker, often reminiscent of *Sterna* species, but rump and slightly notched tail with white outer edges in all plumages grey. In br pale grey overall and dark grey belly contrast with pale underwings and white sides of head, bill vivid red. Upperwings in non-br paler than in 1 and 2, striated back of crown connected with ear-coverts, patch on side of breast absent or faint. Juv very similar to 2, but broader and paler feather edges on dark mantle, leading edge of inner wing lacks dark bar, more solid area of black on rear of head. **V** Calls loudly and wooden *krrrk*. **H** Inland water bodies of south and east Europe, winters Africa and Asia. **D** V 4-9, rare, a few records each year.

SANDGROUSE

4 Black-bellied Sandgrouse **L** 32 cm

Pterocles orientalis **ID** Pigeon-like with small head, short bill and very short feathered legs; due to cryptically coloured upperparts very hard to see on the ground. In all plumages characterised by rounded black belly, underwings contrasting black and white. ♂ with uniform grey breast, ♀ with sandy-coloured striated breast and upperparts more finely barred. In fast flight with pointed wings more reminiscent of golden plover than a pigeon. **V** Often uttered flight call snorting *tyorrrl*. **H** Breeds mainly in north Africa and Asia, in Europe only on the Iberian Peninsula but also occurs from Turkey to the Caspian Sea in semi-deserts and steppes, does not migrate, but in the morning and afternoon flies in flocks over great distances to drink at water-holes. **D -**.

5 Pin-tailed Sandgrouse **L** 30 cm

Pterocles alchata **ID** Smaller and paler than 4, with white belly and in both sexes greatly elongated central tail feathers as well as rusty-brown breast patch edged with black. ♂ upperparts with yellow-green spots, throat black, ♀ has upperparts barred, throat whitish, breast has additional narrow black band. **V** When disturbed or on the way to water-holes utters guttural *katar katarr*. **H** Dry habitats and semi-deserts in north Africa and Middle East, in Europe only on Iberian Peninsula and in southern France (Crau). **D -**.

6 Pallas's Sandgrouse **L** 30 cm

Syrrhaptes paradoxus **ID** (not illustrated) Shares characteristics of 4 and 5: in both sexes belly black, but central tail feathers elongated, very pointed and wings completely whitish underneath, throat always light. Head pale orange, ♂ with uniform pale-grey breast, ♀ with narrow black neck band and spotted sides of breast. **V** Calls *geeyock* and *kockri*. **H** Breeds central Asian steppes, used to 'invade' western Europe regularly on a vast scale (most recently in 1888). **D** V, extremely rare.

juv
non-br
br
non-br
br
1
br
juv
non-br
2
non-br
br
3
br
juv
non-br
non-br
br
♂
4
♀
♂
♂
♀
5
♂

PIGEONS AND DOVES

1 Rock Dove **L** 33 cm **WS** 65 cm

Columba livia **ID** The wild form of 2, both hybridize freely and are sometimes indistinguishable. Features typical of pure Rock Dove are light-grey upperparts, bright white rump, two black bars on secondaries and white underwings. Body shape and fast flight as feral pigeon, mostly in flocks. **V** Coos like feral pigeon in a dull series *drroo-oo-ooh*, during flight-display glides on wings angled in a V-shape. **H** Locally common in mountains and on rocky coasts, particularly in south Europe, nests in hollows, crevices and on rock ledges. **D** br, local on coasts in west Scotland and west Ireland.

2 Feral pigeon **L** 33 cm **WS** 65 cm

Columba livia variety *domestica* **ID** Originates from domestic pigeons that have gone feral; all were originally bred from 1. Plumage very variable, ranging from pure white through various greys and red-browns to blackish, but often also similar to the original Rock Dove. In flight they are easily confused with a range of other unrelated birds including waders, gulls, sandgrouse and small raptors. **V** Like 1, juv begs with drawn-out high squeals. **H** Common and ubiquitous around buildings. Breeds on ledges on buildings in towns and villages, feeds in streets and fields. **D** BR, abundant.

3 Stock Dove **L** 30 cm **WS** 63 cm

Columba oenas **ID** Grey pigeon with no white on neck, wings or rump. Has two short black bars on closed wing, eye dark, rump and underwings grey – in 1 and (usually) 2 underwings white. Has thick black border to wings. Sometimes found in flocks with 4, conspicuous in flight due to smaller size and shorter tail. **V** Call a dull and hollow *oh-ewoh ohe-woh*, display flight with deep wing-beats and long gliding periods with wings held high. **H** Breeds in forests, old parkland and other places with mature trees, using a tree hollow as a nest (unlike other pigeons). **D** BRMW, common.

4 Woodpigeon **L** 41 cm **WS** 73 cm

Columba palumbus **ID** Largest pigeon, common over almost all of Europe, unmistakable due to broad white bands across wings, ad has large, white patches on sides of neck but these are absent in juv. During breeding season in pairs, otherwise in flocks. **V** Display call a dull *droo-doo, doo doo-doo*, also spring display flight lifts sharply upwards with wing-clapping then glides downwards. **H** Breeds in forests, parks and towns, feeds in fields, meadows and gardens. **D** BRMW, abundant.

5 Turtle Dove **L** 26 cm **WS** 51 cm

Streptopelia turtur **ID** Small, often shy dove, with quite long wings, occurs mostly in lightly wooded landscapes. Ad upperparts rufous with black centres to feathers, red skin around eye and collar barred black and white. Juv plainer and lacks collar. In flight distinguishable from 6 by contrasting pattern – black tail with white band at tip, pale belly and dark underwings. **V** Song is purring *turrr turrr*. **H** Breeds in open forests, thickets, orchards and hedgerows, winters in tropical Africa. Often hunted in Europe during migration. **D** BM 4-9, mainly England, still locally common in east but has undergone a huge decline.

6 Collared Dove **L** 32 cm **WS** 52 cm

Streptopelia decaocto **ID** Small, pale dove, often associated with human settlements. Plumage quite uniform light grey-brown with characteristic white-edged black collar around nape, which is absent in juv. Little contrast in flight with washed-out white band at end of tail (clearer from below), light underwing coverts and uniform beige underparts. **V** Displays with dull (but livelier than 4) three-syllable *doo-dooh doo*, mostly delivered from a raised perch; in flight calls hoarsely *craaaah*. **H** Almost exclusively in towns and villages, may breed from March to November. **D** BR, first arrived in western Europe from Balkans around 1950, now common in most of Britain.

7 Laughing Dove **L** 24 cm **WS** 42 cm

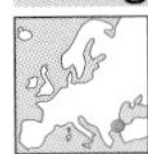

Streptopelia senegalensis **ID** Rather like a small, plain version of 6 but much darker with longer tail and shorter wings and characteristic black-spotted rufous patch on front of neck. Large blue-grey patch on upperwing like 5 but broad white tail-band more similar to 6. Very confiding, often seen in busy towns. **V** Displays with five-syllable fast cooing, third and fourth syllable slightly higher-pitched *dododoodoodo*. **H** Towns, cultivations. Main distribution from north Africa to central Asia, in Europe breeds only in Istanbul on the European side of the Bosphorus (as well as in other Turkish cities, probably mostly introduced). **D** - (occasional records considered escapes).

1
2
plumage
variations
juv
3
4
juv
5
juv
7
juv
6

BARN OWL

1 Barn Owl **L** 36 cm **WS** 88 cm

Tyto alba **ID** Medium-sized owl with very pale plumage overall, prefers open countryside. Pale, heart-shaped facial disc with black eyes, underparts white in western Europe (subspecies *alba*), buff in central and eastern Europe (subspecies *guttata*), upperparts finely patterned grey and yellowish-brown. In flight appears rather uniform, wings lack obvious dark markings above or below. **V** Calls with screeching *shrch* and hoarse *shreee*; juv begs with snoring sounds. **H** Fields, meadows and marshes, often nests on a ledge inside a building. **D** br, uncommon.

OWLS

2 Scops Owl **L** 20 cm **WS** 50 cm

Otus scops **ID** Small owl with yellow irises and broad, short ear-tufts; occurs in open, lightly wooded landscapes of southern Europe. Plumage cryptic and brown overall (can be tinged rufous to greyish), with fine black and white markings – colour and pattern like tree bark. Flight less undulating and more direct than Little Owl (the two often share the same habitat), wings longer and more slender. **V** In display gives soft whistling *piu* every 3 seconds, often from pairs in duet, sounds similar to Midwife Toad. **H** Cultivated lands with trees in southern Europe, also avenues and old gardens; winters in Africa. **D** V 4-9, very rare.

3 Long-eared Owl **L** 34 cm **WS** 92 cm

Asio otus **ID** Superficially similar to 5, but smaller and more slender with narrower wings that produce a light, swaying, gull-like flight. Cryptic brown plumage, long ear-tufts (usually flattened in flight and when relaxed), iris orange. Distinguished from 4 in flight due to more dense streaking on belly, and more finely barred wing-tips and tail. In summer chicks not yet capable of flight often stand on the ground or low in trees uttering begging calls. In winter small flocks roost together in dense copses. **V** Displaying ♂ gives dull *hoo* every 3 seconds, ♀ calls nasally *paah*; alarm call *kweck kreck*, begging call of juv *pee-aah* like a squeaky gate. **H** Coniferous forests, thickets, often breeds in old crows' nests. **D** brmw, uncommon and local.

4 Short-eared Owl **L** 37 cm **WS** 100 cm

Asio flammeus **ID** Lives in open areas such as moors and marshes, hunts at dusk and during the day. Easily confused with 3, but is paler with much less obvious ear-tufts, and has yellow eyes surrounded by black feathers. Can be distinguished from 3 in flight due to more uniform dark wing-tip, white trailing edge to wings, barely any streaking on belly and coarse barring on tail. **V** ♂ calls during display flight *dudududu…*, often combined with wing-clapping, ♀ calls *tchee-op*; alarm call *tcheff*. **H** Moors, heaths, wet meadows, open areas, nests on ground, winters south and west Europe. **D** brmw, uncommon; breeds in north, widespread in winter.

5 Eagle Owl **L** 66 cm **WS** 155 cm

Bubo bubo **ID** Huge owl, heavy with long ear-tufts, could be confused with the much smaller and more slender 3. Upperparts generally grey-brown (can be paler in southern birds) with cryptic markings, underparts rusty-buff, iris orange. Flies rapidly with flat beats of its broad wings, ear-tufts then flattened. **V** ♂ displays mostly at dusk, loud and low-pitched *ooo-hoo*, ♀ answers in slightly higher-pitch and also calls roughly *rreh-he*, warns sharply *kwe kwe*, also repetitive and with bill clacking; juvs beg *tchoo-oosh*. **H** Widespread but thinly distributed in continental Europe, mainly in mountains and isolated forests, often with cliffs (which are used as nesting sites). **D** ir, a few pairs breeding in Britain (mainly in the north) are derived from released captive birds.

6 Snowy Owl **L** 60 cm **WS** 138 cm

Bubo scandiacus **ID** Very large owl of tundra and open mountainous areas in northern Europe, often diurnal, stands prominently on low perches. Unmistakable (except possibly with very pale Common Buzzard or white-morph Gyr Falcon) due to size, overall white plumage and yellow eyes. Old ♂ almost pure white, ♀ faintly barred on belly and clearly barred above, and also obviously larger. Imm has more black-brown barring and spotting. **V** ♂ displays with dull moaning *goh* and warns duck-like *krek-krek-krek*; ♀ warns *byi, byi byi*, hungry juv squeaks. **H** North European tundra, especially regions with many lemmings and voles. **D** V, very rare, mostly northern Scotland (has bred).

alba
guttata
1
grey
rufous
2
3
chick
4
5
6
♂
♂
♀

1 Tawny Owl **L** 40 cm **WS** 90 cm

Strix aluco **ID** A common and widely distributed owl with a compact body, round head and black eyes. Plumage usually reddish-brown but sometimes grey, has line of white spots like a string of pearls on inner scapulars. In flight shows short tail and broad, barred wings without pale area on upper primaries. **V** ♂ displays with hooting *hooh, hu-huhu hooh* (a familiar sound of the night); ♀ calls *kyee-vit*, juv begs with hissing *pseeb*. **H** Resident in forests, woods and parks with mature trees, nests in hollows, during the day often roosts against a trunk. **D** BR, fairly common but strictly nocturnal.

2 Ural Owl **L** 55 cm **WS** 115 cm

Strix uralensis **ID** Large owl of old forests, can only be confused with 1 and 3. Larger, paler and greyer than 1, with a longer slightly wedge-shaped tail and small black eyes which stand out because they are surrounded by pale facial disc. In buzzard-like flight, tail and upperwings appear evenly barred. Bill yellowish, even in juv. **V** Displays with seven-syllable *voohoo, voohoo o-voohoo*; ♀ calls croaking *kruaw*. **H** Breeds in north European taiga and locally in mountains in south-east Europe, uses nest boxes, tree hollows or old raptor nests, extremely aggressive towards intruders when defending nest and young. **D -**.

3 Great Grey Owl **L** 64 cm **WS** 138 cm

Strix nebulosa **ID** Second-largest owl. Has massive round head, facial disc with narrow concentric dark rings and yellow eyes. Overall grey with dark grey and white patterning. In flight can only be confused with 2 and Eagle Owl, but has pale buff panel in primaries and broad dark band at end of tail. **V** Displays with a series of 10-12 low-pitched pumping sounds, decreasing at the end, only audible for 400 m, ♀ answers with thin *tchepp-tchep-tchep*; alarm call low-pitched sullen *grrroou*. **H** North European taiga with open areas, often breeds on tree stumps or in old raptor nests. Distribution erratic and depends on availability of rodent prey. **D -**.

4 Tengmalm's Owl **L** 25 cm **WS** 56 cm

Aegolius funereus **ID** Small owl of dense forests. Has large, slightly square head with pale face, yellow eyes and startled expression, upperparts dark brown with rows of large whitish spots, underparts dark with diffuse spotting. Chicks are uniquely solid dark brown on upper- and underparts. **V** Song far-carrying slightly ascending *pu pu pu-pupupupu* with certain variations, call snapping *tsyuck*; chicks beg with short *ksi*. **H** Dense coniferous and mixed forests, often in mountains, breeds in tree hollows, often in old Black Woodpecker holes. **D** V, extremely rare.

5 Little Owl **L** 25 cm **WS** 53 cm

Athene noctua **ID** Small owl with long legs, short tail and broad, flat, rounded head. Grey-brown above with small white spots, underparts whitish with broad brown streaks, facial disc indistinct but yellow eyes and frowing white 'eye-brows' conspicuous. Often stands with body almost horizontal and bobs when excited. Diurnal and crepuscular, often seen on exposed perches or in undulating flight during the day. **V** Displays with drawn-out and ascending *guh-ug*; calls sharply *kiyu* and warns with hard and high-pitched *ki kikit*, juvs utter hissing begging calls. **H** Open areas, often with willow trees or old buildings as breeding sites, also in villages. **D** iBR introduced, fairly common in England and Wales but population decreasing.

6 Pygmy Owl **L** 17 cm **WS** 35 cm

Glaucidium passerinum **ID** Smallest European owl, barely Starling-sized and almost entirely crepuscular. Small round head, yellow eyes with short white supercilium produce a fierce facial expression, grey-brown plumage pearled and barred with white. Often perches with tail slightly cocked. Flight rapid and undulating over great distances, reminiscent of Lesser Spotted Woodpecker or Starling. **V** Autumn display a series of scale-like ascending whistles, otherwise Bullfinch-like whistling *hyuk* repeated every second, sometimes with a *soft huhuhu* in between; ♀ calls long and thin *tseeeh*, juv begging call similar, but shorter. Silent after dark. **H** Coniferous and mixed forests with clearings and old woodpecker holes for nest, mainly in mountains in south of range. **D -**.

7 Hawk Owl **L** 39 cm **WS** 76 cm

Surnia ulula **ID** Barred underparts, long tail and pointed wings give this northern owl a hawk-like appearance. Often diurnal, it can easily be confused with a Sparrowhawk in flight, but head large and face white with a bold dark edge and fierce expression. **V** Displays with long trill; warns with falcon-like *kikikiki*, begs *pssee-ip*. **H** Open taiga. **D** V, extremely rare.

1
2
3
4
5
6
7

SWIFTS

1 Common Swift L 18 cm WS 42 cm

Apus apus **ID** Commonest and most widespread swift, usually seen in flight and in groups. Often hunts with hirundines, but is larger, has faster and stronger flight and wings sickle-shaped. Overall blackish with some white on throat, tail slightly forked. **V** Call shrill *srreeh*. **H** Nests under eaves of buildings, also cliffs and tree hollows; hunts flying insects over all habitats, travels many miles on foraging flights, winters Africa. **D** BM 5-8, common.

2 Pallid Swift L 17 cm WS 42 cm

Apus pallidus **ID** South European swift, hard to distinguish from 1, but slightly browner with a larger white throat patch, dark area around eye contrasting with paler sides of head, wings less pointed and paler secondaries and inner primaries contrasting slightly with the darker outer primaries and mantle. **V** Lower-pitched than 1, descending *freeeye*. **H** Towns and cliffs in southern Europe, winters Africa. **D** V 4-10, very rare.

3 Alpine Swift L 22 cm WS 55 cm

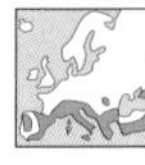

Apus melba **ID** By far the largest swift, can appear almost falcon-like. Similar in all plumages, unmistakable with pale brown upperparts, white chin and white underparts separated by a brown breast-band. **V** Calls trilling, rising and falling in pitch, *tritritri-titi*. **H** Mountains, cliffs and towns in southern Europe, winters Africa. **D** V 3-10, rare but annual, mainly southern England.

4 White-rumped Swift L 15 cm WS 35 cm

Apus caffer **ID** Small, fork-tailed, black swift with contrasting white throat, trailing edge to inner-wing and narrow rump patch. Beware partially albino Common Swift. **V** Calls rather low-pitched and in short bursts starting *tchit-tchit-tchit-tyirr*. **H** African species, breeds in Europe only locally in southern Spain in old nests of Red-rumped Swallows. **D** -.

5 Little Swift L 13 cm WS 33 cm

Apus affinis **ID** Distinguished from 4 by shorter square-ended tail, larger square white rump wrapping round to back of flanks and lack of white trailing edge to inner wing. **V** Calls brightly chirping. **H** African and Asian species found in towns and on cliffs, in Europe has recently started to breed in isolated areas of southern Spain. **D** V, extremely rare.

CUCKOOS

6 Cuckoo L 34 cm WS 57 cm

Cuculus canorus **ID** Upperparts, head and breast grey, belly barred. ♀ also rusty-yellow band on breast, in rare 'hepatic' morph upperparts and breast rusty-brown and barred black overall. Juv sometimes brownish and always shows white nape-patch. Flight falcon-like with pointed wings and long tail, but fast, shallow wing-beats, small head stretched out and lifted slightly, does not glide. **V** ♂ sings the familiar *cook-coo* in sequences, when chasing calls hissing *gowch*; ♀ calls gurgling *bubububu*, juv begs with high-pitched *sree*. **H** Lives in a wide variety of habitats, wherever there are small birds (especially Reed Warbler, Meadow Pipit or Dunnock) suitable for nest parasitization. **D** BM 4-9, fairly common but decreasing.

7 Great Spotted Cuckoo L 37 cm WS 60 cm

Clamator glandarius **ID** Tail longer than 6, upperparts covered in white spots and bars, underparts uniform pale yellow. In ad crown grey with slight crest. From juv to 1s crown and upperparts blackish, primaries conspicuously rusty-brown instead of grey. Often seen on the ground. **V** Calls loudly rattling *tyerr tyerr tyerr tye tye*. **H** Open landscapes of south-west Europe and east Greece, lays eggs mainly in Magpie nests. **D** V 4-7, extremely rare.

NIGHTJARS

8 European Nightjar L 27 cm WS 56 cm

Caprimulgus europaeus **ID** During day relies on cryptic camouflage to remain concealed on ground or branch. Hunts insects at night, flight falcon-like, ♂ with white spots on outer primaries and outer corners of tail. **V** ♂ sings at night, steady, deep, rather mechanical churring; in flight *fiorr-fiorrr-fiorr* and claps wings; also calls frog-like *kruu-ik*. **H** Breeds heaths, moors, forest edges and clearings, winters Africa. **D** bm 5-9, uncommon but increasing.

9 Red-necked Nightjar L 32 cm WS 62

Caprimulgus ruficollis **ID** Larger and longer-tailed than 8, with a reddish collar, grey carpals and broad, even bars on wing-coverts; both sexes have white flashes on wings and tail, but fainter in ♀. **V** ♂ song a persistent two-syllable *kyotok-kyotok*..., ♀ calls softer *tshe-tshe-tshe*..... **H** Heath with scattered shrubs and pine forests. **D** -.

1
2
3
4
5
6
7
8
9
juv Cuckoo in
Reed Warbler
nest
♀ hepatic morph
juv
♂
♂
♀
♂

ROLLER

1 European Roller **L** 30 cm **WS** 55 cm

Coracias garrulus **ID** Mainly bluish bird, the size and shape of a Jackdaw, often perches on a post or telegraph wires. Mantle, tertials and scapulars rufous, otherwise mainly turquoise-coloured with darker blue sections on wings and tail. Juv paler and more brownish with mottled breast. **V** Calls croaking *rak-ak, rrahk*, sways during Lapwing-like 'rolling' display-flight. **H** Open habitats with old trees and perches in south and east Europe, nests in tree hollows and catches insects and small vertebrates on the ground. Winters Africa. **D** V 4-9, very rare.

BEE-EATERS

2 European Bee-eater **L** 26 cm **WS** 38 cm

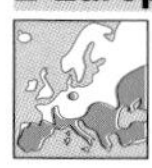

Merops apiaster **ID** Medium-sized, slender and exotic-looking bird with long, slightly decurved bill, narrow wings and long tail with pointed central tail feathers elongated up to 3 cm. Red, yellow and green above, turquoise below. Yellow throat bordered by dark collar, upperparts plainer greenish in paler juv. Social, often sits on wires and hunts insects in flight. **V** Often first noted by call, rolling *prrit* and liquid *glitt*. **H** Open habitats with steep sand banks for breeding tunnels, nests colonially. Winters in Africa. **D** V 4-9, rare but annual (has bred).

3 Blue-cheeked Bee-eater **L** 24 cm **WS** 37 cm

Merops persicus **ID** Similar to 2, but mainly emerald-green without rufous on crown and back, throat orange, central tail feathers pointed and elongated up to 8 cm. In flight underwing coverts copper instead of pale, trailing edge of wing has uniform narrow black band (broader in 2). **V** Calls slightly harder and more rolling than 2. **H** Breeds in semi-deserts of North Africa and central Asia. In Europe regular on passage only in Cyprus, vagrant elsewhere. **D** V, extremely rare.

KINGFISHER

4 Kingfisher **L** 18 cm **WS** 22 cm

Alcedo atthis **ID** Small and stocky with large head, long dagger-like bill, short, coral-red legs and short stumpy tail, exotic-looking with metallic blue upperparts and orange-red underparts. In ♀ lower mandible red, juv slightly less bright and has a shorter bill. Hunts small fish by plunge-diving from a perch close to the water or after hovering. Flies very rapidly and straight low over surface of water. **V** Call a high-pitched and penetrating *tee-eee* and *tsee*. **H** Rivers, streams and lakes, excavates breeding tunnels in steep sand banks. **D** BRMW, fairly common, absent from north Scotland. Population crashes in harsh winters.

HOOPOE

5 Hoopoe **L** 27 cm **WS** 46 cm

Upupa epops **ID** Unmistakable with erectable fan-like crest, long gently decurved bill, cinnamon-pink plumage with black-and-white barring on rounded wings. Digs for invertebrates, undulating flight usually low and clumsy. **V** Song a three-syllable hollow *hoop-hoop-hoop*; calls hoarsely *shaar* and dryly *terr*. **H** Open landscapes with thickets, vineyards or meadows with grazing animals, breeds in tree-hollows, stables, rock piles or earth heaps, winters south Spain and Africa. **D** V, rare but annual, occasionally breeds.

PARROTS

6 Ring-necked Parakeet **L** 40 cm **WS** 45 cm

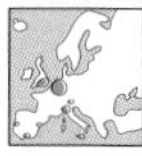

Psittacula krameri **ID** Medium-sized and brilliant green in colour with a long tail and bright red hooked upper mandible. ♂ with black chin, black neck-ring bordered pale blue above and orange-pink below and tail up to 28 cm. ♀ and juv with uniform green head and neck and shorter tail. Usually occurs in flocks and often forms large roosts. **V** Calls loud screeching *keeo, ki-ak*. **H** Native to Asia and tropical Africa, introduced in many parts of Europe, mainly in parks with old trees, nests in tree hollows. **D** ibr south-east England, locally common and increasing, particularly London.

7 Alexandrine Parakeet **L** 58 cm

Psittacula eupatria **ID** Larger than 6, tail up to 35 cm long, red stripe on carpals and lower mandible red. **V** Calls *trrriu, keearr*. **H** Native south Asia, introduced in parts of Europe. **D** i, escapes, no self-sustaining population.

8 Monk Parakeet **L** 33 cm

Myiopsitta monachus **ID** Smaller than 6 and 7, green, forehead and breast grey, wings blue, bill orange. **V** Rasping *tchep*. **H** Native to South America, introduced to several European countries. **D** ir, breeds locally in England.

juv
1
2
juv
4
♂
♀
3
5
6
8
♂
7
♂

WOODPECKERS

1 Green Woodpecker **L** 33 cm **WS** 48 cm

Picus viridis **ID** A large woodpecker with mostly green plumage, whitish eye, bright red cap reaching down to nape and black mask. Yellowish rump and barred outer tail feathers visible in undulating flight. In ♀ submoustachial stripe completely black, in ♂ red in centre. Juv is spotted all over – whitish spots on green above and blackish spots on pale below. Spends a lot of time on the ground searching for ants. **V** Song loud and brightly laughing *kluekluekluekluekluekiue,* not clearly descending but towards end more rapid, flight call *kyukyukyuck*; rarely drums but at 1.5 seconds drumming bursts are twice as long as those of Great Spotted Woodpecker and much softer. **H** Hedgerows, open woodland, old orchards and parks, often found on golf courses. **D** BR, common.

2 Iberian Woodpecker **L** 32 cm

Picus sharpei **ID** Previously regarded as a subspecies of 1, which it replaces in Spain and Portugal. Overall rather similar to 1, but black mask replaced by grey around eyes, barring on flanks and vent faint or lacking, bill slightly shorter, and in ♂ submoustachial stripe only bordered black below or not at all. Occasionally hybrids between 1 and 3 occur which may look very similar. **V** Like 1. **H** Woodland from the Pyrenees across the entire Iberian Peninsula. **D** -.

3 Grey-headed Woodpecker **L** 30 cm

Picus canus **WS** 39 cm **ID** Rather green overall and within range can be confused only with larger 1. Head grey with only thin black lores and submoustachial stripe, eye brownish. Green upperparts duller than 1, underparts greyish with no barring on flanks and in flight no barring on outer tail feathers. In ♂ forehead red, in ♀ grey. Juv like ad, only duller. Frequently feeds on ground, but more likely than 1 to be seen in trees. **V** A series of decreasing whistles getting slower towards the end *kyukyukyu-kyu-kyu-kyu-kyu,* sweeter and more mournful than 1, also calls *tik* and loudly *kya* in series; drums often, evenly rapidly and quite loud, drumming sequence takes 1.2-1.5 seconds. **H** Old forests and parks, often with more coniferous trees and at higher altitudes than 1. **D** -.

4 Black Woodpecker **L** 43 cm **WS** 70 cm

Dryocopus martius **ID** By far the largest European woodpecker, crow-sized and with unmistakable black plumage. Bill and eye are ivory-white; in ♂ entire cap bright red, in ♀ back of the crown only. Juv like ad, only slightly duller slate-black and shorter-billed. Flight more direct than other woodpeckers, slightly unbalanced and crow-like, shows long neck and tail, and strongly notched base of wings. Nest-hollow has large vertical oval entrance hole, not round like other woodpeckers. **V** A loud, unrestrained, laughing *kloy-kloy kleklekle-kle,* starting more hesitantly than 1, but remaining constant at the end, also calls in flight *grigrigri* and long *klee-oh*; drumming loud, rather slow and lasting 2-3 seconds. **H** Old deciduous, mixed and coniferous forests. Occurs across Europe but absent from Britain and Ireland and much of Iberia and Italy. **D** -.

5 Wryneck **L** 17 cm **WS** 26 cm

Jynx torquilla **ID** More reminiscent of a smallish passerine than of other typical woodpecker species. Has a rather weak bill and cryptic, tree bark-coloured plumage that gives excellent camouflage. Does not cling to tree trunks but sits on branches (often hidden high in tree tops, when ochre-yellow throat and whitish belly with narrow barring is characteristic) and hops on the ground hunting for ants (its principal food). Further features are the broad, dark eye-stripe reaching to the side of the neck, the three dark lengthways stripes on the upperparts (the central one from the crown and running down the back is obvious in flight), barred tail and fast and low undulating flight. **V** Call is nasal, a loud croaking *vaahd vaahd vaahd vaahd…*, warns with harsh *teck* and hisses when alarmed at the nest hole; does not drum. Silent on migration. **H** Inhabits open forests, orchards, old parks and gardens, as long as there are enough ants to provide food. Does not excavate its own nest hole, will move into nestboxes. The only migratory woodpecker species, winters in Africa south of the Sahara. **D** m, scarce on south and east coasts. Formerly a common breeding bird, a few pairs may still breed in Scottish Highlands.

♀
4
♀
juv
♂
♂
1
♂
2
♂
3
5
♂
♀

1 Three-toed Woodpecker **L** 23 cm

Picoides tridactylus **WS** 33 cm **ID** Black-and-white woodpecker without any red, ♂ finely streaked golden-yellow on crown (white in ♀), slightly smaller than 3. Head with badger-like stripes, wings mainly black with rows of white spots, underwings evenly barred. North European subspecies *tridactylus* has broad white band from nape down to rump – this is narrower and densely barred in central and south European subspecies *alpinus*. Has only one toe pointing backwards. **V** Calls softer than 3, *kip*; drumming sequence lasts 1-1.5 seconds and lies between species 2 and 3, stronger and slower than 3 and slightly faster at the end, similar to Black Woodpecker but only half as long. **H** Undisturbed mature forests with many conifers and much dead wood, often in northern taiga, in the south almost only in mountains. **D** -.

2 White-backed Woodpecker **L** 26 cm

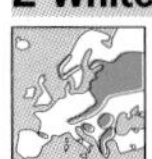

Dendrocopos leucotos **WS** 39 cm **ID** Largest black-and-white woodpecker in Europe, characterized best by broad white barring on the wing-coverts, scapulars and back (instead of the white oval patch on the scapulars in 3, 4 and 5). Vent pinkish-red, flanks streaked, crown red in ♂, black in ♀, but in juv always red. White back and rump usually inconspicuous, in the south European subspecies *lilfordi* rump black and back barred black. **V** Calls *gug*, lower-pitched and softer than 3; drumming longer than in 3, sequence lasts about 1.5-2 seconds, accelerating towards end (like ping-pong ball dropping on table). **H** Old deciduous and mixed forests with lots of dead wood, often close to water or in mountains, especially in eastern Europe. Generally scarce and localized. **D** -.

3 Great Spotted Woodpecker **L** 24 cm

Dendrocopos major **WS** 36 cm **ID** By far the most common, widespread and familiar woodpecker in Europe. Has conspicuous black, white and red plumage. Typical long, oval-shaped white shoulder patches and extensive bright red area from vent to undertail coverts. ♀ lacks small red nape-patch of ♂, juv is characterized by a completely red crown which can lead to confusion with 2 and 5. **V** Calls short and sharp *kik*, also in series; also harsh chattering; drumming rapid and quite short, ends abruptly (sequence lasts for only 0.5-0.8 seconds). **H** All habitats with trees, from forests to gardens, in winter visits bird-tables and -feeders. **D** BR, common.

4 Syrian Woodpecker **L** 24 cm **WS** 36 cm

Dendrocopos syriacus **ID** Occurs alongside 3 in south-east Europe and is very similar to it in all plumages, but only shows minimal white on the two outer tail-feathers (see illustration), has no connecting bar between black moustachial stripe and black on nape, vent is paler red, flanks often faintly streaked towards the back, often only three (not five) rows of white barring in the brownish outer wing and bristles covering upper mandible whitish (not black). In juv breast often tinged reddish. Fairly frequent hybrids with 3 are often recognizable only by the greater extent of white on tail. **V** Calls softer than 3, *pig*; drumming higher-pitched, increasing in tempo and almost twice as long as 3, sequence lasting 0.8-1.4 seconds. **H** Generally lives in more open areas than 3 such as parks, orchards, vineyards and avenues in south-east Europe, but gradually expanding its range north-westwards. **D** -.

5 Middle Spotted Woodpecker **L** 21 cm

Dendrocopos medius **WS** 33 cm **ID** Only slightly smaller than the very similar 3, but with smaller and weaker bill, moustachial stripe that neither reaches bill nor back of neck, vent pale pink and flanks streaked. Almost identical in all plumages, therefore entire crown red in ♂, ♀ and juv, ♀ slightly paler than ♂. **V** Displays with croaking *vaad vaad vaad...*, calls *kik gagagagag* and *kik-goog*; drums only rarely, then rather slowly, with sequence lasting 2 seconds. **H** Prefers oak forests, also very old beech forests. **D** -.

6 Lesser Spotted Woodpecker **L** 15 cm

Dendrocopos minor **WS** 26 cm **ID** Smallest woodpecker, shape reminiscent of a squat passerine, especially in flight. Upperparts with white barring, vent lacks red (otherwise a miniature version of 2), flanks streaked, ♂ has red crown, ♀ black. **V** Song bright *keekeekeekeekee*, reminiscent of Kestrel, sometimes calls *gig* more softly than 3; drums longer (1-2 seconds), but softer and higher-pitched than 3, but with up to 20 beats per second, and bouts often interrupted by a series of calls. **H** Deciduous forests, parks, gardens, often close to wetlands and in winter also in reedbeds. **D** br, England and Wales, uncommon, declining.

alpinus
1
2
lilfordi
3
juv
5
4
6

ORIOLE

1 Golden Oriole L 24 cm

Oriolus oriolus **ID** Blackbird-sized and also looks thrush-like in flight. ♂ unmistakable black and yellow, ♀ yellowish-green, rump, vent and tail-tip yellow, juv duller greenish, 1s ♂ similar to ♀. Often difficult to see in tree tops and best detected by voice. **V** Song loud, flutey whistling *dode-lio*, call hoarse croaking *khraayk*. **H** Old deciduous forests, poplar stands, parks. Winters Africa. **D** bm 5-8, rare breeder in East Anglia and coastal migrant.

SHRIKES

2 Red-backed Shrike L 17 cm

Lanius collurio **ID** Summer visitor. Upright stance on elevated perch while looking for insect prey, often swivels tail when perched. ♂ with red back, blue-grey crown and nape, black mask and black tail with broad white sides at base; ♀ dark brown back and ear-coverts, finely barred below and with little white on tail; juv similar, but also with upperparts barred. **V** Song soft chattering with mimicry, calls hoarse nasal *waad* and *shuck-shuck*. **H** Breeds hedges and forest edges, often near thorn bushes (creates 'larder' by impaling prey). Winters Africa. **D** m 5-10, formerly bred, now very scarce migrant mainly to coasts.

3 Woodchat Shrike L 18 cm

Lanius senator **ID** Crown and nape red-brown, mantle, wings and face-mask black and underparts, rump and scapulars white, ♀ generally paler. Juv similar to 2, but greyer with poorly defined pale patches on scapulars and rump. Subspecies *badius* on western Mediterranean islands lacks white at base of primaries. **V** Song loud and variable, also mimics; warns with hoarse *shrrrt* and *wa-wa-wa*. **H** Open forests, avenues, olive groves and orchards in south Europe. Winters Africa. **D** V 4-9, rare, mainly south coast.

4 Masked Shrike L 18 cm

Lanius nubicus **ID** Slender. Upperparts black with only supercilium, lores, scapulars and primary bases white; flanks orange; ♀ paler, juv similar to 3 but paler grey without brown tinge, rump dark and tail longer. **V** Song harsh, repetitive; calls dry rattling and *tsh-raaah* similar to Common Snipe. **H** Open forests and thickets, in Europe only in east Greece and south-east Bulgaria. Winters Africa. **D** V, extremely rare.

5 Lesser Grey Shrike L 20 cm

Lanius minor **ID** Similar to 6 but smaller, grey with black mask, but in ad forehead black and pink tinge on underparts. Wings relatively longer than in 6 (primary projection more than half length of tail), but tail shorter. In juv forehead grey and upper-parts scaled due to pale fringes – distinguishable from 6 by proportions. **V** Song similar to 3, also with screeching; warns *tshek*. **H** Summer visitor to open habitats with thickets in south and east Europe, often seen perching on cable lines. **D** V 4-9, very rare, mainly east coast.

6 Great Grey Shrike L 24 cm

Lanius excubitor **ID** The only shrike that winters in north and central Europe, sits prominently on bushes and cables. Large, long tail, plumage grey, white and black, forehead grey. Juv barred grey below. **V** Simple song shrill and harsh; calls *shrrrp*. **H** Open areas with hedges or bushes. Winters from Britain and Baltic to Black Sea. **D** wm 10-4, scarce and local.

7 Southern Grey Shrike L 24 cm

Lanius meridionalis **ID** Similar to 6, Iberia and south France only. Darker grey above, underparts tinged pink, lacks white on secondaries. **V** Like 5. **H** Dry plains, semi-desert. Resident. **D** V, very rare (paler Asian subspecies *pallidirostris*).

CROWS

8 Jay L 34 cm

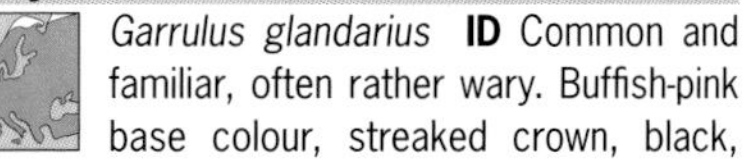

Garrulus glandarius **ID** Common and familiar, often rather wary. Buffish-pink base colour, streaked crown, black, white and blue pattern on wing and black tail and submoustachial stripe. Rounded wings, flappy flight when shows white patches on rump and secondaries. **V** Calls with harsh scolding *khraa* and buzzard-like *heeah*, rarely a soft chatting song. **H** Forests, parks, often most conspicuous in autumn when storing food. **D** BRMW, common.

9 Siberian Jay L 28 cm

Perisoreus infaustus **ID** Only slightly larger than a thrush with dusky grey-brown plumage (darker on head, warmer on belly) and rufous on wings, rump and tail reminiscent of a redstart. Secretive but inquisitive. **V** Mostly silent, call slightly moaning *keeaa*. **H** Resident in Scandinavian coniferous forests and taiga. **D** -.

1
♀
♂
♂
2
♂
♀
juv
3
♂
♂
juv
4
♂
♂
juv
5
juv
6
juv
7
8
9

1 Magpie **L** 46 cm

Pica pica **ID** Attractive black-and-white plumage with metallic green-and-violet sheen; extremely long tail, wings short and round, silhouette unmistakable. **V** Softly chattering song seldom heard, but often loud hoarse *tchek-tchak-tchak*. **H** Open areas with thickets, also in towns, domed nest of brushwood also closed on top. **D** BR, abundant.

2 Azure-winged Magpie **L** 33 cm

Cyanopica cyanus **ID** Seen mostly in flocks moving through scrub and immediately recognizable by the long azure-blue tail and similarly coloured wings. Has pinkish-buff mantle, breast and belly, black cap (mottled paler in juv) and white throat. **V** Vocal, range includes harsh *vruee* similar to Jay, bright *kooee* and rolling *krr-ree*. **H** Resident in open forests and scrub on the Iberian Peninsula. **D** -.

3 Nutcracker **L** 33 cm

Nucifraga caryocatactes **ID** About the size of a Jay, but with longer and more slender bill and in flight conspicuous short tail with white band at tip. Overall dark brown with large white spots (not unlike a massive Starling). Plain dark brown on crown, nape and wings, white on lores and vent. The Siberian subspecies *macrorhynchos* has a longer, straighter, more slender bill and a broader tail-band and is less shy. **V** Calls wooden *rrraaa*, softly chattering song rarely heard. **H** Coniferous forests of taiga and mountains, in autumn sometimes also in gardens. **D** V, very rare.

4 Jackdaw **L** 33 cm **WS** 68 cm

Corvus monedula **ID** Small crow with grey nape, short bill and pale iris, conspicuous within flocks of other crows through smaller size, call and faster wing-beats. Subspecies *soemmerringii* ('Eastern Jackdaw') in eastern Europe greyer below with paler nape and whitish crescent on side of neck. **V** Calls bright and short *jack jack*. **H** Fields, woods, farmland, towns, breeds in tree hollows or on ledges of buildings and cliffs, either in pairs or small colonies. **D** BRMW, common.

5 Chough **L** 39 cm **WS** 74 cm

Pyrrhocorax pyrrhocorax **ID** Rather small crow with slender body, metallic black plumage, red legs and slender, slightly decurved red bill (orange-yellow in juv). Further distinguished from 6 by longer wings protruding beyond tail at rest, in flight squarer wings with six (not five) deeply fingered primaries and straight (instead of curved) trailing edge to wings. **V** Calls *keeach*, more whip-like than 4. **H** High mountains in southern Europe, coastal cliffs in western Europe and always with adjoining short meadows; breeds in pairs or loose colonies. **D** br, west coast only, scarce; has recently recolonized Cornwall.

6 Alpine Chough **L** 38 cm **WS** 70 cm

Pyrrhocorax graculus **ID** Glossy black with yellow bill and red legs, superficially like a giant Blackbird. Wings narrower that 5. Social, very confiding, often attracted to resting hikers. **V** Calls piercing *tsee-aah*, bright jingling *shirrrr*. **H** High mountains; breeds mostly in colonies. **D** -.

7 Rook **L** 45 cm **WS** 87 cm

Corvus frugilegus **ID** Large crow with conspicuous triangular head profile and shaggy 'trouser' feathers on back of flanks, bill in ad pale grey with bare whitish base, also longer and more slender than 8. **V** Calls hoarsely and nasally *gaah* and *grah*. **H** Open cultivated landscapes with thickets; breeds in colonies. **D** BRMW, common.

8 Carrion Crow **L** 47 cm **WS** 92 cm

Corvus corone **ID** Most common and best-known crow in western and central Europe, plumage and bare parts black. Occasional hybrids with 9. **V** Calls croaking *caw caw* and guttural *grrrr*. **H** All types of landscapes, including towns; not colonial. **D** BR, abundant.

9 Hooded Crow **L** 47 cm **WS** 92 cm

Corvus cornix **ID** Replaces 8 in north and east Europe. Black with contrasting grey mantle, scapulars, neck sides and belly. **V** Similar to 8. **H** All habitats; not colonial. **D** br, common in north-west Scotland and Ireland; w, rare on east coast of England.

10 Raven **L** 61 cm **WS** 122 cm

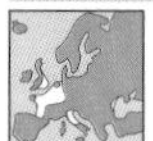

Corvus corax **ID** Largest crow and largest passerine; about the size of Common Buzzard, with powerful bill and prominent shaggy throat feathers. In flight shows wedge-shaped tail, long wings and protruding head. Long-lived and mates for life, therefore mostly seen in pairs or family groups. Soars in flight. **V** Calls very deep and croaking *korrk*, resounding *klong* and repetitive *korrp korrp korrp*. **H** Quiet forests, mountains. **D** BR, fairly common in west.

2
1
macrorhynchos
3
5
juv
soemmerringii
4
6
7
juv
8
juv
juv
9
10

TITS

1 Great Tit L 14 cm

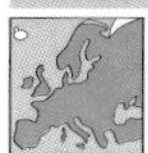

Parus major **ID** Widespread and familiar. Yellow underparts with black stripe from chin to vent (broader in ♂), black head with white cheeks (in juv yellowish without lower black border), moss-green mantle, blue wings and tail and white wing-bar. **V** Sings brisk two-note *teacher teacher* or *tsitsideh tsitsideh*; calls also *pink* and *tsi-tsuhi*, scolding *tsehtsehtseh*. **H** Gardens, parks, forests. **D** BR, abundant.

2 Blue Tit L 12 cm

Parus caeruleus **ID** Widely distributed and common. Has blue crown bordered white, black eye-stripe, blue on wings and tail and yellowish underparts with faint black stripe on belly. Juv paler and yellowish on the head. Very agile in branches, often in flocks. **V** Song silvery bell-like *tsi tsee tsirrr*; calls variable, often *sisididi* and *tsi-tshirr*. **H** Gardens, parks, hedgerows, forests; often visits bird-feeders. **D** BR, abundant.

3 Azure Tit L 13 cm

Parus cyanus **ID** Very pale eastern tit, like a white and blue-grey version of 2, crown white, broad white wing-bars and tips to tertials, tail white-edged but blue at base and in centre. Occasional hybrids with 2 show less white and usually bluish crown or yellowish underparts. May be confused with Long-tailed Tit. **V** Similar to 2. **H** Deciduous and mixed forests, often close to water. **D** -.

4 Coal Tit L 11 cm

Parus ater **ID** Smallest tit, has black crown, chin and throat, white ear-coverts and long white nape-patch (pale yellowish in juv). Dull grey-green above with double white wing-bar and pale grey-buff below. Head relatively large, often has slightly crested appearance. Irish birds have white on head replaced by pale yellow. Continental birds have bluer-grey upperparts and warmer below. **V** Sings *veetse veetse* like higher, faster version of 1; calls with sharply upslurred whistling *stui* and sad *tooh*. **H** Coniferous and mixed forests, also coniferous tree groups in parks and gardens. A shy visitor to bird-feeders. **D** BR, common.

5 Crested Tit L 12 cm

Parus cristatus **ID** Long pointed crest and black-and-white head, light-brown above with no wing-bar, pale buff below. **V** Song whistling *didu-didu-didu-dyoo*, mixed with *tsitsi-gurrrl*; calls low-pitched trilling *si si prroeeoo*. **H** In Britain restricted in range and habitat; found more widely in coniferous and deciduous forest on Continent, can excavate own nest hole. **D** br, only in coniferous forests in Scottish Highlands.

6 Marsh Tit L 12 cm

Parus palustris **ID** Small grey-brown tit with glossy black cap, pale whitish cheeks, plain wings and small black chin-spot. Easily confused with 7. **V** Song a sequence of about 6 equal sounding, *tyuptyuptyup....* or *titatitatita.....*; calls sneezing *pitshoo* and *tsi-tshoo*. **H** Forests, gardens. **D** BR, England and Wales, fairly common but declining.

7 Willow Tit L 12 cm

Parus montanus **ID** Widespread grey-brown tit, very similar to 6. Best separated by call, but also has cleaner white cheeks, matt black cap, longer bill, bigger black chin-patch, pale wing-panel and more bull-necked look. Western subspecies is browner, eastern greyer. **V** Sings melancholic whistling *tyu tyu tyu ....*; calls low-pitched nasal, sneering, down-slurred *zurr* or *si-si-zur zur zur*. **H** Forests, scrub, parks, excavates nest-hollow itself; occasionally visits bird-feeders. **D** br, England and Wales, uncommon and declining.

8 Sombre Tit L 13 cm

Parus lugubris **ID** Brown-grey tit of Balkans with shabby plumage compared to 6 and 7, black bib even more extensive, cap dull brown-black (browner in ♂) and reaching far down sides of head, therefore only narrow wedge of white on cheeks. Rather shy and not social. **V** Song harsher and slower than 6: *tshirf-tshirf-tshirf...*; calls *tsrih-tsrih-tsrih* and rattling *tsherrrrr-rr*. **H** Open deciduous and mixed forests in Balkans, also in cultivated and mountainous areas. **D** -.

9 Siberian Tit L 13 cm

Parus cinctus **ID** Warm-brown tit of northernmost Europe, with rusty-yellow flanks, dull black-brown cap and large black bib on chin, otherwise similar to 7; plumage 'fluffier' than other tits. **V** Sings thinly whirring *tshi-urrr tshi-urrr...*; calls not as drawn-out as 7, *ti-ti taaah taah*. **H** A rare breeder in the northernmost mature coniferous forests of Scandinavia and the Russian taiga up to upland birch-zone. **D** -.

♀
♂
juv
1
2
juv
4
5
3
6
8
7
eastern
western
9

PENDULINE TIT

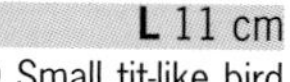

1 Penduline Tit L 11 cm

Remiz pendulinus **ID** Small tit-like bird with grey head and black mask, rufous mantle and thin bill. ♀ slightly paler, juv has head sandy-brown and lacks mask. **V** Sings softly and high-pitched *tsiu-siu sirr seeeu*; calls drawn-out and descending *tseeeeeu* like very high-pitched Reed Bunting. **H** Bushes beside wetlands or in marshes and reedbeds; weaves elaborate hanging nest with tunnel-shaped side entrance, mostly hanging on tips of branches over water (like a woollen sock). **D** V, rare but annual.

BEARDED TIT

2 Bearded Tit L 15 cm

Panurus biarmicus **ID** Somewhat tit-like with roundish body and short yellow bill, but with very long, broad tail and orange-brown plumage. Only ♂ has grey head and black 'moustache'; in juv mantle and tail-sides black. Very agile on reed stems, often conspicuous through call. **V** Song softly chirping *tship tship tshir*; typical calls distinctive 'pinging', often in chorus. **H** Dependent on extensive reedbeds, where it builds an open nest of stems. **D** br, locally fairly common in south-east England.

LONG-TAILED TIT

3 Long-tailed Tit L 14 cm

Aegithalos caudatus **ID** Unmistakable small bird with round, whitish body, tiny bill and a long narrow tail. Most subspecies, including west European *rosaceus*, have dark lateral crown-stripes and pink-flushed scapulars and underparts. Subspecies *caudatus* in north-eastern Europe has completely white head, some of the southern subspecies such as *irbii* (southern Spain) have grey scapulars. Mostly seen in restless, constantly calling flocks. **V** Song thin trilling *veeveeveeveevee*; calls dry buzzing *tsrrr* and high-pitched *see-see-see-see*. **H** Forests with plenty of undergrowth, hedges, parks and gardens; builds ball-shaped nest in branch forks, camouflaged with lichens. **D** BR, abundant.

HIRUNDINES

4 House Martin L 14 cm

Delichon urbicum **ID** In flight easily recognizable by narrow, triangular, swallow-like wings, forked tail and the contrast between white underparts (including throat) and blackish upperparts with white rump; close views show upperparts have a metallic blue-black sheen. **V** Calls short *prrit*, repeated in twittering song. **H** Breeds towns and villages, hunts over open areas, often very high in air; builds rounded mud nest under eaves and protrusions on buildings, also on cliffs in some places. Winters Africa. **D** BM 4-10, common.

5 Swallow L 19 cm

Hirundo rustica **ID** Long, pointed wings and deeply forked tail with rows of white spots near tip and narrow, elongated outer tail feathers, especially in ♂, produce distinctive silhouette. Upperparts uniform metallic blue-black, underparts creamy white with dark breast-band and rusty-red throat and fore-crown. Juv has duller, washed out plumage and shorter tail. **V** Twittering, fluid song with scratching sounds and ending in a purr; calls liquid *vit*, alarm call sharp *tsli-fit*. **H** Summer visitor. Barns, stables, villages, hunts in open areas and over wetlands; cup-shaped clay nest is built inside buildings; in autumn forms enormous flocks which roost in reedbeds. Winters southern Africa. **D** BM 4-10, abundant.

6 Red-rumped Swallow L 17 cm

Cecropis daurica **ID** South Europe, can be confused with 5 but rump and nape pale orange, tail, vent and lower rump uniform black, throat light and underparts faintly streaked. **V** Song like 5, but lower and coarser; calls sparrow-like *chree-up*, *shreep*. **H** Summer visitor. Rocky areas, nest with funnel-shaped entrance under bridge or in building. **D** V 4-10, rare.

7 Sand Martin L 13 cm

Riparia riparia **ID** Small, brown above, white below with brown breast-band, tail has shallow fork. **V** Call rapid, dry *tre-tre-tre-tre*, given in sequence when singing. **H** Wetlands; breeds in colonies, excavates nest tunnels in vertical sandy bank. **D** BM 4-9, common.

8 Crag Martin L 14 cm

Ptyonoprogne rupestris **ID** Brown, larger than 7, but lacks breast-band, underwing coverts darker, white spots near tip of square-ended tail and dark undertail coverts. **V** Chattering song; calls *pit*, *trit* and *tsriy*. **H** Cliffs and mountains in south Europe; nests on ledges, rarely on buildings. Summer visitor Alps and Balkans, resident elsewhere. **D** V, extremely rare.

caudatus
3
juv
1
juv
♀
2
♂
4
juv
5
♂
7
6
8

LARKS

1 Skylark L 17 cm

Alauda arvensis **ID** Common and familiar lark, grey-brown and buff overall with white trailing edges to wings, medium-long tail with white edges and a small crest. Primaries protrude beyond tertials at rest. Feathers scaled in juv. **V** Song long and jubilant with high-pitched rolling sounds and mimicry, delivered mainly in flight from great height; calls *dr-rip*. **H** Open fields and meadows. **D** BRMW, common but declining.

2 Woodlark L 14 cm

Lullula arborea **ID** Small lark, much shorter tail than 1, whitish supercilium joining at the back of the head, white patch on leading edge of outer wing, tips of outer tail feathers white. Flight shows more pronounced undulation than 1. **V** Song mostly given in flight, a soft, melodious sequence becoming faster and louder, *li li lililililooloolooloolulu iloo iloo*…. , especially at dusk and night; call a melodic *doodeloi*. **H** Heathland, mountain meadows, clearings. **D** br, uncommon and local but population increasing in south England.

3 Crested Lark L 17 cm

Galerida cristata **ID** Has conspicuous pointed crest, broad and round wings without white trailing edge, relatively short tail with warm brown edges and long, pale, pointed bill. Can be confiding but runs rapidly. **V** Song simple, made up from single calls and mimicry, given from elevated perch or in flight; calls melancholic *dooi* and *di di dooh*. **H** Dry, open areas, also streets and industrial areas. **D** V, extremely rare, although common on the Continent right up to Channel ports.

4 Thekla Lark L 16 cm

Galerida theklae **ID** Similar to 3, both occur together in Iberia and far south-west France. Slightly smaller with shorter bill, greyer plumage overall but reddish uppertail coverts contrast with colder rump, neat and profuse streaking on breast, greyer underwing coverts and blunter crest. **V** Softer than 3. **H** Often in drier, hillier, rockier places than 3. **D** -.

5 Short-toed Lark L 15 cm

Calandrella brachydactyla **ID** Smaller and paler than 1, underparts are unstreaked, dark spot on side of neck (often hard to see), clear supercilium, crown rufous after moult, unmarked pale lesser coverts and dark median coverts, very long tertials. **V** Sings twittering song in erratic flight, *tshut tshut tshull-tshill-ill-ill drro drri dooe tshullullull*; calls dryly *drut* or *trulp*. **H** Summer visitor to open dry areas. **D** V 4-10, rare but annual.

6 Lesser Short-toed Lark L 14 cm

Calandrella rufescens **ID** Differs from similar 5 in having finely streaked breast-band, tertials that fall well short of tail-tip, plumage darker and more grey-brown and stubby, finch-like bill. **V** Sings longer, less monotonously and with more mimicry than 5; calls buzzing *drrrd*. **H** Open areas in Spain, Turkey and south Russia. **D** V, extremely rare.

7 Calandra Lark L 19 cm

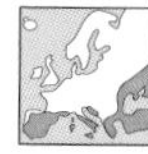

Melanocorypha calandra **ID** Large, chunky lark with relatively short tail, long thick bill and large black spots on sides of breast. In flight shows black undersides to long, broad wings and white trailing edges above and below. **V** Melodious song with mimicry delivered in circling flight from height, during which wing-beats slow and undulating; call loud and hard, rolling *tshuritt*. **H** Steppe-like areas in south Europe. **D** V, extremely rare.

8 Dupont's Lark L 17 cm

Chersophilus duponti **ID** In Europe only in Spain, very shy and tends to run rather than fly. Similar in colour to 1, but more grey-brown overall and slimmer with longer legs, no white trailing edge to wing and distinctive longer bill which is clearly decurved. **V** Sings at dusk and night at great height with short flute-like sounds and nasal end tone; calls *tyu-tyoo*. **H** Dry steppe-like areas in central Spain. **D** -.

9 Shore Lark L 17 cm

Eremophila alpestris **ID** Distinctive black and yellow head pattern, even when feathered ear-tufts or 'horns' are not visible. Body streaked brown, legs and bill black. ♀ and 1w paler, juv spotted and with faint moustachial stripe. Black moustachial stripe and breast band merge in Balkan subspecies *balcanica*, separated by yellow in northern subspecies *flava*. **V** Sings short, stuttering sequences; calls high-pitched *pee, eeh-dudi*. **H** Breeds mountain meadows, fells and tundra, winters mainly on North Sea coasts. Resident in the Balkans. **D** w 10-4, scarce, usually on east coast, very rare inland.

1
juv
2
3
4
5
6
7
8
9
♂
balcanica
juv
♀ non-br
♂ br

PHYLLOSCOPUS WARBLERS

1 Willow Warbler L 11.5 cm

Phylloscopus trochilus **ID** Very common but inconspicuous greenish bird that moves with agility among branches and is best recognized by its song. Very similar to both chiffchaffs, but has longer wings with primaries projecting far beyond tertials, more intensely greenish above, supercilium clearer and legs pale. Juv, 1w and ad winter yellow below. North-east European subspecies *acredula* greyer. **V** Song starts with high notes followed by thin, melancholy, descending refrain; call clearer than 2, with two-syllable upslurred *hoo-eet*. **H** Woodland edges, bushes and thickets, winters Africa. **D** BM 4-9, common.

2 Common Chiffchaff L 11 cm

Phylloscopus collybita **ID** Very common, greenish brown above, pale below. Less yellow than 1. Pale eye-ring. Dips tail downwards. Wings shorter than 1, legs dark, plumage more brownish. North-east European subspecies *abietinus* paler and browner, north Russian *tristis* (Siberian Chiffchaff) lacks yellow-green tinge. **V** Sings *chiff-chaff-chiff-chaff-chaff* with subdued growling *perre perre* in-between; calls monosyllabic upslurred *huit*, juv in autumn has higher-pitched *heet*. **H** Forests, woods and thickets. Winters south and west Europe. **D** BM 3-10, common; w, uncommon.

3 Iberian Chiffchaff L 11 cm

Phylloscopus ibericus **ID** Replaces 2 as breeding bird in Iberia, has slightly longer wings and is more greenish, but certain identification only possible through song. **V** Song divided into three parts and often ends in trilling, *tyip-tyip-tyip-huid-huid-tirrr;* call descending and nasal *pioo*. **H** Similar to 2. **D** V 4-6, very rare.

4 Wood Warbler L 12 cm

Phylloscopus sibilatrix **ID** Long wings, yellow-green above, yellow breast, white belly, clear yellow supercilium and dark green eye-stripe, legs pale; often in treetops. **V** Two song types, a series ending in high trill *tsip-tsip-tsip-tswirrrrrrr* and a melancholic whistling sequence *duh duh duh duh*; calls sharply *tsip* and melancholy *pew*. **H** Old deciduous forests, winters Africa. **D** bm 4-8, more common in north and west.

5 Western Bonelli's Warbler L 11 cm

Phylloscopus bonelli **ID** Upperparts olive-grey with yellowish rump, flight feathers with green edges and conspicuous pale edges to tertials, head pattern very faint creating an open facial expression with obvious dark edge and underparts completely whitish in contrast to 4. **V** Song a clear, laughing trill lasting 1 second, slower than the end sequence of 4, *svisvisvisvisvi....;* calls two-syllable *doo-it*. **H** Mountain forests in south-west Europe, prefers oaks. Winters Africa. **D** V 5-9, very rare.

6 Eastern Bonelli's Warbler L 11.5 cm

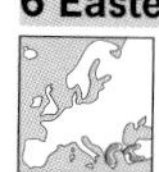

Phylloscopus orientalis **ID** Slightly larger than 5, greyer above with slightly longer wings and greater coverts often clearly paler, but most easily distinguished by voice. **V** Sings slightly faster than 5 and in between sequences calls contrasting crossbill-like *chip* and wooden *tut*. **H** Summer visitor to mountain forests in the Balkans, present from 4-9. **D** V, extremely rare.

7 Greenish Warbler L 10 cm

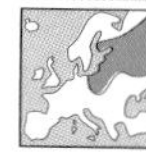

Phylloscopus trochiloides **ID** Similar to 1 with grey-green upperparts, but has a short, clear-cut whitish wing-bar (which is often inconspicuous, sometimes with a second faint bar on the median coverts), whitish supercilium clearer and longer, legs grey-brown. Lower mandible pale. **V** Song short, loud, high-pitched, fast, includes Wren-like trill; calls similar to Pied Wagtail: *si-litt*. **H** Breeds east European forests, winters south Asia. **D** V, rare but annual, mainly east coast in autumn.

8 Arctic Warbler L 12 cm

Phylloscopus borealis **ID** Has one wing-bar (sometimes a hint of a second), plumage similar to 7, but larger, heavier, wings longer, supercilium does not reach the base of bill but eye-stripe does (reverse is true in 7), tip of lower mandible dark, legs brown-pink. **V** Sings a whirring *sresresresresre*; calls sharply *djik*. **H** Breeds forests in north-east Europe, winters south Asia. **D** V, rare but annual.

9 Yellow-browed Warbler L 10 cm

Phylloscopus inornatus **ID** Small, moss-green above with two clear yellow wing-bars, long supercilium, diffuse crown-stripe. **V** Calls clear *tseeooit*. **H** Breeds Siberia, vagrant to Europe. **D** V 9-10, rare but increasing, sometimes winters.

10 Pallas's Warbler L 9.5 cm

Phylloscopus proregulus **ID** Very small, two wing-bars, told from 9 by yellow median crown-stripe and rump, long yellow supercilium; often hovers. **V** Call squeaky *cho-it*. **H** Breeds Siberia, vagrant Europe. **D** V, mostly 10-11, rare but increasing.

acredula
1
1w
2
abietinus
4
3
5
7
6
8
9
10

LOCUSTELLA WARBLERS

1 River Warbler L 15 cm

Locustella fluviatilis **ID** Much more often heard than seen. Upperparts uniform grey-brown, breast faintly striated, supercilium unclear, flanks darkish olive-brown, legs pink, undertail coverts long and brown with broad white crescent-shaped tips. **V** Sings much more slowly than 3 with clearly defined separate syllables, persistent mechanically reeling *tse-tse-tse-tse-tse*, delivered especially at night; calls *tsr* and *dshik*. **H** Thickets near water. Winters Africa. **D** V 5-9, extremely rare, occasionally holds territory in spring.

2 Savi's Warbler L 14 cm

Locustella luscinioides **ID** Easily confused with Reed Warbler, but darker red-brown above, usually without rusty-brown rump, breast and flanks darker brown-beige, tail broad and rounded with long, uniform rusty-beige undertail coverts (different to 1). Walks on ground and vegetation (reed-hops). **V** Reeling song similar to 3, but lower-pitched, harder and faster, often introduced with ticking sounds; calls similar to Great Tit *tshing, pvingt*. **H** Breeds larger reedbeds, winters Africa. **D** bm 4-9, very rare breeding bird in Britain.

3 Grasshopper Warbler L 13 cm

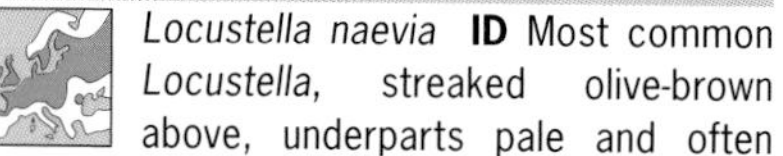

Locustella naevia **ID** Most common *Locustella*, streaked olive-brown above, underparts pale and often with unclear streaks on breast, supercilium faint, broad, rounded tail with long irregularly spotted undertail coverts (compare with 5). Usually hidden in low vegetation, moves mouse-like on or near ground. **V** Grasshopper-like reeling *serrrrrrrrrrrrrrrrr* lasting minutes, also at night; call short *pritt*. **H** Dense cover in open habitats. **D** BM 4-9, locally fairly common.

CISTICOLA

4 Zitting Cisticola L 10 cm

Cisticola juncidis **ID** Small with short wings, short, rounded tail with black-and-white tips and slightly decurved bill. Upperparts with clear light and dark streaking overall. Usually stays hidden in thickets close to ground. **V** Sings monotonous *tsrip tsrip tsrip* even in the midday heat during typical undulating song-flight at a height of about 10 m, calls loudly *tship*. **H** Open areas in south Europe, occasionally breeds further north. **D** V, extremely rare, most records on south coast.

ACROCEPHALUS WARBLERS

5 Sedge Warbler L 12 cm

Acrocephalus schoenobaenus **ID** Most common of the streaked *Acrocephalus* warblers, although dark stripes often weak and diffuse. Long creamy supercilium accentuated by dark sides of streaked crown. In juv breast striated. Like other 'acros', tail tapers to a point. **V** Sings night and day, reminiscent of Reed Warbler but faster and more varied with mimicry and crescendo of excited notes, which change to melodic whistling, for example, *tsrutsru-trett krukrukrupsi trutru-perrrrrr-errrrrr vi-vi-vi lululu zetre zetre…*; calls harsh *trrr* and *tyeck*. **H** Reedbeds, marshes and vegetated margins. Winters Africa **D** BM 4-9, common.

6 Aquatic Warbler L 12 cm

Acrocephalus paludicola **ID** Rare warbler with a restricted range, can easily be confused with 5. Characteristic are the lighter yellowish base colour, boldly striped mantle and rump, pale lores, faint streaking on breast and flanks (ad only) and dark cap with neat, narrow, pale median crown-stripe (sometimes present in 5 in juv). Juv even paler ochre-yellow with unmarked underparts (in contrast to 5 in juv). **V** Sings more sluggishly and monotonously than 5 *err-didi err-dudu err….*; calls *errrr* and *teck*. **H** Summer visitor to wet sedgy grassland in east Europe. Migrates through west Europe en route to Africa. **D** V 8-9, rare but annual, mostly at sites on south coast.

7 Moustached Warbler L 13 cm

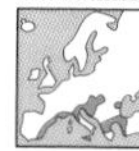

Acrocephalus melanopogon **ID** Streaked above, but in contrast to 5 has rather rusty-brown base colour and crown and ear coverts darker, accentuating the broad, square-ended whitish supercilium and the white throat. Flanks and sides of breast plain, tinged rusty-brown, undertail coverts whitish, wings shorter with primaries only projecting slightly beyond tertials. Behaviour recalls Cetti's Warbler, cocks tail. **V** Song slightly softer and livelier than Reed Warbler, includes ascending fluty *loo loo looo loooh* notes reminiscent of Nightingale; calls smacking *tcheck* and *krrk*. **H** Reedbeds and rushy marshes. Resident around Mediterranean, summer visitor elswhere. **D** -.

1
2
3
4
5
juv
6
juv
7

1 Reed Warbler **L** 13 cm

Acrocephalus scirpaceus **ID** Most common unstreaked *Acrocephalus* warbler – has angular head and long bill. Upperparts olive- to rust-brown, rump warmer rufous, underparts whitish with buffy flanks and undertail coverts, but often cinnamon- to rust-coloured, supercilium faint and not reaching beyond eye, legs are grey-brown. **V** Song is a rhythmic sequence of repetitive grumpy churring notes, *trr-trr-trr-tri-tri-tri-tiri-tiri*, occasionally broken by mimicked whistles, slower and more simple than Sedge Warbler; call short *chrer*. **H** Large and small reedbeds. Winters Africa. **D** BM 4-9, common.

2 Marsh Warbler **L** 14 cm

Acrocephalus palustris **ID** Very similar to 1 but less bound to reedbeds and wetlands. Plumage dull olive-brown above, rump not rust-coloured (except in juv), buff-grey tinge below with throat often whitish, supercilium and eye-ring often clearer, tertials and primaries more obviously paler edged, alula conspicuously dark, legs light brown, wings slightly longer (but in both species the tips of 7-8 primaries are visible). **V** Variably rapid song delivered day and night with changes in speed, harsh, whistling, squeaking and creaking notes, full of excellent mimicry of European and African species, in between the characteristic nasal *ti-tzaaa* or tit-like *tse-bi*; warns long *karrr* and *tshrrr*. **H** Thickets, swamps, other tall dense vegetation, nettle stands, not only near water. Winters Africa. **D** bm 5-8, very scarce migrant, very rare breeding bird in Britain.

3 Paddyfield Warbler **L** 13 cm

Acrocephalus agricola **ID** Eastern species, similar to 1 but smaller, with longer, rounder, more mobile tail and shorter wings. Upperparts quite variable rusty to light grey-brown, underparts whitish with brownish flanks and undertail coverts, supercilium long and conspicuous, accentuated above by dark sides of crown. Eye-ring faint, sides of neck paler, tertials broadly edged rusty-brown, bill shorter, lower mandible with dark tip, legs flesh- to horn-coloured, primaries protrude less over tertials and only 6 tips are visible. **V** Song full of mimicry and therefore similar to 2, but with constant tempo, softer, slower, without coarse elements and without the characteristic *tse-bi* of 2; calls differ from 1, *dsack*, *tchick* and rapid chattering. **H** Mostly on drier edges of reedbeds from Black Sea eastwards. Winters south Asia. **D** V 9-10, very rare.

4 Blyth's Reed Warbler **L** 13 cm

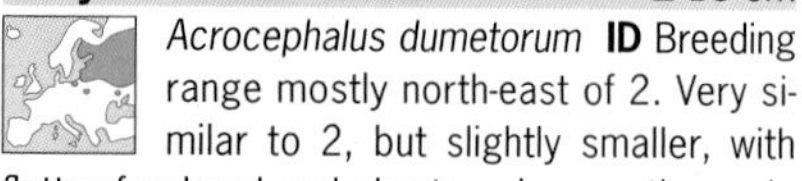

Acrocephalus dumetorum **ID** Breeding range mostly north-east of 2. Very similar to 2, but slightly smaller, with flatter forehead and shorter wings, rather pale olive-brown to grey-brown above, chalk-white below (including undertail coverts) with only faint tinge of colour on flanks, clear eye-ring and conspicuous elliptical supercilium. The wings are uniformly coloured, primary projection reaches only halfway along the uppertail coverts (not two-thirds), legs are grey and the tips of 6-7 primaries are visible. **V** Song, mainly given at night, is similar to 2 with mainly brilliant mimicry, but is slower and phrases are repeated Song Thrush-like up to 10 times. Often blends in a clear ascending *low-loo-lee-a*, but the typical snapping *check check* is always present; commonest call hard *chack* recalling Blackcap. **H** Similar to 2, often in even drier areas, fond of bramble thickets. Winters south Asia. **D** V 5-6 and 9-10, very rare, mainly east coast.

5 Great Reed Warbler **L** 19 cm

Acrocephalus arundinaceus **ID** A huge version of 1, supercilium clear, bill large and thrush-like, wings very long. **V** Sings with a loud and creaking *karra-keet-karra-keet-keet*; calls include *krek* and *kerrr*. **H** Reedbeds and wetland margins. Winters Africa. **D** V 5-9, rare but annual.

CETTI'S WARBLER

6 Cetti's Warbler **L** 14 cm

Cettia cetti **ID** Usually hidden in dense vegetation, hard to see but has loud and distinctive voice. Compact with red-brown upperparts, underparts tinged greyish, pale supercilium, short, round frequently raised tail (with only 10 tail-feathers), short rusty-beige undertail coverts and short, round wings. **V** Song starts abruptly as loud and explosive *plitt-plitt plitti plitti-plittplott;* calls abrupt *pit* and churring *pitititit.* **H** Resident in dense vegetation beside water in south and south-west Europe, in some years breeding further north. **D** br, colonized south Britain in 1970s, increasing.

1w
1
1w
2
1w
3
4
1w
5
1w
6

1 Icterine Warbler **L** 13 cm

Hippolais icterina **ID** The most common *Hippolais* in much of central and north-east Europe. Compared to *Acrocephalus* warblers has more angled head, broader bill and shorter undertail coverts. Greenish above, yellowish below, supercilium indistinct and lores pale, giving 'open' facial expression; secondaries edged paler creating a wing panel, grey legs. Juv often more 'washed out' and greyer. Moves sluggishly, less active than *Phylloscopus* warblers. **V** Varied song with sequences resembling Marsh Warbler, but delivered from higher vegetation and not at night, blended in typical meowing *gheeaah*; usual call *tetero-it* or *didero-id*; also calls *tetete* and *teck*. **H** Open forests, parks, gardens, winters Africa. **D** V 5-9, rare, mostly east coast.

2 Melodious Warbler **L** 13 cm

Hippolais polyglotta **ID** Replaces 1 in south-west Europe, head slightly rounder, on the greenish upperparts tinged brown rather than grey, pale yellow below, no obvious pale panel on secondaries and brownish legs. Most important difference apart from song and call is the shorter primary projection, not reaching the uppertail coverts and only half the length of the tertials (more than three-quarters in 1). **V** Sings more melodically, more chattery and faster than 1 at the beginning, repeating the typical sparrow-like chirping call *trrrt*, never meowing *gheeaah*; calls also *tet* and *chret*. **H** Often warmer, drier bushy habitats and lower thickets than 1. Winters Africa. **D** V 5-9, rare, mostly in south-west.

3 Olive-tree Warbler **L** 17 cm

Hippolais olivetorum **ID** The largest *Hippolais* with heavy, long bill and very long wings, brown-grey above, whitish below, legs grey. Can only be confused with much smaller 4, but has a pale wing panel like 1, dusky undertail coverts and very dark flight- and tail feathers. **V** Loud, husky song reminiscent of Great Reed Warbler with repetitions, for example, *kutshok tshu tshi tshack kerr kerr;* call low-pitched and hard *tshack*. **H** Summer visitor to Balkans. Open forests with ground cover, including almond- and olive-groves. **D** V, extremely rare.

4 Eastern Olivaceous Warbler **L** 12 cm

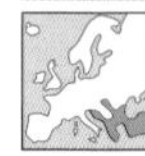

Hippolais pallida **ID** More like a pale Reed Warbler than other *Hippolais* warblers, but has square-ended tail with pale edges, and a broader bill base. Upperparts grey with olive tinge (never rusty), underparts uniform whitish, supercilium distinct, lower mandible yellowish, legs grey-brown and primaries not projecting quite as far beyond tertials. Dips tail downwards. **V** Song lacks mimicry and is similar to that of Reed Warbler, but rougher chattering and more monotonous, sometimes with the ascending sequence repeated; calls snapping *tsack* and rattling *krrrt*. **H** Summer visitor from Hungary to Balkans, breeds in scrub, open forests and orchards. **D** V 8-10, very rare.

5 Western Olivaceous Warbler **L** 13 cm

Hippolais opaca **ID** Spanish counterpart of 4. Can only be confused with Reed Warbler (but occupies different habitat), otherwise very similar to 4, but slightly larger, with longer legs, sandy-brown upperparts, fainter supercilium, longer bill which is broader at base, with sides appearing convex from below and not concave. **V** Sings more rapidly and melodically than 4 with more flute-like notes. **H** Open forest, plantations, gardens. Winters Africa. **D** -.

6 Booted Warbler **L** 11 cm

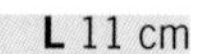

Hippolais caligata **ID** The smallest *Hippolais* warbler, similar in size to a *Phylloscopus*, pale brown above, pale supercilium accentuated by dark lores and dark lateral crown stripes (similar to Paddyfield Warbler). Tail edges whitish, legs brownish-pink, lower mandible pale with dark tip, flicks tail slightly upwards. **V** Song soft, fast, chattering, bubbling, without mimicry, similar to soft Garden Warbler, often starts with *di-di-di*; calls rasping *dsrak*. **H** Breeds in north-east Europe in thickets, low scrub, herbaceous plants along waterways and in forest steppe. Winters Asia. **D** V 8-9, very rare.

7 Sykes's Warbler **L** 12 cm

Hippolais rama **ID** Similar to 6, slightly larger, longer tail, upperparts greyer, whiter below, with short supercilium and longer bill which lacks dark tip to lower mandible. Therefore also quite similar to 4, but flicks the tail upwards (not down), has shorter wings with usually only 5 (instead of 6) primary tips visible and no distinct olive tinge to upperparts. **V** Sings more rapidly and with more structure than 6, reminiscent of Sedge Warbler; calls *tsak*. **H** Breeds south-east of 6 in semi-deserts and steppes with bushes and scattered trees from Volga Delta to central Asia. Winters south Asia. **D** V 8-9, extremely rare.

1
1w
1w
2
1w
3
1w
4
1w
7
6
5
1w

SYLVIA WARBLERS

1 Blackcap L 14 cm

Sylvia atricapilla **ID** The most common and widespread *Sylvia*, frequently breeds in gardens. Grey overall with a brownish tinge above, lighter below, flanks darker olive-grey and tail plain grey. Immediately recognized by cap, which is black in ad ♂ and brown in ♀ and juv. ♂ could be confused with Marsh or Willow Tit, but they have white cheeks and black chin. Secretive during breeding season, otherwise often seen on berry bushes. **V** Pleasant, melodious but discordant high-pitched whistling song; warns harshly *teck* and *tack-ack-ack*. **H** Gardens, parks, forests, woods, summer visitor in north and east of range. **D** BM 4-10, very common; w, small numbers in south.

2 Garden Warbler L 14 cm

Sylvia borin **ID** Least distinctive of the *Sylvia* warblers with uniform grey-brown plumage, lacking any bold markings. Common across almost all of Europe. Quite heavily built, head rounded, sides of neck lighter grey, dark eye, faint eye-ring, legs and bill dark grey. Secretive, mostly stays hidden in foliage. **V** Song rich, deep and mellow compared with 1, lacking high-pitched whistling phrases; warns distinctive deep *vid vid vid vid.* **H** Breeds in open forests, areas of scrub and parks. Winters Africa. **D** BM 5-9, common.

3 Barred Warbler L 16 cm

Sylvia nisoria **ID** Eastern species, large with long tail, tips of tail and fringes of tertials and greater coverts pale, uppertail and undertail coverts always scaled. In ad iris pale (yellow in ♂, beige in ♀), upperparts grey and underparts barred. In juv iris dark, upperparts grey-brown, underparts cream, but has – in contrast to the otherwise similar 2 – pale edges to tertials and greater coverts. **V** Scratchy, short song including the species-specific rattling *rrrt-t-t-t-t.* **H** Open areas with thickets, often in thorn hedges, summer visitor from east-central Europe eastwards. **D** V 9-10, rare, especially east coast, nearly all British records are of 1w.

4 Lesser Whitethroat L 13 cm

Sylvia curruca **ID** Small, common *Sylvia* with short tail and similar appearance in all plumages. Upperparts, including wings, grey-brown, head paler grey with ear-coverts darker, sometimes faint white supercilium, underparts silky white, legs dark grey, iris dark; never shows rufous in plumage. **V** Song a simple, monotonous, wooden 'rattle' on one note *de-dede-dede-de*, sometimes with soft chattering prelude, often alternating with high-pitched, mouse-like *tsit-sitsitsitsi*; warns snapping *tett.* **H** Summer visitor to large gardens, parks, hedgerows, scrub, forest edges. **D** BM 4-10, common in England.

5 Common Whitethroat L 14 cm

Sylvia communis **ID** Common *Sylvia* warbler found in open areas across Europe. In all plumages has broad rufous edges to wing coverts and tertials, light yellow- to orange-brown legs, pale lower mandible and in ad also light brownish iris. ♂ with grey head, prominent white throat and pinkish breast, ♀ slightly duller with grey-brown head and beige breast, juv often has head and mantle uniform pale grey-brown. Can be confused with Spectacled Warbler and 4. **V** Short, scratchy, twittering song with jerky rhythm is often given in flight; calls *churr* or *churrit;* scolding *vit vit vit vit.* **H** Breeds in bushes in open landscapes, often in thorny hedgerows. Winters Africa. **D** BM 4-9, common.

6 Western Orphean Warbler L 15 cm

Sylvia hortensis **ID** Large south-western *Sylvia* warbler with grey-brown upperparts, underparts grey with brown-pink tinge, plain undertail coverts and cap and ear coverts dusky, blackish in ♂. Larger than Sardinian Warbler, legs blackish, iris pale in ad with no red eye-ring. **V** Loud, thrush-like song consisting of regularly repeated quite low-pitched syllables, for example, *turo-turo-turo tshree-tshree pyupyupyu;* calls *chack*, warns rattling *trrrrr.* **H** Open forests, high maquis and bushes in south-west Europe. Winters Africa. **D** V, extremely rare.

7 Eastern Orphean Warbler L 16 cm

Sylvia crassirostris **ID** South-eastern counterpart of 6. Very similar to it in all forms, but bill longer and heavier, tail longer, upperparts cleaner grey, head often darker, underparts whiter, undertail coverts scaled, iris often dark. Juv similar to juv 3, but ear-coverts dark and no barring. **V** More melodious song, longer and more varied than 6, often reminiscent of Nightingale, for example, *troo troo troo shiwoo shiwoo yo-yo-yo-broo-treeoo*; calls lower-pitched than 1: *check* and rasping *trrr.* **H** Summer visitor to open deciduous forest and areas with bushes and scattered trees. **D** -.

♀
♂ 1w
♂
1
2
1w
♂
♀ / ♂ 1s
3
1w
4
1w
6
♀
♂
♀ / 1w
5
♂
♂
7

1 Sardinian Warbler **L** 13 cm

Sylvia melanocephala **ID** Common resident in Mediterranean region. Small and in all plumages has clean white throat, white outer tail feathers and red orbital ring. ♂ with black hood and dark smoky-grey upperparts and flanks, ♀ with grey hood and dark brownish upperparts and flanks. **V** Song fast, short, harsh chattering with short whistling and grinding notes in between, uttered from a perch or in flight; warns with rhythmic *terett tret-tret-tret* and *tr-tr-tr*. **H** Often in bushes, scrub and copses in southern Europe. **D** V, very rare, most often on south or east coasts, has wintered.

2 Rüppell's Warbler **L** 13 cm

Sylvia rueppelli **ID** In Europe occurs only in south Greece where it can only be confused with 1, but always shows clear whitish edges to tertials, secondaries and secondary coverts. ♂ with black face and throat divided by white submoustachial stripe, ♀ greyer overall than 1 with inconspicuous orbital ring and throat often speckled grey or dark (but can be plain white). **V** Song similar to 1, but slightly slower and more uniform, often delivered in butterfly-like flight; calls rattling *khrrr* and snapping *tsit*. **H** Open oak forests and dense scrub, often on stony slopes, from 3-9. Winters Africa. **D** V, extremely rare.

3 Cyprus Warbler **L** 13 cm

Sylvia melanothorax **ID** Breeds only on Cyprus and is similar to 1 and 2. ♂ recognizable by rough black scaling on underparts reaching from throat to undertail coverts, this is much fainter in ♀ and usually missing on belly, and only present on undertail coverts in juv, which also differs from 1 in having a pink rather than grey base to the bill and pale edges to the tertials. **V** Song slow, bumpy and dry, like the call *khrr khrr* but less harsh than in 1. **H** Breeds dense scrub on Cyprus, winters Middle East. **D** -.

4 Subalpine Warbler **L** 12 cm

Sylvia cantillans **ID** Common in south Europe. ♂ blue-grey above and bright pink-red underneath with contrasting white submoustachial stripe and red orbital ring (submoustachial stripe broader in the eastern subspecies *albistriata*, but belly and flanks paler). ♀ has similar coloration but is paler overall with a whitish eye-ring. Juv browner, tertials fringed brown. Juv has white throat and is told from juv of 5 by grey-brown rather red-brown wings. **V** Song more varied than 1, also with clear, bright note sequences, delivered from top of bush or in flight; calls *che* and *kherr tetet*, duller than 1. **H** Breeds scrub, also in mountains. Winters Africa. **D** V 5-9, rare, mostly south and east coasts.

5 Spectacled Warbler **L** 12 cm

Sylvia conspicillata **ID** Reminiscent of the much larger Common Whitethroat due to rusty-brown wings, grey or brown head and white eye-ring, but ♂ has black around eye and on lores and a more intensely pinkish breast, ♀ has shorter primary projection, primaries are also more extensively rufous. **V** Sings often in flight, high-pitched twittering and starting with clear notes; calls Wren-like *trrrrtrrr*. **H** Summer visitor to low scrub and semi-dry saline steppes in west Mediterranean and an isolated resident population on Cyprus. **D** V 5-10, extremely rare.

6 Dartford Warbler **L** 13 cm

Sylvia undata **ID** Small, dark *Sylvia* of south and west Europe. Has long, often cocked tail. ♂ grey-brown above, claret below with white specks on throat and red orbital ring, ♀ duller overall, juv browner above and greyer below with brown-beige throat. Subspecies *dartfordiensis* occurs from south England to north Portugal and is browner above. **V** Delivers short and scratching song from top of bush or in flight; call hoarse and scolding *tkhaa-ar*. **H** Resident in gorse and heather heathland and scrub. **D** br, locally fairly common in south England and East Anglia.

7 Marmora's Warbler **L** 13 cm

Sylvia sarda **ID** Western Mediterranean island counterpart of 6, similar to it but underparts including throat completely grey. Sexes rather similar, ♂ darker on head and throat. Juv greyer than juv of 6, throat more whitish. **V** Song a short chattering with end trill; call hard *tek*. **H** Resident on Sardinia and Corsica in habitats from from maquis to mountains. **D** V, extremely rare.

8 Balearic Warbler **L** 12 cm

Sylvia balearica **ID** Limited to Balearic Islands, closely resembles 7 but is smaller, with longer tail, sharply demarcated whitish throat and base of bill yellow-orange (not pink). **V** Song similar to 6, but ending with rolling trill; calls disyllabic, softer and nasally *tsr-ek*. **H** Resident on bushy, stony hill slopes and coastal rocks on the Balearics (except Menorca). **D** -.

1
2
3
4
albistriata
5
dartfordiensis
6
♀ Common Whitethroat for comparison
JK
7
8

KINGLETS

1 Goldcrest L 9 cm

Regulus regulus **ID** Smallest bird in Europe, very tiny, greenish with whitish wing-bars. In ad crown bordered black with central stripe orange in ♂ and yellow in ♀, pale eye-ring accentuates the relatively large, dark eye. In brief juv plumage, head greyish and without pattern. Moves actively through bushes and tree-tops and its high-pitched voice is conspicuous. **V** Song high-pitched on two notes *sisisisisi*, often ending with short trill; call very thin, high-pitched *sri-sri-sri*. **H** Coniferous and mixed forests, also in gardens. **D** BRMW, very common, breeding population supplemented by continental migrants in autumn and winter.

2 Firecrest L 9 cm

Regulus ignicapilla **ID** As small as 1 and very similar, but in all plumages has bold black eye-stripe and white supercilium. In brief juv plumage has eye-stripe and supercilium but no dark crown markings. **V** Song very high-pitched, getting faster and ascending *si si-sisisisisihrr*; call slightly lower-pitched than 1, rising in pitch when notes consecutive. **H** Coniferous, mixed and partially deciduous forests and parks. Also found in more open, bushy places in winter. **D** brmw, scarce and local, mainly England and Wales.

TREECREEPERS

3 Treecreeper L 13 cm

Certhia familiaris **ID** Small mouse-like bird, streaked brown above and plain white below, with white supercilium and pale wing-bars. Climbs jerkily and in spiral up tree trunk and along branches, using tail as a prop and probing bark for insects with the slender, slightly decurved bill. Very similar to 4, but flanks cleaner white, supercilium more distinct and pale fringes (not spots) on primary tips. **V** Song high-pitched and sharp, much longer than 4 and ending with a Blue Tit-like trill *tsi tsi tsisirri-tsisirirr*; call slower than 4, a high-pitched, sibilant *srri srri* and *ti*. **H** Parks and mixed forests, often in mountains where it lives alongside 4. **D** BR, common.

4 Short-toed Treecreeper L 13 cm

Certhia brachydactyla **ID** Upperparts streaked like 3, underparts dirty white with brown-tinged flanks, supercilium indistinct and often not reaching bill, unbroken buff wing-bar and white spots on primary tips. **V** Song short, jerky, high-pitched and slightly ascending *ti ti ti-terit sri*; calls similar to Coal Tit with clear *tit* and *ti-tioo*, also in 'dripping' series, sometimes *srri* similar to 3. **H** Forests, parks, gardens. **D** V, extremely rare.

WALLCREEPER

5 Wallcreeper L 16 cm

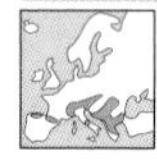

Tichodroma muraria **ID** Small, white spots on wings and tail and crimson wing-patches stand out from otherwise grey plumage. ♂ in br with black throat. **V** Song *too troo tsryoo*; calls thinly *tsui*. **H** Steep mountain faces, often close to water, in winter also at lower altitudes. **D** V, extremely rare.

NUTHATCHES

6 Nuthatch L 14 cm

Sitta europaea **ID** Climbs on trunks and branches. Very distinctive with short tail, chisel-like bill, blue-grey upperparts, black eye-stripe and reddish vent. Underparts orange, in ♂ flanks darker. North-east European subspecies whiter below, in Italy more intensely orange. **V** Sings loud whistling *tioo tioo tioo* and *weeweeweeweewee*; calls loud fruity *twitt twitt twitt* and soft *tsit*. **H** Forests, parks and gardens. **D** BR, England, Wales and south Scotland, common.

7 Rock Nuthatch L 15 cm

Sitta neumayer **ID** Larger and paler than 6 with longer bill and no rusty shades below. **V** Very vocal, song and calls with variations from loud and clear whistling to trilling. **H** Mountains and cliffs, climbs on rocks, also on old ruins. **D** -.

8 Corsican Nuthatch L 11 cm

Sitta whiteheadi **ID** Corsica only; white supercilium, crown black in ♂, grey in ♀. Very agile and tit-like in the crowns of trees, excavates own nest hole. **V** Sings trilling *dudududididi*; calls hoarsely *cheh cheh*. **H** Old pine forests in mountains. **D** -.

9 Krüper's Nuthatch L 12 cm

Sitta krueperi **ID** In Europe breeds only on Lesvos. Has distinctive rufous spot on breast; ♀ has less black on forehead. **V** Song fast and nasally variable *tutituti…*; calls Greenfinch-like *dwui* and hoarsely scolding *tsha-tsha*. **H** Pine forests on Lesvos, otherwise Turkey to Caucasus. **D** -.

♂
♀
1
juv
♂
♀
2
juv
3
4
5
♀ / ♂ non-br
♂ br
♀
6
♂
7
9
♂
♂
north-east
8
♂

WAXWING

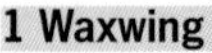 

1 Waxwing L 20 cm

Bombycilla garrulus **ID** Pink-brown starling-sized bird, with long crest, black chin and mask, and yellow band at end of tail. Outside breeding season mostly in flocks in berry bushes. Ad has yellow line down centre of primaries and white primary fringes, 1w has white central line only. In flight similar to 2, but more slender and triangular, wings pale below (dark in 2) and tail square (slightly notched in 2). **V** Song simple, slow and soft with bell-like trill and rougher notes; calls high-pitched sibilant trill: *sirrrr*. **H** Breeds taiga with coniferous forests. In winter also in gardens and parks south to Britain and the Balkans, occurring wherever there are berries. **D** w 10-4, uncommon mainly in east.

STARLINGS

2 Starling L 21 cm

Sturnus vulgaris **ID** Common and well known over almost all of Europe. In non-br black iridescent feathers have clear pale spots, in br these are reduced. Bill yellow in br, otherwise blackish, in ♂ has blue base. Unspotted juv variably light to dark grey-brown, during the moult to 1w unusually bi-coloured. Triangular flight profile. **V** Varied song, twittering, chattering, whistling, much mimicry; calls whirring *tyurr*, juv hoarse *staaar*. **H** Breeds in holes in residential areas, gardens, forests, meadows, outside the breeding season often in huge flocks, roosting in reedbeds or trees. Winters south to Spain. **D** BRMW, abundant.

3 Spotless Starling L 21 cm

Sturnus unicolor **ID** Replaces 2 on the Iberian peninsula. Plumage looks 'oily' with more uniform purple sheen, legs paler pink, in br lacks white spots (♂ has longer feathers on the throat than 2), in other plumages only small pale spots on the undertail coverts and belly, never on the crown, as well as narrow pale fringes to the flight feathers. The unspotted juv is darker overall than juv of 2. **V** Like 2, song is simpler and more penetrating. **H** Residential areas, mainly breeding in colonies, gardens, forest edges and plantations. **D** -.

4 Rose-coloured Starling L 21 cm

Sturnus roseus **ID** Ad pink body, black head with drooping crest and black wings and tail. Juv sandy, much paler than 2, lores pale (dark in 2), rump paler than rest of upperparts, bill yellowish, shorter and stouter, legs stronger. **V** Song chattering with harsh and grinding notes like 2, but without mimicry; calls also similar. **H** Breeds in open landscapes in south-east Europe, occasionally west to Hungary, follows locust swarms and often breeds in huge colonies on cliffs, in quarries, also on houses and stables. Winters south Asia. **D** V, rare but annual, ads in summer, juvs in autumn, sometimes winters.

5 Common Myna L 23 cm

Acridotheres tristis **ID** Slightly larger than 2 but much more robust, feathers darker grey-brown with blackish head. Bill, legs and bare skin around eye yellow, in flight shows conspicuous white patch on primaries. **V** Very noisy, song reminiscent of Song Thrush with similar repetitions, but rougher and more croaking; calls *chaak*. **H** Asian species, introduced to several locations in Europe (for example, Moscow, eastern Black Sea coast), mostly in groups near human habitation. **D** -.

WREN

6 Wren L 10 cm

Troglodytes troglodytes **ID** Tiny bird with short tail often held cocked above back. Round-bodied and short-necked. Feathers brown with fine dark barring, bill quite narrow and long. **V** Song is amazingly loud, alternately sweet and rattling with end trill; *ti loo ti-ti-ti-ti-ti turr-yu-too-loo tell-tell-tell-tell-tell yu terrrrrrr-tsill*; calls grating *tsrrr* and hard *tseck*. **H** Forests, parks, gardens, bushes, often close to water. **D** BR, abundant.

DIPPER

7 Dipper L 19 cm

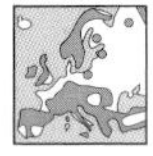

Cinclus cinclus **ID** Seen bobbing on stones in fast-flowing water, diving or swimming, or following stream in rapid whirring flight. Starling-sized with short tail often cocked, outline Wren-like. Large white bib distinctive, in most regions belly red-brown, but especially in north Europe black-brown (Black-bellied Dipper). Juv grey and barred all over. **V** Soft twittering song; calls penetrating *tsrrt*. **H** Fast-flowing streams and rivers, especially in mountains. **D** BR, fairly common in north and west; Black-bellied Dipper rare migrant to east coast.

1w
1
non-br
juv
♂ br
2
juv
br
4
3
non-br
♂ br
5
Black-bellied
7
6
juv

THRUSHES

1 Blackbird L 25 cm

Turdus merula **ID** The most widespread and familiar thrush in Europe, found in a wide range of habitats including residential areas in almost all regions. Typical posture when hopping across lawns shows raised tail and slightly sagging wings. ♂ completely black with yellow bill and eye-ring, ♀ dark-brown to blackish, variably rusty-brown, slate-grey or black-brown below, breast often washed out, mottled or streaked, bill yellowish. Juv mottled brown, warmer and paler than ♀. In 1w and 1s as in ad but flight feathers paler and appear brown. **V** Song beautiful melodic whistling, loud, varied, often slightly melancholy with higher- and lower-pitched notes, sometimes ending with twittering. Calls from raised perches at dawn and into late winter, calls diverse, for example, *tchack-ack-ack*, low-pitched *gock*, very high-pitched *tseeeh* and harsh *srrri*. **H** Gardens, copses, parks and forests. **D** BRMW, abundant.

2 Song Thrush L 23 cm

Turdus philomelos **ID** Small, common thrush with warm brown upperparts and creamy white underparts marked with dark spots that sometimes merge together. Sexes similer, juv has small beige spots on upperparts and wing coverts. More secretive than 1, in jerky flight shows short tail and ochre-brown underwing coverts. **V** Beautiful and loud song of whistling and liquid notes, with each repeated several times, for example, *diudut-diudut-diudut kuklivi kuklivi kroo kroo kvi-kvi-kvi pio pio*, mostly delivered from tree tops; calls short *tsip*, also on migration at night, and warns sharply scolding *xixixixi*. **H** Woodland, parks and gardens. **D** BRMW, common but declining.

3 Redwing L 21 cm

Turdus iliacus **ID** From similar 2 by bold head pattern with cream supercilium and submoustachial stripe as well as red flanks, and in flight by red underwing coverts. **V** Song of two to five flute-like tones followed by soft chirping, *dri dru dru drudro, tyerre-tyurre-tyo*; calls high-pitched and penetrating *tzeee*, which can often be heard on migration at night. **H** Breeds open forests, during migration and winter visits berry bushes and meadows. Winters south and west Europe. **D** MW 10-3, very common, often in flocks; b, rare breeder in north Scotland.

4 Mistle Thrush L 28 cm

Turdus viscivorus **ID** Large, bold, upright thrush, superficially similar in colour to the much smaller 2, but has longer tail, greyer upperparts with pale edges to flight feathers, large dark spots on underparts, and in flight shows pure white underwing coverts and white corners to tail tip. Alert and shy. **V** Song like 1, but verses shorter, faster, more monotonous, mostly without the soft chirping end, *truitrufu tyuriityuroo*; call wooden rasping *tserrr*. **H** Forests, parks, often in areas where mistletoe is common. **D** BRMW, common but declining.

5 Fieldfare L 26 cm

Turdus pilaris **ID** Large with contrast between chestnut mantle and grey head and rump. Breast buff to rusty-yellow, breast and flanks heavily spotted, underwings white and tail black. **V** Song chirping and chiding; call a dry, Magpie-like *tchack-tchack-tchack* and pressed *gheeeh*. **H** Forest edges, meadows, parks, breeds in loose colonies. In winter widespread in central, south and west Europe. **D** MW 10-3, common, mostly in flocks; b, rare breeder north Scotland.

6 Ring Ouzel L 24 cm

Turdus torquatus **ID** Breeds uplands, similar to 1, but less rounded shape, in all plumages with pale breast-band and pale fringes to flight feathers. Ad ♂ black with white crescent, ♀ and 1w brownish-black with beige crescent (can be hard to decipher in 1w). Underparts scaled, less so in north Europe subspecies *torquatus*, much more in central and south European *alpestris*. **V** Simple, melodious song of 2-4 repeated flute-like tones like *trub-trub-trub* or *sivooh sivooh*; calls *tack tack* or *chock*, harsher than 1. **H** Breeds forested fells in north Europe and mountainous conifer forests in central and south Europe. Found in lowland fields, bushes and forest edges during migration and winter. Winters south Europe. **D** bm 4-10, uncommon.

7 White's Thrush L 29 cm

Zoothera dauma **ID** Large with conspicuous dark, half-moon-shaped spots and long bill, in flight shows white underwing bisected by broad black stripe; similar in all plumages. Juvs of 1 and 4 may be mistaken for this extreme rarity. Shy, mostly hidden in undergrowth. **V** Song a monotonously repeated long whistle. **H** Breeds moist taiga with undergrowth from western Urals eastwards. Vagrant elsewhere. **D** V 10-11, extremely rare.

juv
♀
♂
1
juv
2
3
4
5
♀
6
torquatus
♂
alpestris
♂
7

ROCK THRUSHES AND FLYCATCHERS

1 Blue Rock Thrush L 22 cm

Monticola solitarius **ID** Usually in rocky habitat and almost as big as Blackbird, with long, dark bill and long, dark tail, which is moved slowly up and down. ♂ very dark blue overall with wings and tail blackish, ♀ plain dark-brown above and barred paler below, but from a distance both sexes often appear dark. Shy and alert, regularly perches high on rocks but also hides quickly behind them when disturbed. **V** Typical sad, fluty, loud, clear thrush-like song, with shaky notes in between, uttered from perch or in flight; calls moaning *uib uib* and low-pitched *choock*. **H** Resident in sunny, rocky slopes in south Europe, also on rock walls and sometimes in hill-towns. **D** V, extremely rare.

2 Rock Thrush L 19 cm

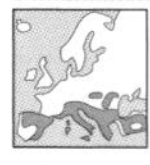

Monticola saxatilis **ID** Sturdy with short rufous tail and quite long bill. Br ♂ unmistakable with blue-and-orange plumage and white patch on back, ♀, non-br ♂ and juv brown and similar to 1, but barred above, tinged orange below and with rusty-brown tail. **V** Whistling, Blackbird-like song, softer than 1 and often starting with descending trill, delivered from perch or in high song-flight; calls softly *dyu* and *hu-dshak*. **H** Summer visitor to stony mountain meadows and rocky scree in southern Europe north to southern Alps and Hungary. **D** V, extremely rare.

3 Spotted Flycatcher L 14 cm

Muscicapa striata **ID** Rather plain grey-brown, mostly sits upright on perches, from where it hunts flying insects, is conspicuous by its call. Upperparts light grey-brown with dark streaks on crown, underparts whitish with diffusely streaked breast. Juv has ochre spots above and on tips of greater coverts. **V** Weak song high-pitched and sharp with harsh and forced notes, for example, *tsi tsvit tsrri..*; calls sharp, abrupt and high-pitched chirping *tsrri, tsit*. **H** Open forests, parks, and gardens, breeds in hollows or dense vegetation such as ivy. Winters Africa. **D** BM 5-9, fairly common but declining.

4 Red-breasted Flycatcher L 12 cm

Ficedula parva **ID** Difficult to see as often stays hidden in tree-tops. Small and agile, in all plumages with pale brown upperparts, whitish underparts, pale eye-ring and broad white patches at base of tail. Only ad ♂ has grey head and orange throat, ♀ has buff tinge to breast and flanks. 1w like ♀, but buffy with pale tips to greater coverts. ♂ in 1s still like ♀, in 2s with a little orange on the throat and barely grey on head, attains full coloration only in 3s. **V** Song begins with sharp notes, followed by rhythmic disyllabic elements and descending, something like *sri sri wud wud aida aida du du dooh*; calls Wren-like *srrrt*, also *tck tck*, warns whistling *ilu ilu*. **H** Breeds in mature deciduous and mixed forests, often with beeches. On migration in hedges and copses. Winters south Asia. **D** m 9-10, very scarce, mainly on east coast.

5 Pied Flycatcher L 13 cm

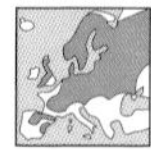

Ficedula hypoleuca **ID** Quite robust, often flicks wings and tail. In all plumages whitish below, white patch on wing and white bases to outer tail feathers. Br ♂ variable above, ranging from blackish (especially in north) to grey-brown (central to east European form *muscipeta*). ♀ and 1w brown above, breast and flanks often beige, no or small white spot on forehead. **V** Rhythmic and variable song, for example, *tsivi tsivi tsuli tsuli vutee vutee tsuli sri*; calls sharply *pit*. **H** Deciduous and mixed forests, breeds in hollows (also nestboxes). Winters Africa. **D** BM 4-9, locally fairly common in north and west.

6 Collared Flycatcher L 13 cm

Ficedula albicollis **ID** Similar to 5, br ♂ recognized by broad white collar, larger white spot on forehead and completely black tail, also upperparts always black with whitish rump. ♀ slightly greyer than 5 with larger white patch at base of primaries. **V** Totally different song to 5, slow with long drawn-out squeezed notes, like *truh tseet tru sidi*; call a long sucking *heeep*. **H** Breeds deciduous forests and parks in east Europe. Winters Africa. **D** V, extremely rare.

7 Semi-collared Flycatcher L 13 cm

Ficedula semitorquata **ID** Breeds in south Balkans and intermediate in plumage between 5 and 6. ♂ upperparts blackish with slightly more white on side of neck than 5, more white at the base and edges of tail, white-tipped median coverts and more white on base of primaries. ♀ grey-brown above, sometimes shares the last two features, also tertials often paler and with narrower and more even white on edges than 5 or 6. **V** Sings more slowly than 5, calls lower-pitched than 6. **H** Breeds deciduous and mixed forest and orchards. Winters Africa. **D** -.

1
♀
♂
2
♀
♂
3
juv
4
1w
♂ br
♀ / ♂ 1s
5
♂
♂
♀
muscipeta
6
♂
♀
7
♂

1 Robin L 13 cm

Erithacus rubecula **ID** Familiar and often confiding, frequently seen in towns and gardens. Forehead, sides of head and breast orange-red, belly off-white, upperparts brown with greyish border between red and brown feathers. Sexes similar, in brief juv plumage mottled all over with rich buff and lacks red. Often hops on ground. **V** Song silvery, and melancholy high-pitched notes, long and sweet at first, then becoming more chattery and ending in a pearly trill, also sings in winter; calls *tick*, also in fast sequence, warns high-pitched *tsi-eeh*. **H** Woods, gardens, parks. **D** BRMW, abundant.

2 Bluethroat L 13 cm

Luscinia svecica **ID** Body shape similar to 1, always has whitish supercilium and rufous patches at base of tail. Throat of br ♂ blue, divided from whitish belly by black and rufous breast-bands. Contrasting spot in the centre of throat is variable in size and colour, being red in Scandinavian subspecies *svecica* (Red-spotted Bluethroat) and white in western subspecies *cyanecula* (White-spotted Bluethroat). ♀ has cream throat bordered by black and sometimes with a scattering of blue or rufous feathers. **V** Song silvery with mimicry, often starting with high-pitched *tri tri tri* and accelerating in pace, frequently delivered at night; calls harshly *track*. **H** Summer visitor, *cyanecula* to swamps, marshes and reedbeds (winters Spain and Africa), *svecica* to mountains, moist thickets and forests (winters Africa and Asia). **D** m 5 and 9-10, very scarce, mainly on east coast.

3 Red-flanked Bluetail L 13 cm

Tarsiger cyanurus **ID** Inconspicuous bird, in all plumages with small white throat-patch neatly defined by dark edges, orange flanks and bluish upperside to tail. ♂ uniform dark blue above, ♀ and young up to 1s olive-brown above with whitish eye-ring. **V** Often sings from top of tree with a sad *tyulu-tyulu-tyulurr*; calls *hooeed* and *track*. **H** Breeds dense taiga forest from east Finland eastwards. Winters Asia. **D** V 5 and 9-11, extremely rare.

4 Nightingale L 16 cm

Luscinia megarhynchos **ID** Uniform rufous-brown above with a brighter red-brown tail, whitish below except for beige breast. Mostly stays hidden in thickets. Compare with 5. **V** Sings day and night with flute-like sequences and whistling crescendos, for example, *diu-dut diu-dut tshurrtshrrtshurr diudi doo doo-doo-doo-dee diudut*; calls ascending *hweet* and croaking *karr*. **H** Breeds forests and thickets with dense undergrowth, winters Africa. **D** bm 4-9, breeds locally in southern England.

5 Thrush Nightingale L 16 cm

Luscinia luscinia **ID** North-eastern counterpart of 4, similar but darker grey-brown above with breast clouded grey and faintly streaked and eight (instead of seven) primary tips visible projecting beyond tertials. **V** Sings lower and more slowly and powerfully than 4, whistling crescendos replaced by low-pitched *tshook-tshook-tshook*; calls flat *heet* and rolling *errr*. **H** Similar to 4 but often in moister places such as swamp forest. **D** V 5 and 9, extremely rare.

6 Rufous Scrub Robin L 16 cm

Cercotrichas galactotes **ID** Vaguely resembles 4 but has striking head pattern and longer tail which is often raised or fanned to display prominent black-and-white tips. Subspecies *galactotes* in south-west is rufous above, *syriacus* in south-east is brown-grey. Often sits in open or hops on ground. **V** Hurried, short song is musical and thrush-like; calls hard *tack* and *bzzzzz* like a buzzing insect. **H** Summer visitor to dry, open landscape with bushes. **D** V, extremely rare.

7 Black Redstart L 14 cm

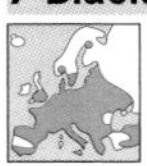

Phoenicurus ochruros **ID** Frequently shimmers orange-red tail, mature ♂ blackish with white wing-patch; ♀ and juv to 1s dusky grey-brown with no white. **V** Short song consisting of whistling and clattering sounds, with typical grinding notes in between, often delivered at dusk from roof or aerial; call *visd tek-tek*. **H** Towns, cities, rocky areas; often nests in wall cavities, found in flatter, more open areas during migration and winter. **D** brmw 3-10, scarce and local in England and Wales.

8 Common Redstart L 14 cm

Phoenicurus phoenicurus **ID** Constantly quivers bright orange-red tail. Br ♂ very distinctive, non-br and 1w are paler versions. ♀ paler and browner with warmer tinges, paler buff below than 7. **V** Short, variable, song is delivered from dawn and often includes mimicry, for example, *huid trui-trui-trui-suru*; calls *huid tick-tick*. **H** Breeds open forests, parks and gardens, nests in tree hollow. Winters Africa. **D** BM 4-9, fairly common in west.

juv
1
2
♂
svecica
♀
♂
cyanecula
4
3
♀
♂
5
galactotes
6
syriaca
♂ 1w/
non-br
7
8
♀/♂ 1s
♂ br
♀
ad ♂

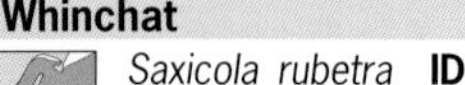

1 Whinchat **L** 13 cm

Saxicola rubetra **ID** Often perches in prominent position. Supercilium long and whitish, throat and breast orange (in juv and non-br spotted brown), upperparts brown with darker markings and base of tail white on outer corners. **V** Chirping song with mimicry delivered day and night; call *yu teck-teck*. **H** Breeds wet meadows, pastures and heaths. Winters Africa. **D** BM 4-9, locally fairly common but declining.

2 European Stonechat **L** 12 cm

Saxicola rubicola **ID** Similar to 1, breast orange or orange-brown, but head and throat uniform dark, white patch on side of neck, tail all dark and rump paler, throat whitish in 1w. **V** Chirping song, calls *weet chack-chack*. **H** Breeds moors, heaths, dunes, mountains, winters also fields and marshes. **D** BR, locally common.

3 Siberian Stonechat **L** 12 cm

Saxicola maurus **ID** Replaces 2 from western Urals eastwards, ♂ has extensive pure white rump, black (instead of dark grey) underwing coverts, more white on the sides of the neck and less orange on breast. ♀ and 1w in contrast to 2 paler, with unstreaked, beige rump, pale throat and faint supercilium. **V** and **H** Like 2. **D** V, extremely rare.

4 Northern Wheatear **L** 15 cm

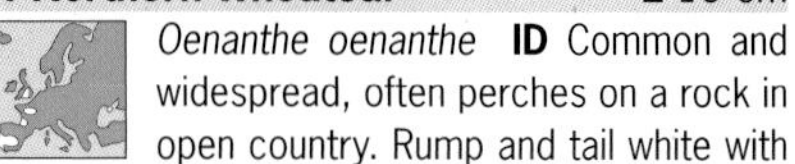

Oenanthe oenanthe **ID** Common and widespread, often perches on a rock in open country. Rump and tail white with black pattern like an inverted T. In br grey above, pale orange below, ♂ with black mask and wings, ♀ paler. Non-br and 1w more brown-grey above and buff-beige below. **V** Short song is grinding and harsh; calls include sucking *heet* and hard *tshak*. **H** Moors, heaths, rocky fields. Winters Africa. **D** BM 4-10, fairly common breeder in north and west, widespread during migration.

5 Isabelline Wheatear **L** 16 cm

Oenanthe isabellina **ID** Only in south-east Europe. Very similar to 4 in non-br but slightly larger and more upright posture with shorter tail, shorter wings and longer legs. Uniform sandy-brown overall, including wings, with a prominent black alula (in 4 greater coverts also dark), clear pale supercilium broadest in front of eye (in 4 broadest behind eye), pale (instead of dark) underwings and a broader black band on tip of tail. **V** Long chatting song with typical series of whistles and mimicry; call high-pitched, flute-like *huit*. **H** Summer visitor to steppe. **D** V, extremely rare.

6 Western Black-eared Wheatear **L** 15 cm

Oenanthe hispanica hispanica **ID** More slender than 4 with band on tip of tail narrower and irregular. Occurs in two morphs, either with dark throat or dark eye-mask. Warm ochre above, fading to beige, ♀ duller and less contrasting. **V** Song short and dry chirping with some mimicry, delivered from a perch or in flight; calls rasping *gshr*. **H** Breeds south-west Europe in open, rocky landscapes with light scrub. Winters Africa. **D** V, extremely rare.

7 Eastern Black-eared Wheatear **L** 15 cm

Oenanthe hispanica melanoleuca **ID** The south-eastern counterpart of 6. Similar, but feathers less warm and greyer and in br ♂ pale plumage often bleaches to white. ♀ has broader black mask or more extensive black throat than 6 and black extends onto forehead as narrow black band above bill. **V** As 6. **H** Summer visitor to open, rocky areas. **D** V, extremely rare.

8 Pied Wheatear **L** 15 cm

Oenanthe pleschanka **ID** ♂ in br immediately recognizable by black mantle and throat always black and reaching far onto the breast. After moulting ♀ has breast intensely reddish-ochre. In all other plumages hard to distinguish from the very similar 7, but upperparts darker and colder grey to earth-brown with clearer pale fringes to feathers, throat dusky grey-brown and diffusely demarcated, reaching further down onto the often dark ochre-grey breast. **V** Similar to 7, but often with shorter phrases. **H** Summer visitor to rocky places such as coastal cliffs and mountains in south-east Europe. **D** V, extremely rare.

9 Cyprus Wheatear **L** 14 cm

Oenanthe cypriaca **ID** Breeds only on Cyprus and is very similar to 8, but with larger head, shorter wings and tail, often broader black band on tip of tail, less white on rump and nape and darker orange-buff underparts. Br ♀ barely duller than ♂, in non-br and 1w browner above with brown-grey crown and nape and more intensive reddish-beige below. **V** Song a cicada-like *bizz bizz bizz bizz…*; calls *bzru*. **H** Breeds in stony regions, winters Africa. **D** -.

10 Black Wheatear **L** 17 cm

Oenanthe leucura **ID** Plumage black overall except for white on rump, vent and sides to base of tail, ♀ slightly duller brown-black. **V** Melodious song with loud whistling and chirping; call a descending *puip*. **H** Resident in rocky regions. **D** -.

1
2
3
4
5
6
7
8
9
10
♀/1w

ACCENTORS

1 Alpine Accentor L 17 cm

Prunella collaris **ID** Robust, Skylark-sized bird of high mountains, much larger than 2. Blackish median and greater coverts, white tips form two wing-bars, rufous streaking on flanks, finely spotted throat visible only at close range. Flight slightly undulating; in winter quite tame, often in flocks and around mountain huts. **V** Song lark-like with low-pitched trills; calls *dshurr, dyurr-rrup* and *tyup*. **H** Rocky areas with meadows in mountains, in winter also at lower altitudes. **D** V, extremely rare.

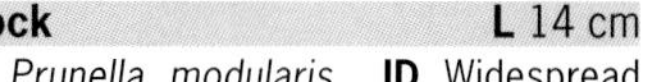

2 Dunnock L 14 cm

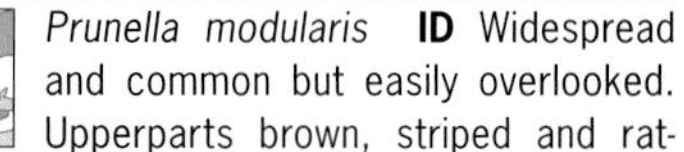

Prunella modularis **ID** Widespread and common but easily overlooked. Upperparts brown, striped and rather sparrow-like, but with slender bill, much grey on head and breast and heavily streaked flanks. Often creeps jerkily and mouse-like on ground, but quickly moves into low cover. **V** Sweet-noted, rapid and unvaried song, most often delivered from top of a bush; calls metallic *steeeh* and ringing *dsidsidsi*. **H** Woodland, scrub, parks, gardens. **D** BRMW, abundant.

SPARROWS

3 Snowfinch L 18 cm

Montifringilla nivalis **ID** Large sparrow of high alpine regions. Shows much white on belly, inner wings and outer tail feathers, differs from Snow Bunting by fairly plain brown mantle and plain grey head. Flight feathers and central tail feathers black. In br has black throat and bill, otherwise throat white and bill yellow. ♀ slightly paler than ♂. **V** Stuttering sparrow-like song *tshi-tui tshi-tui* given from perch or in flight; calls out of tune *psheeah* and rolling *prrt*. **H** Rocky mountains above tree line, also at mountain huts. **D** -.

4 House Sparrow L 15 cm

Passer domesticus **ID** Familiar and common. ♂ with grey crown, chestnut crown-sides and nape, grey rump and black throat and bib, the intensity and extent of which change with state of wear of the plumage (showing little black when fresh and much when worn). ♀ and juv grey-brown on head and rump, with buff supercilium. Almost always seen in flocks. **V** Song a sequence of *tshilp* and *tshurrp*-calls; also calls: familiar chirping *tsherr, tshetsherett, kurr,* but mostly *tshilp*. **H** Usually found close to human habitation, breeds mostly on buildings. **D** BR, common but declining.

5 Tree Sparrow L 13 cm

Passer montanus **ID** Smaller than 4, sexes similar with rusty crown restricted by pale grey collar broken at nape, ear-coverts white with neat black spot. Juv has fainter version of same head pattern. Outside breeding season mostly in flocks, also associated with 4. **V** Song slightly higher-pitched and faster than 4, *tship tship....* ; calls in flight *tek-tek-tek* and *twit*, nasal *toto*, also *tsuit* and *trrrt*. **H** Cultivated land, villages, open forest, parks; will use nestboxes. Widespread and common in places, in Europe rarely in towns but often in villages. **D** br, uncommon, may be stabilizing after recent severe decline.

6 Spanish Sparrow L 15 cm

Passer hispaniolensis **ID** Often occurs alongside 4 and is very similar to it. ♂ has all chestnut crown, white supercilium and ear-coverts, extensive black throat and breast and black striping on mantle and flanks, although this is restricted in fresh moult. ♀ very similar to 4, but with faint streaking on breast and flanks, paler belly and heavier bill. **V** Song similar to 4, but slightly higher-pitched and more complicated in parts, often disyllabic notes ascending and emphasised at the end; typical flight call *teefuid*. **H** Towns, cultivated lands, steppe and semi-deserts close to water; breeds in colonies in bushes. **D** V, extremely rare.

7 Italian Sparrow L 15 cm

Passer italiae **ID** A stable hybrid population between 4 and 6, ♂ differs from 4 by having completely chestnut-brown crown, pure white ear-coverts, mostly clearer white supercilium and pattern on mantle richer in contrast. ♀ cannot be differentiated from 4. Is regarded by some as a subspecies of 6. **V** Like 6. **H** Breeds from Italy to the southern edge of the Alps as well as on Crete; like 4 lives only close to human habitation. **D** -.

8 Rock Sparrow L 16 cm

Petronia petronia **ID** Superficially similar to ♀ of 4, but more robust with conspicuous stripes on head, thick bill and white tip to tail, yellow patch at base of throat often difficult to see. **V** Song consists of different calls, for example a nasally ascending *bai, tvayuid*. **H** Stony areas. **D** V, extremely rare.

1
3
non-br
♂ br
2
juv
4
♀
♂ fresh
♂ worn
juv
5
7
♂
♀
♂ worn
8
6

PIPITS

1 Meadow Pipit L 15 cm

Anthus pratensis **ID** Common and widespread but lacks striking features. Depending on the degree of wear, upperparts grey- to olive-brown with more or less clear streaking, underparts whitish to buff with bold blackish streaking on breast and flanks (on breast only in juv). Legs pale flesh-coloured, in flight shows white outer tail feathers. Compare with 2. **V** Sings high-pitched and monotonous *tsip tsip tsip tsi tsi tsirr tsia tsyup* mostly in flight; best characteristic is the high-pitched thin call *sip sip sip*, warns *tsip tsrip* in breeding season. **H** Breeds in open, mainly moist areas, meadows. Winters south and west Europe **D** BRMW, common.

2 Tree Pipit L 15 cm

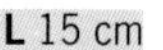

Anthus trivialis **ID** Generally common and widespread summer migrant, very similar to 1 and most easily identified by voice. Overall buff-brown and cleaner looking than 1, head pattern clearer, streaking on flanks narrower, often with stronger contrast between yellowish breast and whitish belly, bill heavier and hind claw shorter. **V** Song varied and trilling, delivered mainly in flight, starting with *tsi tsi tsi* and ending in a descending *tsia tsiya tsiya*; call incisive *zeep* or *speez*, very different from 1, warns *supp supp* when breeding. **H** Forest edges, clearings, meadows and heathland with trees or copses. Winters Africa. **D** BM 4-9, locally common.

3 Olive-backed Pipit L 15 cm

Anthus hodgsoni **ID** Siberian pipit, similar to 2, but upperparts only faintly streaked and with olive tinge, streaking on breast darker, clearly defined supercilium yellowish in front of eye and whitish behind, black-and-white spot at back edge of ear coverts. Wags tail more vigorously. **V** Song shorter and drier than 2; calls *zeep* slightly higher-pitched and rougher than 2, similar to 4 but shorter. **H** Breeds taiga from Urals eastwards, winters south Asia. **D** V 9-10, very rare, occasionally winters.

4 Red-throated Pipit L 15 cm

Anthus cervinus **ID** Rather similar to 1. Ad has unmistakable brick-red throat, breast and sides to head (slightly paler in ♀). 1w lacks red and can be told from 1 by two broad whitish longitudinal stripes on mantle (accentuated as they are bordered by dark stripes), finely streaked rump and heavy flank streaking. **V** Often sings in flight, usually a long sequence of whistling, trilling, rattling and rasping themes; call high-pitched, sharp and long *spee-eeh*. **H** Breeds wet meadows, winters eastern Mediterranean. **D** V 5 and 9-10, annual.

5 Water Pipit L 16 cm

Anthus spinoletta **ID** Breeds alpine meadows, has dark legs and is more robust than 1. In br breast pink and unstreaked, head grey with white supercilium, mantle brownish. Non-br dusky brown above, white underparts well streaked, supercilium and wing-bar whiter than in 1, bill longer. Wary. **V** Song similar to 1, but more powerful; call stronger than 1: *veest veest*. **H** Breeds mountain meadows above tree line, winters wetlands and coasts in lowlands from south England to Mediterranean. **D** w 10-4, uncommon and local, mainly in south.

6 Rock Pipit L 16 cm

Anthus petrosus **ID** Similar to 5, also with dark legs but pale grey (not white) outer tail feathers. Plumage uniform dusky dark grey-brown with heavily mottled buff underparts, non-br and 1w with olive tinge above. Scandinavian subspecies *littoralis* has pinkish breast in spring. **V** Song and call as 5. **H** Rocky coasts of north and west Europe. **D** BRMW, fairly common on coasts.

7 Tawny Pipit L 17 cm

Anthus campestris **ID** Large, pale pipit with almost wagtail-like appearance, often wags its long tail. Ad sandy and lightly streaked above, streaked below only thinly on sides of breast, dark centres to the median coverts and loral stripe prominently dark. Juv at first similar to 1w of 8 with striped mantle and well-marked breast, but with dark loral stripe, paler bill and shorter curved hind claw. **V** Monotonous song of repetitive *tsir-li* notes; call a sparrow-like *tshilp*. **H** Summer visitor to dry, sandy, open areas. Winters Africa. **D** V, rare but annual, mainly south coast.

8 Richard's Pipit L 18 cm

Anthus richardi **ID** Largest pipit, slender with long neck and legs. Flanks rusty-beige, breast band of narrow streaks. Juv sometimes similar to 7 but lores pale and hind claw longer and straight. Could be confused with Skylark. **V** Sings in flight with monotonous *dsh-dshe-dshe … tshia-tshia-tshia*; typical call loud sparrow-like *tshreep* **H** Breeds Siberian steppe, autumn visitor to Europe. **D** V 9-10, rare but annual, sometimes winters.

worn
1
fresh
2
3
1w
4
ad
1w
1w
br Britain
6
br Scandinavia
1w
br
5
juv
7
br
8
1w

1 White Wagtail **L** 18 cm

Motacilla alba alba **ID** Striking small, slender bird of open areas that continuously wags its long tail. Plumage black, white and grey. Always with black breast-band, grey mantle and white wing and outer tail feathers. In br throat black and ♀ has less black on nape than ♂. In non-br and 1w head paler, throat white, only breast-band black; juv more uniform grey including head and breast. **V** Song a chirping sequence of calls; call a sharp disyllabic *tsi-litt* and shorter *tslit*. **H** Wetlands, meadows, open areas, towns. **D** mw, much less common than 2.

2 Pied Wagtail **L** 18 cm

Motacilla alba yarrellii **ID** Replaces 1 in Britain and Ireland, familiar in town and country, occasionally breeds in Norway and north-west France. Br ♂ with all black mantle, in ♀ and 1s ♂ upperparts grey-black, white wing-bars broader. In non-br and 1w often recognizable by almost black (not grey) rump and dark grey flanks. Often forms large roosts in town-centre trees. **V** and **H** Like 1. **D** BR, abundant.

3 Grey Wagtail **L** 19 cm

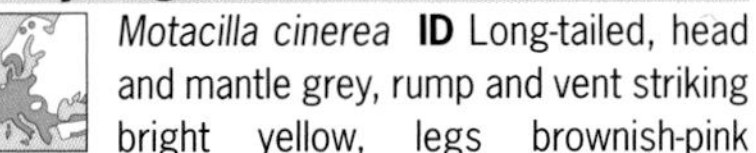

Motacilla cinerea **ID** Long-tailed, head and mantle grey, rump and vent striking bright yellow, legs brownish-pink (blackish in all other wagtails), in flight broad white wing-bar visible from above and below. Throat solid black only in br ♂, otherwise whitish, breast and belly vary from whitish in juv to yellow in br. **V** Simple, metallic song; call sharper and more metallic than 1 *tsis-iss*, warns high-pitched, ascending *tsooh-it*. **H** Most often near running water, from mountain streams to towns. **D** BR, common.

4 Citrine Wagtail **L** 17 cm

Motacilla citreola **ID** Eastern wagtail of open wetlands, with slightly longer tail and legs than the similar 5, in all plumages with broader white edges to tertials and double white wing-bars, mantle always grey, rump never yellow. Breast and belly yellow, head in br ♂ yellow bordered by black collar, in ♀ and non-br greyish with a yellow border around ear-coverts. Juv and 1w lack yellow but recognizable by whitish 'ear-covert surround' and pale lores. **V** Song similar to 1, distinctive call a buzzing *dzeep*. **H** Summer visitor to eastern European wetlands, extending its range westwards. **D** V 5-10, very rare, mainly Northern Isles and east coast.

5 Blue-headed Wagtail **L** 16 cm

Motacilla flava flava **ID** Continental subspecies of 8. Relatively shorter tail than 1-4, in ad mantle greenish, underparts all yellow, head blue-grey with white supercilium, this coloration most intense in ♂ in br, duller and paler in ♀ and in non-br. In 1w pale olive-brown above, beige with yellow tinge below, especially on vent, in juv additionally a narrow dark collar. **V** Very simple song, a scratching *sri-srit sri...*, from elevated perch or in flight; calls a rather soft *swe-up*. **H** The most widely distributed of the yellow wagtail complex (5-11), summer visitor to meadows and wetlands, often with domestic animals, in autumn can form large roosts in reedbeds. **D** m 4-9, uncommon migrant.

6 Black-headed Wagtail **L** 16 cm

Motacilla flava feldegg **ID** South-eastern form of 8, ♂ easily recognized by extensive black cap reaching to the nape, supercilium absent and clear green tinge to mantle. ♀ with dark-grey cap, but white chin and paler overall, but differences quite clear in contrast to other forms. **V** Call more buzzing than 5: *tzeeup*. **H** Breeds from Balkans to the Black Sea. Summer visitor. **D** V 5-6, extremely rare.

7 Grey-headed Wagtail **L** 16 cm

Motacilla flava thunbergi **ID** Breeds north-east Europe, ♂ has dark-grey head, blackish ear-coverts, yellow throat, often white moustachial stripe. **V** and **H** As 5. **D** V, rare.

8 Yellow Wagtail **L** 16 cm

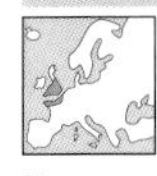

Motacilla flava flavissima **ID** Breeds in Britain, locally also on neighbouring European coasts from France to Norway. Head green with yellow throat and supercilium, mantle brighter yellow-green. **V** and **H** As 5. **D** BM 4-9, locally common but declining.

9 Iberian Wagtail **L** 16 cm

Motacilla flava iberiae **ID** Iberia only. Head grey, throat and narrow supercilium white. **V** and **H** Like 5. **D** V, extremely rare.

10 Ashy-headed Wagtail **L** 16 cm

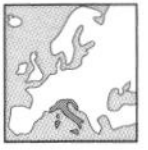

Motacilla flava cinereocapilla **ID** Breeds mainly Italy. Head dark-grey, throat white, supercilium faint or absent. **V** and **H** Like 5. **D** V, extremely rare.

11 Yellow-headed Wagtail **L** 16 cm

Motacilla flava lutea **ID** Lower Volga to north Kazakhstan. Head often all yellow, otherwise similar to 8. **V** and **H** Like 5. **D** -.

♂ br
♀ br
1w
non-br
1
2
♀ br
♂ br
♂ non-br
♂ br
1w
3
4
♀
♂
1w
7
8
9
all ♂ in br
10
11
♂
♀
6
♀
♂
5
1w

FINCHES

1 Chaffinch L 15 cm

Fringilla coelebs **ID** Perhaps best-known finch and one of commonest birds in Europe. About the size of House Sparrow and characterized in all plumages by double white wing-bar, white outer tail feathers and greenish rump. ♂ with blue-grey crown and nape, chestnut mantle and pink-red ear-coverts, throat and breast, duller in non-br. ♀ and juv olive-brown and grey above and greyish buff below. Outside breeding season often in flocks and on ground. **V** Loud descending song with final flourish *dsedse-dsedserit-tscherrit*, in many regions with additional Great Spotted Woodpecker-like *kick*; calls metallic *pink*, rolling *rrrooh*, long *heeeep* and in flight *yupp*. **H** Woodlands, parks, gardens. **D** BRMW, abundant.

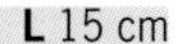

2 Brambling L 15 cm

Fringilla montifringilla **ID** Breeds northern forests, but occurs widely as winter visitor across much of Europe. In all plumages shows orange breast and large white patch on rump and lower back. Br ♂ has black head and bill, in non-br head and mantle mottled due to paler feather fringes, bill yellow. Head of ♀ always brown-grey. Mostly in flocks. **V** Song very simple and monotonous, like a distant saw *rrrrrhoo*; typical call loud rasping *zwee-ik*, in flight also harder and more nasal than 1: *yack yack*. **H** Breeds north European forests, winters beech forests south to Mediterranean. **D** mw 10-4, usually uncommon but numbers vary greatly from year to year.

3 Hawfinch L 18 cm

Coccothraustes coccothraustes **ID** Big with short tail and heavy triangular bill, large head and thick neck with grey collar, in flight shows white wing-bars and broad white tail-tip. Bill silver in br, yellowish in non-br, secondaries bluish-black in ♂, grey in ♀. Juv paler and mottled below. **V** Softly grinding song; calls loud *see-ut* and Robin-like *tsick*. **H** Forests, especially hornbeam, shy, more widespread and confiding on Continent. **D** brmw, scarce and local.

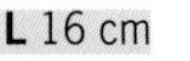

4 Bullfinch L 16 cm

Pyrrhula pyrrhula **ID** Rotund finch with short, black bill, bright white rump and vent, completely black tail, grey mantle and white wing-bar. In ad cap and chin black, ♂ bright pinkish-red below, ♀ brownish-grey. Northern birds larger and brighter. In juv (plumage for short period only) whole head grey-brown with conspicuous black eye. Not particularly shy, outside breeding season in small flocks. **V** Unremarkable, soft chirping song with a few low-pitched flute-like tones; call wistful whistling *duh* and *pyuh*, in Scandinavian birds slightly lower-pitched and in north Russian populations calls nasally *daaah*. **H** Woodland, parks, gardens; seldom visits bird-tables. **D** BRMW, common.

5 Common Rosefinch L 14 cm

Carpodacus erythrinus **ID** Eastern species which has expanded westwards. Br ♂ (only from 2s) has red on head, breast and rump, belly white. However, ♀, 1s ♂ and juv are overall brown-grey with olive tinge, faintly and diffusely streaked above and below. They have two faint wing-bars, a beady black eye that stands out against the unpatterned head and a short, stumpy, 'roundish' bill. Very secretive, often noticed only when the ♂ sings for a short time at the start of the breeding season. **V** Sings a loud whistling *tute-hutya* or *vidye-vidye-woo*; calls *zoo-eet* and warns like Greenfinch: *dyai*. **H** Breeds bushes, forest edges and thickets near water. Winters south Asia. **D** V 5 and 9-10, rare but annual, mainly Northern Isles and east coast. Has bred.

6 Pine Grosbeak L 21 cm

Pinicola enucleator **ID** Largest finch, breeds northern taiga forest. Stocky body with short neck, but tail quite long and can be quite agile when foraging among twigs. Wings blackish with two narrow white wing-bars and narrow white fringes to tertials, bill short, deep and round. ♂ carmine red, ♀ and 1w yellowish-green. **V** Light, almost yodelling flute-like song *dideliy dyidelu pulipiy*; call a bright whistling *tyulidih* and softer *boott-boott*. **H** Northern taiga, in winter sometimes moves a bit further south and found in rowan trees. **D** V, extremely rare.

7 Trumpeter Finch L 13 cm

Bucanetes githagineus **ID** Small with a large head and usually pale bill. Plumage brown-grey. Br ♂ has red bill and pink tinge to plumage, non-br and ♀ with bill and plumage slightly pinkish, juv more uniform buff. **V** Song a nasal trumpeting *aaaaahp oooooop*, calls like child's trumpet *ahp*. **H** North African and Asian deserts, in Europe breeds only south Spain (Almería, Murcia). **D** V, extremely rare.

♂ br
♂ non-br
♀
1
♂ br
♂ non-br
♀
2
♀ non-br
♂ br
3
juv
♀
♂
4
♀
♂ br
5
♀
♂
6
♀
♂ br
7

1 Greenfinch **L** 15 cm

Carduelis chloris **ID** Robust sparrow-sized finch with overall predominantly green plumage, conical pink-grey bill and prominent yellow patches at the base of the primaries and base of the tail. Br ♂ has a lot of grey on the wing and side of head, ♀ duller brownish-green and faintly streaked, juv more beige with stronger streaking. **V** Trilling song delivered from perch or in bat-like flight with chirping and rolling tones, a nasal sneering *shwoo-insh* and often mimicry within song; calls *djuweee*, *yup* and *dyurrurrurrt*. **H** Gardens, parks, farmland, scrub; visits bird-tables. **D** BR, common.

2 Siskin **L** 12 cm

Carduelis spinus **ID** Small bird with relatively long, pointed bill, short tail with yellow on sides at base, yellowish rump and conspicuous yellowish wing-bars. Overall yellowish-green (juv more brown-grey) with whitish belly and heavily streaked flanks, in ♂ crown and chin black. Outside of breeding season mostly in flocks, tit-like and very agile on outer twigs of alders and birches when foraging. **V** Rapid, rolling, chirping song, also with mimicry, often started with *tlui* and ending in *knaatsh*; calls high-pitched, sweet and musical *tlui* and, when flying off, soft chattering *tetetet*. **H** Conifer forests, in winter parks and gardens with birch and alder. **D** BRMW, common, more widespread in winter.

3 Citril Finch **L** 12 cm

Carduelis citrinella **ID** Small finch of south European mountains, yellowish-green and unstreaked with uniform dark tail, paler greenish rump and two inconspicuous yellowish wing-bars. ♂ with grey nape and more intense yellow tinge especially on the face, ♀ slightly duller with more streaked mantle and greyer flanks. **V** Short, chirping song with Goldfinch-like beginning and compressed end notes; calls *dyit*, *dyi-di-di*, slightly nasally and with metallic ringing. **H** Resident in open coniferous forests up to tree line. **D -**.

4 Corsican Finch **L** 12 cm

Carduelis corsicana **ID** Apart from very limited distribution also identifiable by pale brown (instead of grey-green) streaked mantle and brighter yellow underparts in comparison to similar 3. **V** Song better structured, lower-pitched, more flute-like than 3, more like Linnet; calls more drawn out and clearer and warns with Bullfinch-like *duh*. **H** Resident only on Corsica, Sardinia and Elba. **D -**.

5 Serin **L** 11 cm

Serinus serinus **ID** Smallest finch, has tiny conical bill on comparatively large head, bright yellow rump, completely dark tail and only narrow yellowish wing-bars. In ♂ head and breast yellow, at early stages partly hidden by greenish feather edges, as plumage becomes worn breast wears to brighter yellow. ♀ paler yellow and more streaked. **V** Sings from perch or in swaying flight, ringing on one level; calls brightly ringing *tililit* (or *girr-lits*). **H** Parks, gardens, forest edges. **D** V, rare, annual (has bred), mainly south coast.

6 Common Crossbill **L** 16 cm

Loxia curvirostra **ID** Sturdy with crossed bill-tip adapted to feed on spruce cones. Large head, no bold markings. Ad ♂ red, imm and ♀ grey-green with yellowish rump. Mostly in flocks. Several subspecies have larger bill and similar to 7: *balearica* (Majorca), *corsicana* (Corsica), *mariae* (Crimea). **V** Sings from tree-top similar to 1, chirping and trilling, mixed with slightly metallic call *chip chip* or *jip jip*. **H** Fir and spruce forests; breeds also in winter. **D** brmw, uncommon and local but irruptive.

7 Scottish Crossbill **L** 16.5 cm

Loxia scotica **ID** Size, bill size and call between 6 and 8. **H** Caledonian pine forest only. **D** br, scarce, restricted to north Scotland.

8 Parrot Crossbill **L** 17 cm

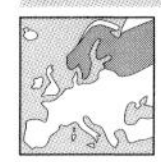

Loxia pytyopsittacus **ID** Very similar to 6, but bill heavier and deeper, crossed tip of lower mandible does not protrude beyond upper mandible, head and neck thicker; prefers pine cones. **V** Sings like 6; calls slightly lower-pitched and stronger, rather like *gop* or *tup*. **H** Taiga. **D** brm, very rare, a few pairs breed in pine forest in Scottish Highlands. Irruptive.

9 Two-barred Crossbill **L** 15 cm

Loxia leucoptera **ID** Characterized by two broad white wing-bars and white tips to tertials (but note two wing-bars sometimes present, though narrow, in variant '*rubifasciata*' of 6). Bill a little less deep than 6, ♂ often more raspberry-red, ♀ more yellowish. **V** Song variable, rattling, reminiscent of 2; calls similar to Mealy Redpoll, dry *tyeck tyeck* and nasally trumpeting *aaaap*. **H** Taiga with abundant larches. **D** V 10-3, very rare.

1
♀
♂
♂
juv
2
♂
♀
3
♂
♀
♂
4
5
♂
♀
6
♂
♀
7
♂
juv
8
♂
♀
9
♀
♂

1 Goldfinch **L** 13 cm

Carduelis carduelis **ID** Common and attractive finch with pale buff-brown body, black wings with white spots on tertials and broad yellow wing-bar, white rump and black tail with white spots near tip as well as long, pointed, grey-pink tweezer-like bill. Ad unmistakable with black-and-white head pattern and red face, in juv head and body streaky grey-brown up to early winter. Outside breeding season mostly in flocks, often on and around thistles. **V** Trilling and chirping song, immediately recognizable by continuous species-specific call: tinkling *tililit*, or only *litt*. **H** Open ground with bushes, forest edges, hedgerows, parks, gardens. **D** BRMW, common.

2 Linnet **L** 13 cm

Carduelis cannabina **ID** Small finch with longish tail, overall grey-brown plumage, grey bill, whitish edges to outer tail feathers and outer primaries appear as pale areas on otherwise fairly plain upperparts when bird flies up. Breast and forehead of ♂ pink-red (in non-br partly hidden by beige feather edges), head grey, mantle brown. ♀ and early winter ♂ without red, duller and diffusely streaked above and below, head brown-grey, lighter beige areas immediately above and below the eye and in centre of ear-coverts (as in ♂) create a characteristic 'facial expression'. **V** The attractive, canary-like song consists of chirping and rolling sounds and is sung from the top of a bush; flight call a dry *d-dip* or *dip*, contact call soft whistling and questioning *peeoo*. **H** Open fields with bushes, waste ground. Often breeds in loose colonies **D** BRMW, common but declining.

3 Twite **L** 13 cm

Carduelis flavirostris **ID** The least distinctive small finch, breeds only in the north. Similar to ♀ of 2, but pale patch on primaries fainter, pale wing-bar slightly clearer, unstreaked throat and finely streaked breast ochre-yellow, bill in non-br yellow, in br blackish, legs black. Rather similar in all plumages, only ♂ has a barely discernable pinkish tinged rump. Outside the breeding season in flocks close to seashore. **V** Song chirping and trilling with scattered species-specific calls and rattling *trrrt*; distinctive nasal *tchooit* and Linnet-like calls. **H** Breeds moors and heaths, winters North Sea and Baltic coasts. **D** brmw, uncommon.

4 Mealy Redpoll **L** 13 cm

Carduelis flammea **ID** Active, social, grey-brown, heavily streaked small finch with red forehead, black chin and tiny yellow bill. Grey-brown upperparts and flanks streaked dark, belly white, whitish wing-bar quite broad and clear. Ad ♂ breast tinged pink-red. North-east European breeding birds of subspecies *flammea* greyer with whitish rump and white wing-bars. Icelandic (*islandica*) and Greenland (*rostrata*) subspecies similar size but darker. **V** Sings mainly in flight *tettetett tsrrrr*; calls dry, rhythmic *ju-ju-ju-jut* and musical *soo-e*. **H** Breeds forests (especially birch), heaths. Winters north and central Europe, often in alder and birch. **D** w 10-3, uncommon winter visitor, mainly in north and east.

5 Lesser Redpoll **L** 12 cm

Carduelis caberet **ID** Very like 4, which it replaces as a breeding species in Britain and central Europe (included on map of 4), but slightly smaller, darker and browner overall with buff wing-bar and brownish streaked rump. **V** and **H** Like 4. **D** BR, fairly common but declining.

6 Arctic Redpoll **L** 13 cm

Carduelis hornemanni **ID** Small, pale finch. Very similar to 4, sometimes almost impossible to separate, but pale, 'fluffy' plumage can give 'snowball' appearance. Has even smaller, stubbier yellowish bill than 4, while unstriped white rump, unstreaked underwing coverts, minimal streaking on flanks, cinnamon tinge to face and breast and in ad ♂ the pink-tinged (not red) breast are typical features. **V** All vocalizations slightly softer and higher-pitched than 4. **H** Breeds tundra, willow-thickets and birches. Local movements in winter. **D** V 10-3, very rare, mainly north and east coasts. Usually with flocks of 4 and 5. Irruptive.

7 Common Waxbill **L** 11 cm

Estrilda astrild **ID** (not illustrated) Tiny finch introduced into reedbeds in Portugal and Spain. Brown-grey and finely barred dark overall with black vent and red bill (black in juv), lores, eye-stripe and belly (plain in juv). **D -**.

8 Red Avadavat **L** 10 cm

Amandava amandava **ID** (not illustrated) Another waxbill introduced to Spain, Portugal and north Italy. In all plumages with rump and bill red, lores, wings and tail black, ♂ with red head and body, ♀ brown-beige. **D -**.

juv
1
2
♀
♂
3
♀ br
♂ non-br
5
♀
♂
4
♀
♂
6
♀
♂

BUNTINGS

1 Lapland Bunting L 15 cm

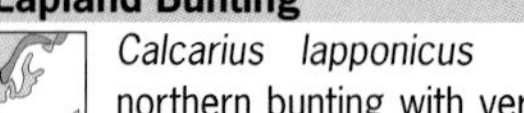

Calcarius lapponicus **ID** Lark-like northern bunting with very long wings, yellow bill with black tip and black legs with very long hind claw. Ad always has rusty-brown nape, ♂ with distinctive black head and breast markings, these are paler in ♀ and very faint in non-br. Non-br and 1w have rusty-brown patch on greater coverts bordered by narrow white wing-bars, pale median crown stripe and cinnamon-brown sides to head. **V** Song short and with typical ring; calls dry, rattling *prrrt*, mostly followed by high-pitched *teu*, also harsh *dyub*. **H** Breeds tundra, winters on fields and dunes around North Sea and northern Black Sea. **D** mw 9-4, scarce, almost always at coast.

2 Snow Bunting L 17 cm

Plectrophenax nivalis **ID** Much white on tail and inner wings. Br ♂ only black on mantle, primaries and central tail, otherwise almost all white, br ♀ has mantle black-brown and head with grey-brown markings. In 1w and non-br bill yellow, underparts white, flanks, breast sides, crown and sides of head buff, upperparts sandy-brown with blackish streaking. Usually in flocks on sparsely vegetated ground, often confiding. **V** Song short chirping; call *prirrrit*, also soft, mellow *teu*. **H** Breeds mountains and tundra, winters North Sea and Baltic coasts. **D** mw 10-3, uncommon, mainly coasts; b, rare on high peaks in Scottish Highlands.

3 Corn Bunting L 18 cm

Emberiza calandra **ID** Large and heavy, rather nondescript plain grey-brown, brown with dark streaks above, underparts pale and boldly streaked, heavy bill with pink base, tail lacks white edges. Flies clumsily with dangling legs. **V** Simple song with ticking introduction vaguely recalls jangling keys: *tick tick-tick-tsick tsrrrrrs*; quiet call short and sharp *tsick*. **H** Open cultivated areas with available song perches. **D** brm, uncommon and declining.

4 Yellowhammer L 16 cm

Emberiza citrinella **ID** Familiar bunting, easily recognized by its more or less yellow plumage, unstreaked rufous rump and the lack of a clear head pattern. ♂ has bright yellow head and breast, ♀ paler with washed-out olive-brown head-stripes, in non-br similar but in 1w sometimes shows very little yellow. **V** Sings from an elevated perch, often for long periods, *see-see-see-see-seesee soooor*; calls *metallic tzik, till-it*. **H** Open fields with hedges, forest edges. **D** BRMW, common but declining.

5 Pine Bunting L 16 cm

Emberiza leucocephalos **ID** Siberian counterpart of 4. All yellow tones are replaced by white and rufous. ♂ has unmistakable head pattern with white cheek patch (less distinctive in ♀). In 1w like a whitish version of 4 without yellow and green tones. **V** Similar to 4. **H** Like 4, breeds east of Urals. **D** V 10-3, extremely rare.

6 Cirl Bunting L 16 cm

Emberiza cirlus **ID** West and south European species, in contrast to 4 has olive-green rump. ♂ with black chin, throat and eye-stripe, ♀ differs from 4 by olive rump colour, clearer face-stripes, finer streaking on underparts and rusty-brown scapulars. **V** Sings a monotonous rattling *tetetetete* and slightly more whirring *dsredsredsredsredsre*; calls very soft Song Thrush-like *dsib* and descending *tsee*. **H** Open landscapes, farmland with bushes and hedgerows. **D** br, much declined, now a local breeder in south Devon and Cornwall.

7 Yellow-breasted Bunting L 15 cm

Emberiza aureola **ID** ♂ has black face, chestnut crown, mantle and breast-band and white patch on median coverts, but often attains full ad plumage only in 3s. ♀ and 1w rather plain, but with pink bill, very broad beige supercilium and median crown-stripe, faint or absent lateral throat stripe, pale yellow breast, only slight streaking on flanks, grey-brown rump and beige and blackish 'tiger-striped' mantle. **V** Song similar to Ortolan Bunting but softer and more melodic with ascending flute-like notes, but very variable, for example, *trutru treetree trutratro-tri*; call short and sharp *tsick*. **H** Open forests, meadows, moist thickets. Breeds north-east Europe, winters tropical Asia. **D** V 9, very rare, most frequent on Shetland and east coast.

8 Rock Bunting L 16 cm

Emberiza cia **ID** Distinctive in all plumages due to grey head and breast with black lateral crown-stripe, eye-stripe and moustachial stripe and orange belly, ♀ and 1w slightly duller. **V** Long, rapid, ringing song reminiscent of Dunnock; calls high and short *tsip* and longer *tsee*. **H** Rocky slopes in south Europe, also vineyards. **D** V, extremely rare.

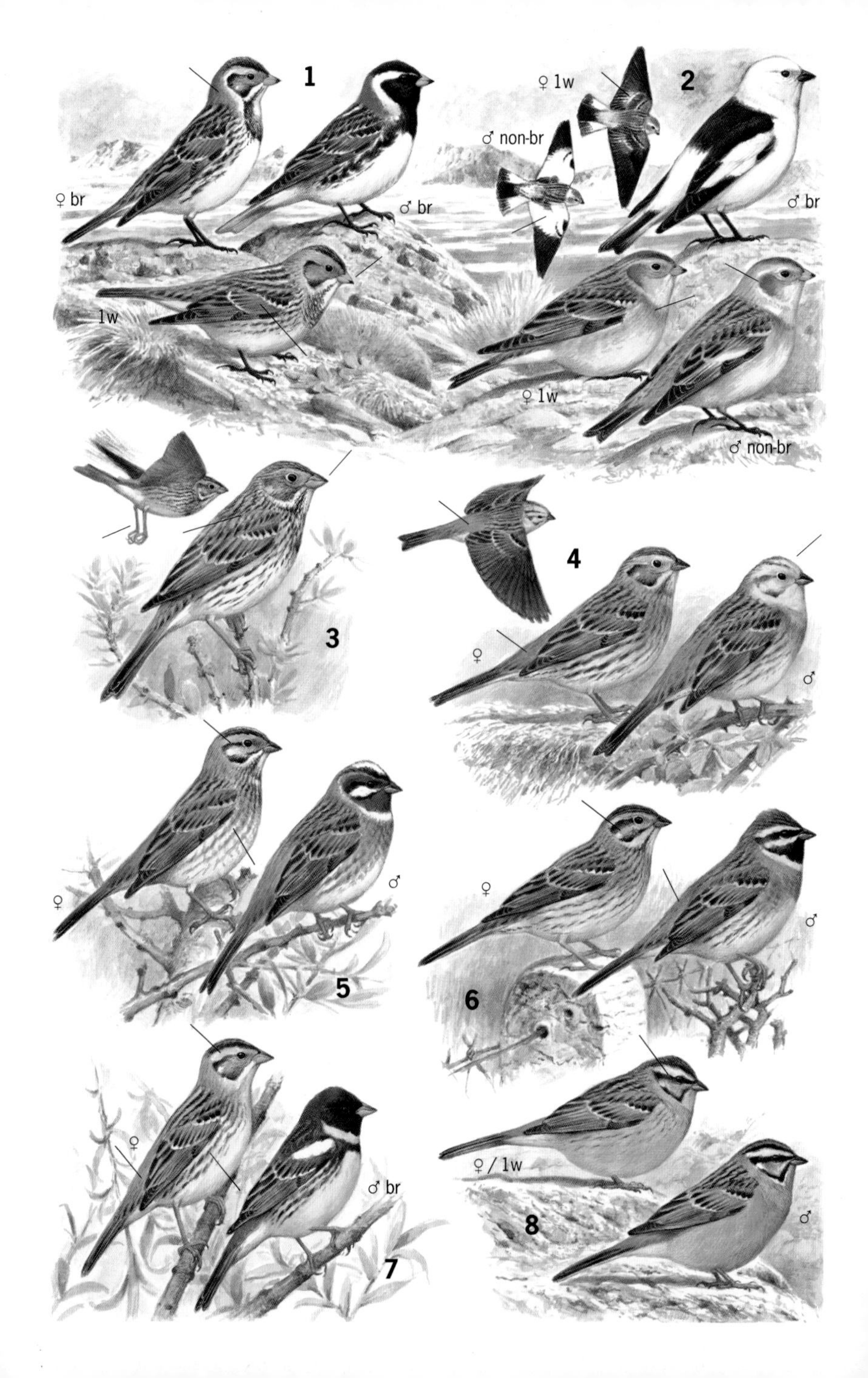

1
2
♀ br
♂ br
1w
♀ 1w
♂ non-br
♂ br
♀ 1w
♂ non-br
3
4
♀
♂
5
♀
♂
6
♀
♂
7
♀
♂ br
♀ / 1w
8
♂

1 Ortolan Bunting L 16 cm

Emberiza hortulana **ID** Widespread but local in continental Europe. Always has pink bill, conspicuous pale eye-ring, yellow throat and submoustachial stripe and rusty-orange belly. In ♂ head and broad breast-band olive-green, underparts unstreaked, in ♀ and non-br duller and streaked on crown and breast, in 1w head is more brownish, streaking more pronounced and extending onto flanks. **V** Has a large repertoire, but always quite mournful ringing with lower-pitched second half, for example, *tsee-tsee-tsee drudrudru*; calls soft, liquid *plip* as well as alternating *see* and *tyuh*. **H** Open cultivated lands, often sandy ground. Winters Africa. **D** V, rare, mainly south coast.

2 Cretzschmar's Bunting L 15 cm

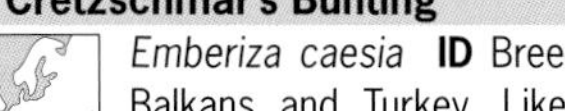

Emberiza caesia **ID** Breeds southern Balkans and Turkey. Like a brighter version of 1: head and breast blue-grey, throat and underparts rusty-red, eye-ring white. ♀ paler, in 1w compared with 1 has darker rufous rump, eye-ring cleaner white, underwings white with rusty and not tinged yellow. **V** Song similar to southern dialects of 1, less melodious and with only one long end-note, for example, *si si si sooh*; calls similar to 1, *dsip* and *dyu*. **H** Stony slopes, mainly near coasts. **D** V, extremely rare.

3 Cinereous Bunting L 16 cm

Emberiza cineracea **ID** Very restricted range. Has rather plain grey plumage with grey bill and yellowish throat, moustache and eye-ring as well as a lot of white on the tips of the outer tail feathers. **V** Song similar to 1: *tsitsitsi tsutsa*; calls *tsik* and *tship*. **H** Stony slopes, summer visitor. In Europe only on Greek islands of Lesvos, Chios, Ikaria and Skyros. Also Turkey. **D** -.

4 Black-headed Bunting L 17 cm

Emberiza melanocephala **ID** Large south-east European bunting with no white on long tail, ♂ unmistakable with black head, rufous mantle and completely yellow underparts. ♀ noticeably paler and duller, mantle slightly streaked, in non-br and 1w even less contrast, rump brownish, underparts pale yellow and unstreaked. **V** Song hard, like jumbled call notes: *tup tup ti ti ti ti djup*. Calls varied, soft metallic *tlip*, deep *djup*. **H** Breeds open landscapes with scattered bushes, also areas under cultivation. Winters Asia. **D** V, extremely rare.

5 Red-headed Bunting L 16 cm

Emberiza bruniceps **ID** Central Asian counterpart of 4. Head and breast of ♂ red-brown, mantle streaked greenish, rump yellow. ♀ and 1w almost identical to 4, but slightly smaller, shorter primary projection, rump tinged greenish. **V** Like 4 but weaker. **H** Breeds open areas and steppes east of lower Volga. Winters south Asia. **D** V or escapee. Extremely rare.

6 Reed Bunting L 15 cm

Emberiza schoeniclus **ID** Common bunting in wetlands, coloured brown, buff, black and whitish. Br ♂ unmistakable with black head and throat and white submoustachial stripe and collar, ♀ streaked brown with pale submoustachial stripe and blackish lateral throat stripe. Only a hint of ad ♂ head pattern seen in non-br and 1w. Several very similar subspecies, but in south with clearly thicker bill, for example, *reiseri* (southern Balkans) and *tschusii* (Black Sea). Often perches on reed stems, conspicuous on the ground and often fans tail. **V** Sings a monotonous *tsit tsrit tsrit tsrelitt*; calls drawn out and descending *schwee* as well as harsh *dsu*. **H** Reedbeds, moist thickets, farmland in winter. **D** BR, common.

7 Little Bunting L 13 cm

Emberiza pusilla **ID** The smallest bunting, similar in all plumages: supercilium, ear coverts and median crown-stripe rusty-brown, clear whitish eye-ring, fine streaking on underparts. In autumn sometimes difficult to tell from 6, but smaller, plain lores, moustachial stripe and supercilium do not reach bill and legs pink. **V** Song short, high-pitched, melodious, variable with typical bunting themes; calls sharply with short *tsick*. **H** Breeds arctic willow thickets, winters south Asia. **D** V, rare.

8 Rustic Bunting L 14 cm

Emberiza rustica **ID** In br distinctive black-and-white head pattern, rufous breast, collar and streaking on flanks, ♀ often barely paler. In 1w similar to 6 and 7, note bill with straight culmen and pink base, un-striped red-brown nape and rump, white wing-bars, white spot on hind ear-coverts, white belly, red-brown streaks on breast and flanks. Slight crested effect to crown. **V** Short flute-like song with changes in pitch, for example, *didelio-didelio didi-didu*; calls *tsick* like 7. **H** Breeds moist, open forests, winters south Asia. **D** V, rare.

♀
♂
1
1w
♀
♂
2
♀
♂
3
♀
4
♂
reiseri
5
♂
♂ br
6
♀ 1w
♀
♀ br
8
7
♀ 1w
♂ br

1 Blue-winged Teal L 39 cm **WS** 62 cm
Anas discors **ID** American counterpart of the Garganey. ♂ has dark blue head with bold white crescent on face between bill and eye, brown flanks spotted black, undertail coverts black and bordered white. ♀ and juv have pale spot adjoining bill more marked than in Garganey. Both sexes have pale blue upperwing coverts like ♂ Shoveler. **H** As Common Teal. Vagrant from North America. **D** V, rare but annual.

2 Green-winged Teal L 36 cm **WS** 56 cm
Anas carolinensis **ID** Very similar to Common Teal but ♂ has bold vertical white line dividing breast from flanks and lacks horizontal white line on body; ♀ indistinguishable. **H** As Common Teal. Vagrant from North America. **D** V, rare but annual.

3 Lesser Scaup L 42 cm **WS** 62 cm
Aythya affinis **ID** ♂ Very similar to hybrid Tufted Duck x Pochard (see illustration on page 39), but with rather peaked head, vermiculated grey upperparts and black on bill restricted to nail, also white on wing-bar restricted to secondaries. ♀ like Scaup but with less white on face and wing pattern as ♂. **H** As Tufted Duck. Vagrant from North America. **D** V, very rare but annual.

4 Golden Pheasant L ♂ 100 cm, ♀ 65 cm
Chrysolophus pictus **ID** ♂ with gold crown, neck, rump and tail and crimson underparts, ♀ like Pheasant but heavily barred (not spotted) all over. **V** One- or two-note screech. **H**. Asian species introduced to dense woodland in Britain. **D** ibr, rare, local and apparently declining.

5 Lady Amherst's Pheasant L ♂ 105 cm,
Chrysolophus amherstiae ♀ 65 cm **ID** ♂ has black-and-white barred neck and tail, blue-green back and red-and-yellow rump, ♀ like 4 but darker and with blue skin around eye. **V** Three-note screech. **H** Asian species introduced to woodland in Bedfordshire and around. **D** ibr, very rare, population appears to be unsustainable.

6 Wilson's Storm-petrel L 17 cm **WS** 40 cm
Oceanites oceanicus **ID** Rather like European Storm-petrel but larger, lacks white bar on underwing, and legs protrude beyond square tail in gliding (not fluttering) flight. Has pale band on upperwing like Leach's Storm-petrel. **H** Pelagic, breeds southern oceans during austral summer and passes through north Atlantic in small numbers in July and August. **D** m 7-8, rare but regular off Scilly; V, extremely rare elsewhere.

7 Long-billed Dowitcher L 29 cm
Limnodromus scolopaceus **ID** Like a snipe-shaped Bar-tailed Godwit with narrow white oval down back and white trailing edges to wings in flight. Underparts rufous in br, grey in non-br; bill and legs green-grey. **V** Call *kip,* often double or trilled. **H** Breeds North America and east Siberia, vagrant to Europe. **D** V, rare but annual.

8 Lesser Yellowlegs L 24 cm
Tringa flavipes **ID** Smaller and slighter than Redshank with finely streaked brown breast, bright yellow legs and square white rump. **V** High-pitched *tiur tiur.* **H** Breeds North America, vagrant to Europe. **D** V, rare but annual.

9 Laughing Gull L 39 cm **WS** 110 cm
Larus atricilla **ID** Long drooping bill and slate-grey above. Br with dark red bill and legs and black hood extending far down throat and nape. Little obvious white in black primary tips and the contrasting white trailing edge rather broad. Non-br with ear-coverts and hind crown finely streaked, bill and legs blackish; 1w similar and with grey breast and flanks, flight feathers all dark and upperwing coverts brown. **H** Breeds North America, vagrant to Europe. **D** V, rare but annual, most often western coasts.

10 American Herring Gull L 63 cm
Larus smithsonianus **WS** 145 cm **ID** Like Herring Gull and almost impossible to separate in field as ad. 1w and 2w have closed tail solidly black, smooth chocolate underparts, pale inner primaries, often white head and pink-based bill. **H** Breeds North America, vagrant to Europe. **D** V, very rare, mostly west coast.

11 Dusky Warbler L 11 cm
Phylloscopus fuscatus **ID** Like a dark, brownish Common Chiffchaff with no yellow tones, grey-brown underparts and well-marked supercilium that is paler before eye. **V** Diagnostic *tek*, similar to Lesser Whitethroat. **H** Breeds Siberia, winters south Asia, vagrant to Europe. **D** V 10, very rare, mostly Northern Isles and east and south coasts.

12 Radde's Warbler L 12 cm
Phylloscopus schwarzi **ID** Like a stocky, greener and yellower version of 11 with thick bill, bull-neck and thick, pale legs. Thick yellowy supercilium and distinct eye-stripe. **V** Call a soft, low, clucking *qulip.* **H** Breeds Siberia, winters south Asia, vagrant to Europe. **D** V 10, very rare, mostly east and south coasts.

BIRD SOUNDS

The variable vocalizations of birds are among their most remarkable features. It is important, first of all, to distinguish between songs and calls. Songs, which are almost invariably delivered by ♂ birds only, serve the purposes of proclaiming ownership of a territory, attracting females and strengthening the pair bond. Songs often have a complicated structure, but sometimes they are only sequences of simple calls. Some species are able to perfectly imitate the calls of other birds or sounds from their environment and incorporate these into their songs.

Song is not limited only to the passerines ('songbirds'), but is used by many other birds and has exactly the same functions. These songs may even appear to our ears more pleasant and melodious than the songs of many passerines. Although songs are heard mainly before and during the breeding season, in many species they can also be heard during migration, or even in winter. They are then used to proclaim feeding territories.

Calls usually have a simpler structure and consist of only one or a few notes. Many species possess different calls for different purposes – for example contact calls may be used between members of a flock on the move, while alarm calls warn other birds of a predator's presence. Interpreting calls phonetically is difficult, but note whether they are mono- or multi-syllabic, whether they ascend or descend, and also their general tone (harsh, soft, whistling, chirping, etc).

Several bird species also produce so-called instrumental sounds, such as the well known drumming of woodpeckers or bill-clattering of White Stork. In flight, wing and tail feathers can also produce sounds due to vibration.

For the observer a knowledge of vocalizations is not only helpful and important, but often critical for correct identification. Just consider the Willow Warbler and Common Chiffchaff, which are almost identical in appearance but utter totally different songs, while the equally similar Meadow and Tree Pipits have very different flight calls.

Of course, it takes a long time to memorize all the calls and songs of the birds you regularly

encounter. The many CDs of bird sounds that are available are good learning aids, but note that birdsong recordings should not be used in the field to attract birds during the breeding season, as that may disturb them. It is also possible to learn a lot from other birdwatchers in the field. It is time-consuming to follow each unknown bird call until you finally see and identify it, but experience has shown that this is the best way to anchor new-found knowledge in the memory.

It is slightly easier to learn bird calls if you start in winter, when fewer species are present. You can then advance step by step as the summer migrant species begin to arrive, instead of beginning in May and trying to untangle an already complete chorus of birdsong. Therefore the following tables 1 to 3 – created as learning and memory aids – are structured by season and deal with the species that can be heard in gardens, parks or woodland in Britain. Species occurring in other habitats are dealt with separately, as are additional species likely to be encountered in continental Europe, and those likely to be most often heard calling on migration, or at night.

The emphasis lies on passerines, which are mentioned first in all the tables. All the widespread and common breeding species of Britain are dealt with. Then follows a selection of other notable voices from other orders, but these are not complete as these species are in most cases easily seen and can therefore also be identified visually. Owl calls are dealt with in detail within the main text.

Trying to represent bird calls and songs in words is a very difficult task, not least because each person perceives bird sounds slightly differently. The often strange-looking letter-sequences selected here should be read in a loud whisper and not in normal speech strength to best interpret them. In between the different species there is enough blank space to note personal interpretations.

TABLE 1: BRITISH BIRD SOUNDS OF GARDENS, PARKS AND WOODLANDS IN WINTER

Some of the species spending the winter in Britain start to sing very early in the year to establish breeding territories. Calls and songs are listed here.

Song a repeated, whistled, usually two-note rhythmic *teacher teacher* or *seedah seedah*; also calls high-pitched *pink* or *pink pink* like Chaffinch:	Great Tit, p.120
Silvery, bell-like *trill tsi tsee sirrr* as song; also *tyerr err-err* and *tsitsitsidu*:	Blue Tit, p.120
Repetition of similar, full notes such as *tyup-tyup-tyup-tyup* or sneezing *pitshy-pitshy-pitshy-pitshy*; calls explosively *pitshoo*:	Marsh Tit, p.120
Song *teeoo-teeoo teeoo-teeoo* or *tseeh-tseeh-tseeh*, on same pitch or descending; call drawn out, down-slurred, nasal *zurr zurr* or sharply introduced *si-si-zur zur zur*:	Willow Tit, p.120
High pitched and rhythmic *vitse vitse vitse vitse…*; call clear upslurred *stui*; commonest in coniferous forests:	Coal Tit, p.120
Loud, human-like whistle *teeooh-teeooh-teeooh-teeooh*, also faster *vitvitvitvit*; call *twit twit*:	Nuthatch, p.138
High-pitched, thin song, lasting 3 seconds, ending in a trill, reminiscent of Blue Tit *titi-tsitserree tsritsirrr*; call high-pitched and thin *srree*:	Treecreeper, p.138
Very soft and clear, ascending and descending *sisihsisihsisihsisih* – extremely high-pitched, often not audible to elderly people; call thin *sri-sri-sree*:	Goldcrest, p.138
Clear, high-pitched notes increase in tempo and drop in pitch, with pearly trills, silver-clear but sometimes slightly melancholy; call *tick, tick*, warning call high-pitched and thin *seeeh*:	Robin, p.146.
Very loud, clear song lasting 5-6 seconds, with rattling and softer notes and a trill at the end *titi-turrr-lilitutu-turr-looloo-tsett-tsett-tsett-turrrrrrrrr-ti;* call dry, grating *tsrrrrrr* and metallic *tsack*, often in sequence; usually close to ground:	Wren, p.140
Loud chirping calls, also in sequence creating a rather plain song; almost exclusively around human habitation:	House Sparrow, p.150
Nasal *toyt*, rattling *trrretrretrret*, in flight *tek-tek-tek*; gardens, hedgerows:	Tree Sparrow, p.150
Call powerful *pink pink*, in flight softer *yupp yupp*, also harsh and low-pitched *rrooh* ('rain call'):	Chaffinch, p.156

Short, softly whistling, slightly descending *pyuh*: Bullfinch, p.156

Harsh, drawn-out *djuuwee* and *dshoosh*, subdued *duyurrurrurrt*: Greenfinch, p.158

Nasal *zweek-ik*, also *yack* flight call harder than Chaffinch; mostly in flocks, winter visitor: Brambling, p.156

Calls loud *see-ut* and Robin-like *tsick*: Hawfinch, p.156

Clear, sweet and musical *tlui* or *tseelooh*, also sullen *krree* and when flying up dry *ketket*, mainly in flocks near alder trees or scrub: Siskin, p.158

Song-flight in wide circles, dry *tetetet tsrrrr*; call slightly metallic but rather soft, dry, rhythmic *ju-ju-ju-jut* and musical *soo-e*; often in birches: Lesser Redpoll, p.160

Chirping finch-song with *kip*-calls in between: *tsiri-tsiri tshrut-tshrut-shree kip-kip-kip trttrt tshirree*; characteristic call metallic *chip chip* or *jip jip*, warning call lower-pitched *tuck*; coniferous forests only: Common Crossbill, p.158

Call somewhat similar to Magpie *shackshackshack* and *geeaah*: Fieldfare, p.142

Call a high-pitched, drawn-out and penetrating *tzee*. Simple song, heard sometimes later in spring, consists of two to five flute-like tones followed by soft chirping: *dri dru dru drudro, tyerre-tyurre-tyo*: Redwing, p.142

Song heard only near running water, harsh chattering and trilling, rather soft chirping; calls penetrating *tsrrts* in low flight above water. Only in north and west Britain: Dipper, p.140

Sharp, high-pitched and penetrating call *tsitsi* and *tsitsiss*; usually near running water: Grey Wagtail, p.154

Song is pleasant, melodious but varied and discordant whistling, higher-pitched than song of Garden Warbler and more fluty, call hard *teck* and snapping *tett-etetet*; woods, gardens in winter; some birds winter but becomes much commoner from late March when migrants arrive: Blackcap, p.134

Hoarse, rasping *raatsh*, also buzzard-like meowing *heeaaah*: Jay, p.114

Harsh *tshak-tshak-tshak* or *tshakerack*: Magpie, p.116

Hard and powerful *kick*, harsh chattering *kick-ik-ik-ik*... loud, fast drumming of bill on tree lasting almost 1 second: Great Spotted Woodpecker, p.114

Bright *keekeekeekeekee* like Kestrel; long, slow, weak drumming lasting over 1 second, often repeated after short pause: Lesser Spotted Woodpecker, p.114

Loud laughing call, descending and faster at end *glooh glooh glooh gloo-glooglooglooo*; flight call *kyukyukyuck*: Green Woodpecker, p.112

TABLE 2: BRITISH BIRD SOUNDS OF GARDENS, PARKS AND WOODLAND FROM MARCH TO MID-APRIL

Several additional calls now occur as the song activity in the resident birds increases and the first migrants return. First the main song is described, then the calls. In some places notes are added on the typical habitat or favoured time that the species sings.

Full, varied, loud, melodic fluty whistle, often slightly melancholy or pompous, from dawn and mostly from an elevated perch; calls *tshackshak, srri, gock*:	Blackbird, p.142
Loud, short flute-like notes, one- to three-syllabic, also shrill notes, each repeated two to four times, for example, *tatooh-tatooh-tatooh tooteh-tooteh diudit-diudit-diudit dyackdyackteeh tlio-tlio* …; call short *tsip*, warning sharp and penetrating *xixixixixi*:	Song Thrush, p.142
Similar to Blackbird, but shorter, faster 'verses', overall flatter, less varied and more melancholic whistling, rarely sings early in the morning, but often can be heard during the day as the only thrush; call wooden rasping *tserrrrrr:*	Mistle Thrush, p.142
Uttered from an elevated perch, song a rather mixed chattering with whistles and crackles, snapping, hissing, whistling, also mimicking other animal calls or mechanical noises, in between repeatedly a descending whistling *staaar*; call *dyurr*, juv calls *staaah*:	Starling, p.140
Sings monotonous, steady *chiff-chaff-chiff-chaff*, in between softly *trrt trrt*; call a monosyllabic up-slurred *huit*; woods, large gardens, bushes:	Common Chiffchaff, p.126
Soft song, in melody similar to Chaffinch, but slower, descending thinner, softer *hiloo dide-loo-du-du-dooh* without Chaffinch's rapid end flourish; call is a slower, clearly bisyllabic *hoo-it* in comparison to Common Chiffchaff, downslurred *sid-u* in autumn; woods, bushes:	Willow Warbler, p.126
Very high-pitched and thin, a sequence of increasing short notes ascending at the end *si si si-si-sisisseeh*, lacks final flourish of Goldcrest; only in coniferous and mixed forests. Scarce and local in Britain:	Firecrest, p.138
Powerful, short song, slightly descending and ending with rolling flourish of rapid notes, *tsit-tsittsit-tsittsittsitsu-tsitsurria*, may end with an attached *kick* like Great Spotted Woodpecker:	Chaffinch, p.156
A sequence of full trills of different pitch and speed, often good imitations in between as well as nasal and squeezed *dshoo-ee* and *dshaaait*; uttered from singing perch and during butterfly-like display flight:	Greenfinch, p.158
Typical finch-song with chirping and rolling elements, often similar to Greenfinch, but with *stigelitt*-calls in between; call tinkling *stiga-lit* or only *glitt-glitt*; often in gardens:	Goldfinch, p.160

Reminiscent of a canary, chirping, rolling, also partly whistling, varied song; flight call nasal, dry *d-dip* or *dip* as well as whistling *peeooh*; open countryside, heaths, forest edges: Linnet, p.160

Thin, sweet-noted, ringing, high-pitched song lasting about 2 seconds in jumping rhythm remaining on same pitch *witselitselititselwitselit-swits*, mostly calling from a raised perch; call a slightly broken *seeeh* and more ringing *dsidsidsi*: Dunnock, p.150

Disyllabic hollow moaning *oo-ooh, oo-ooh…*; mainly in old deciduous forests and parks: Stock Dove, p.102

Typical dull, cooing, pigeon voice, 4-6 rhythmic deep and hollow-sounding elements *grroo-grooh groo, groo groo*: Woodpigeon, p.102

Hollow and monotonous, trisyllabic, higher-pitched than Woodpigeon *doodooh doo, doodooh do, ….*; flight call hoarse and nasal *khraa*; almost always around human habitation: Collared Dove, p.102

Periodic single deep grunting sounds, followed by high-pitched explosive note, *oooart-oooart-oooart pits*, only at dusk and during 'roding' display flight in spring and early summer; moist forests with clearings: Woodcock, p.76

TABLE 3: BRITISH BIRD SOUNDS OF GARDENS, PARKS AND WOODLAND FROM MID-APRIL TO JUNE

From the middle of April onwards the chorus of birdsong will become very confusing if you are not already familiar with some of the species singing in the previous months. Now many additional species are added, some with beautiful but also complicated songs. Most of these are woodland species rather than garden birds and tend to occur in 'wilder' habitats.

Similar to Blackcap but mellower, more Blackbird-like, with deep, complicated chattering; warning call a distinctive deep *vid vid vid vid*; woods, bushes, overgrown areas: Garden Warbler, p.134

Loud, fast and monotonous wooden 'rattle' *te-dedededede*, sometimes shorter, softer, suppressed chattering song at start (often absent), also mouse-like, high-pitched *tsitsitsitsitsitsi*; call abrupt *teck*; forest edges, bushes, large gardens, hedges: Lesser Whitethroat, p.134

Silvery trilling song, in which single *tsip*-sounds get continuously faster and louder, rush towards an end-trill; alternatively a sadly whistling *pew pew pew pew*, increasing in intensity, also short flight songs; call melancholy *pew*; old deciduous forests, usually hidden in tree-tops: Wood Warbler, p.126

Short, variable song, *huid trui-trui-trui-suru* and occasionally enriched by short mimicry; warning call *hooid tick-tick*; starts singing at dawn. Mainly north and west Britain: Common Redstart, p.146

Starts with *tsi-tsi-tsi* then repetition of several elements at different speeds, from tree-tops or in song-flight, ending in ascending flourish of *tseeah* notes, with this the song flight changes to a parachute-like descent, *dyidyidyi tyatyatya trrritrri trri we we weee tsee-ah tsee-ah tsee-ah tsee-ah*; call buzzy *zeep* or *speez*; forest edges and clearings:	Tree Pipit, p.152
Beautiful flute-like, loud, sensuous song with great tone range, many different 'verses', sometimes reminiscent of Song Thrush with repetitions, characterized by sweet crescendo-notes which grow louder but decrease in pitch, also sobbing and pulsating elements, also sings during the day; warning call slightly ascending *hweet* and low-pitched, frog-like *karr*. South England only:	Nightingale, p. 146
Unremarkable sequence of sharp, high-pitched, chirping sounds, *tsirr, tsitseeht, tsirt tsrt*; call sharp and high-pitched *tsirrt*, warning call *tsrrt-tek*:	Spotted Flycatcher, p.144
Variable unobtrusive song, rhythmical, composed of 3-6 phrases, *si-tsooli-tsooli vritya-vritya-tsilili-tsilili-vree*; short and sharp warning call *pit*:	Pied Flycatcher, p.144
Harmonic, loud fluty whistle, *didlio, doode-lio*; call similar to Jay, croaking *kraaah*; deciduous forest, returns in May. In Britain a very rare breeder in East Anglian poplar plantations. More common on the Continent:	Golden Oriole, p.116
Rolling *turrr-turrr, turrr-turrr….*; open forests, bushy farmland:	Turtle Dove, p.102
Loud *cook-coo* often repeated for minutes; during chases also hoarse *gug-khaa-khaa-khraa*; ♀ utters bubbling, gurgling trill:	Cuckoo, p.108
Continuous deep churring *errrrrrr errrrrr*, like steady radio interference, given at night; sometimes wing-clapping sounds, frog-like *kruu-ik* and louder *fiorr fiorr*; only at night along forest edges, over clearings, heath and moors:	European Nightjar, p.108

TABLE 4: BRITISH BIRD SOUNDS OF FIELDS, MEADOWS AND OPEN LANDSCAPES

Uninterrupted jubilant trilling, first from the ground, later high in the air, starting at dawn; call dry *trrrooloot* and *burrrt*:	Skylark, p.124
Beautiful, long song delivered from the ground or in the air often with descending sequences getting faster and louder towards the end, *loo loo-loolooloooloola … dili dili dilililiiloo*; call soft *didlui, tlooi*; open plains, heath, clearings, often on sandy soils:	Woodlark, p.124
A sequence of fast, sharp tones, often in short song-flight, *tsip tsip tsip tsip tsoo tsoo tsrr tsrr syoo syoo syoo syoo*, without the drawn out final notes of Tree Pipit; call high-pitched *sip sip sip*:	Meadow Pipit, p.152
Drawn-out chirping, with species-specific *tsi-lit* throughout, call also *tsi-lit* or *chi-zick*:	Pied Wagtail, p.154

A short sequence of harsh calls, *psi sri tsurrl srit*; call soft, upslurred *swe-up*; wet meadows, sometimes arable farmland: Yellow Wagtail, p.154

Short sequence of harsh, squeezed and flute-like notes, also mimicry, uttered from low singing perch; warning call *tek* and *you tek-tek*; wet meadows, fallow lands, moorland, from April onwards, can also be heard at night: Whinchat, p.148

Short verses reminiscent of Dunnock; call *weet chack-chack*; moors, heaths, fallow fields: European Stonechat, p.148

Short, chattering verse with grinding sounds, whistling call *heeet* and smacking notes, variable, also in flight and before sunrise; warning call *tck*; bare areas with stones: Northern Wheatear, p.148

In structure, through repetition, similar to Song Thrush, but melancholic sound more like Mistle Thrush, *droodroodroo tyootyootyoo dagagag tshiri tshiri*; call very hard *tack tack tack*; breeds in uplands: Ring Ouzel, p.142

Delivers short and scratching song from top of gorse or heather, or in flight; call drawn out and hoarse *tkhaa-ar*; heathland in southern England and the East Anglian coast: Dartford Warbler. p.136

Dry, scratchy song given from perch or louder and longer in song-flight, often in the rhythm *wanderer, where are you bound?*; call nasal *wheet wheet* and *churr* or *churrit* (similar to Red-backed Shrike), scolding *vit vit vit vit*; bushes in open landscapes, borders, hedgerows: Common Whitethroat, p.134

Grasshopper-like, whirring, monotonous dry song, on even pitch, lasting for minutes, more reminiscent of an insect or an angler's reel than a bird, *sirrrrrrrrrrr…;* warning call harsh *tsik*; also sings at night from dense vegetation or bushes close to the ground in open areas: Grasshopper Warbler, p. 128

Simple monotonous song, stuttering start with short whirring at end, *tsit tsit tsit tsirirr*, or *srip srip srip-srip-sirraah*; call *tsioo* and rougher *schwee*; reed-covered ditches, reedbeds, wet meadows: Reed Bunting, p.164

Rapid rattling series of same-tone notes, at the end descending with a drawn-out note *see-see-see-see-seesee soooor*, commonly described as *a little bit of bread and no cheeeese*, delivered mainly from power cables, high in a bush or from other elevated perches; call metallic *tzik* and *till-it*; farmland with scrub and hedgerows, heaths; still a common and widespread species despite a recent decline: Yellowhammer, p.162

Rattling song at same pitch but slightly more whirring than Lesser Whitethroat, *dsredsredsre…* or varying higher-pitched *tsirrtsirrtsirr-tsirr..*; call *sip*; mainly in south and west Europe on dry slopes and in orchards, in Britain in Devon and Cornwall only; formerly much more widespread and common in south England; sympathetic farming practices recently aided recovery from the brink of extinction in Britain: Cirl Bunting, p.162

Sequence of short, sharp notes, followed by a jangling sound, like a shaken bunch of keys, *tsik tsik tsiktsik tsrrrrrs*; call low-pitched and quiet hard *tstick*: Corn Bunting, p.162

Sharp creaking bisyllabic *kirrr-reck*; when flying up *pick pick pit*, wings produce whirring sound; can also be heard at night: Grey Partridge, p. 44

Loud croaking *gook-gock*, followed by soft *brrrt* caused by the wing beats; when flying up loud *boock* and wing sounds: Pheasant, p. 44

Liquid, loud, continuously repeated tri-syllabic *whip whip-whip (wet my lips)*; especially in the evening but also at night, scarce in Britain: Quail, p.44

Continuous monotonously repeated wooden *rrrp-rrrp, rrrp-rrrp, rrrp-rrrp*, especially at night; wet meadows, fields, from May. In Britain mostly on Outer Hebrides: Corncrake, p.70

TABLE 5: CONTINENTAL BIRD SOUNDS OF GARDENS, PARKS AND WOODLAND

Short, quick and slightly ringing song, lasting 1 second *tit-tit-titeroit-tree*; call high-pitched *teeht*, or slightly dripping *tee tee teetee*, louder and more Coal Tit-like than Treecreeper: Short-toed Treecreeper, p.138

Alternating bright and thin *titisri*, rattling *tulltulltull, tsriwiwi*, dry, growly and grinding *khrrrrkh, krrrrsh* in between; call dry *wit, tick-tick*; often on house roofs in continental Europe, rare breeder in Britain: Black Redstart, p.146

Starts sharply and has bubbly ending *tsitsi-burrrrl* or *gurrr*, lower-pitched than other tits, rarely also whistling notes, call low-pitched trilling *si si prrroeeoo;* widespread in Europe, in Britain only coniferous forests in Scottish Highlands: Crested Tit, p.120

Song similar to Marsh Warbler but uttered from high perch and only during the day, very varied with much mimicry and hurried repetitions, also scattered croaking and *tet*-sounds and meowing *gheeaah* in between; call nasal *dide-roid*, warning *tet tet*; deciduous forests, parks, gardens: Icterine Warbler, p.132

Song reminiscent of Icterine Warbler, but faster, not so coarse, often less mimicry, but instead always contains sparrow-like *trrt*; call trumpeting *trrrt* and *tshet*; open forests, parks, gardens, south-west Europe only: Melodious Warbler, p.132

Similar start to Pied Flycatcher or Wood Warbler, end ascending but very clear, *tink tink tink ydyda yda doo doo dlooh*; call soft and clear *teeyoo* and softer than Wren *trrr*; old deciduous forests, principally in eastern Europe, and only from May onwards: Red-breasted Flycatcher, p.144

Slow song with long drawn-out squeezed notes, something like *truh tseet tru sidi*; call a long sucking *heeep*; deciduous forests, parks in eastern Europe: Collared Flycatcher, p.144

Similar to Nightingale, but more powerful, without crescendo and with lower-pitched *tshook-tshook-tshook-tshook...* (Nightingale softer, Thrush Nightingale more harsh); warning call remains on same pitch *eeeeht* and low-pitched *errr*; lives in moister thickets than Nightingale, from Denmark eastwards:	Thrush Nightingale, p.146
Fast, high-pitched, twittering song, similar to walking on glass-splinters, uttered from high perch or in butterfly-like display flight; calls tinkling *tilililt* (or *girr-lits*); often in gardens:	Serin, p.158
Short, flute-like verse *woodye-woo-woodye, too-te-hootya*; call similar to Greenfinch *zoo-eet*; forest edges, bushes, only from late May, mostly east Europe:	Common Rosefinch, p.156
Song a three-syllable hollow *hoop-hoop-hoop*; calls hoarsely *shaar* and dryly *terr*; open landscapes with thickets, vineyards or meadows; rare in Britain but has bred:	Hoopoe, p.110
Croaking and moaning sequence of 4-10 notes *quaah quaag quaak quaa quaa*; call similar to Great Spotted Woodpecker's *kick*, but often in sequence, drums only rarely; mostly oak forests:	Middle Spotted Woodpecker, p.114
Less pronounced than Green Woodpecker, more like human whistling than laughing, clearly descending and slower towards end *kyukyu-kyoo-kyoo-kyoo kyoo kyoo kyoo*; flight call *kyuck*; drumming lasts at least one second, weaker than Great Spotted Woodpecker:	Grey-headed Woodpecker, p.112
Laughing call like Green Woodpecker but brighter, wilder, on one pitch *kwoik-wikwikwikwikwikwi*; call drawn out and loud *kleeoh*, in flight softer *krikrikrikri*; drumming loud but slow, lasting 2-3 seconds:	Black Woodpecker, p.112
Unusual, nasal squeaking uniform sequences, reminiscent of Middle Spotted Woodpecker *waahd-waahd-waahd-waahd-waahd...* ; parks, orchards, open forests:	Wryneck, p.112

TABLE 6: CONTINENTAL BIRD SOUNDS OF HIGH MOUNTAINS

Included here are the typical birds of the Alps, Pyrenees and Balkans and other high-lying mountain regions. Knowledge of songs and calls is often important for finding species in such vast landscapes. Many species also found in the lowlands may occur in the mountain forests up to the tree-line, or even higher, while some of the woodpeckers, owls and grouse listed in this section also occur at lower altitudes in northern Europe.

Distant similarity to trill of Skylark, in comparison to Dunnock slower and less bright, with low-pitched, hard trills; call rolling *droor, dsheb* and *tooye*; lives above the tree line on meadows in south and central Europe:	Alpine Accentor, p.150
Song *too troo tsryoo*; calls thinly *tsui*; steep cliffs in mountain regions, in winter also at lower altitudes:	Wallcreeper, p.138

Song similar to Meadow Pipit, but longer and uttered in flight; call very similar to Rock Pipit, a single, more drawn-out *weest*, stronger than Meadow Pipit; wet meadows above tree-line, winters south England:	Water Pipit, p.152
Stuttering, chirping, bunting-like song, uttered in gliding display flight or while perched; call *qooaah, psheeoo*; rocks, often around upper cable car stations:	Snowfinch, p.150
Loud flute-like notes, some reminiscent of Golden Oriole, scattered squeezed chirping in between, mostly in high song-flight with spread tail feathers; call loud and bright *dyoo*, also hard *tack*; rare on stony mountain meadows:	Rock Thrush, p.144
Blackbird-like, whistling song, but shorter, from perch or in flight; whistles thinly *dooit*, warning call also thrush-like *tshack*:	Blue Rock Thrush, p.144
Varied whistling and smacking calls, rolling *krooh*, penetrating *tsssseeh*, cutting to tinkling *tshirrl, pyrr*; often circling around mountain peaks, or near mountain huts:	Alpine Chough, p.118
Wooden crowing, sometimes repeated fast *krraah, krraahkraah-kraah*, rasping like old clock and less croaking than Jay; in coniferous forests:	Nutcracker, p.118
Call sounds like Great Spotted Woodpecker *kick*, sometimes a bit softer, more *kyook*; drumming slightly longer, but slower than Great Spotted Woodpecker; old forests, especially conifers:	Three-toed Woodpecker, p.114
Monosyllabic, hard woodpecker calls, softer and lower-pitched than Great Spotted Woodpecker, *kyock*; drumming about 2 seconds long and getting faster; older deciduous forests:	White-backed Woodpecker, p.114
At dusk Bullfinch-like whistling *dyoob dyoob*, in autumn ascending sequence *tyat tyet tyoot tyi tyyt*; old open forests, clearings:	Pygmy Owl, p.106
Song ascending *pu pu pu-pupupupu*, call snapping *tsyuck*:	Tengmalm's Owl, p.106
Very high-pitched and thin, reminiscent of a Goldcrest *tziuhi-tsitsitsit-sitsi-tseritsieh*; coniferous, deciduous and mixed forests, often near moist areas, also in some lower ranges:	Hazel Grouse, p.44
Wooden, burping *aarrr arrr*; above the tree-line, from the ground, often on snow fields, including Scottish Highlands:	Ptarmigan, p.44
Sequence of wooden clapping, gulping and chafing noises, becoming faster; quiet mountain forests, including Scottish Highlands:	Capercaillie, p.44

TABLE 7: CONTINENTAL BIRD SOUNDS OF FIELDS, MEADOWS AND OPEN LANDSCAPES

Song similar to Garden Warbler but shorter and rougher, often with scattered rattling *trrrrr-at-atatat*, delivered from perch or in song-flight; warning call a *rrrrt-t-t-t*; bushes in east Europe:	Barred Warbler, p.134

Song closer to Icterine than other *Acrocephalus* warblers, sings from lower perch, also at night and not as sharp, full of masterful mimicry and with regular speed changes and drier notes in between and a characteristic, nasal *tsabeeh*; call *tyeck* and rattling *tshirrr*; only from mid-May, very rare breeder in Britain: Marsh Warbler, p.130

Short, fast harsh chattering song with short whistling and grinding notes in between, also uttered in flight; warns terett *tret-tret-tret* and *tr-tr-tr*; Mediterranean scrub: Sardinian Warbler, p.136

Song simple, made up from single calls and mimicry, given from elevated perch or in flight; calls melancholy *dooi* and *di di dooh*; dry, open areas: Crested Lark, p.124

Soft, varied, chattering song with mimicry and typical calls in between; call hoarse, nasal and drawn-out *waaahw* and slightly smacking *shack-shackshack*; in bushes and hedges, only from May, extinct as breeding bird in Britain: Red-backed Shrike, p.116

Monotonous sequence of calls, *tsirlooh*, *tsiri* or *tsirlooi*, from an elevated perch or in undulating song-flight, also uttered by ♀; call sparrow-like *shilp*; bare plains and fields: Tawny Pipit, p.152

Starts like Yellowhammer with 3-5 equal notes, but followed by 1-3 lower-pitched notes, very variable and with regional dialects, *tsri tsri tsri tsroo, dri dri dri dri droo droo droo*; call soft liquid *plip* and *spee-eh*; sandy areas, farmland; south and east Europe: Ortolan Bunting, p.164

Starting *tsip tsip* followed by ringing notes similar to Dunnock, from February; call *tsip* higher than Cirl Bunting; warm, often stony slopes and quarries in the southern Europe: Rock Bunting, p.162

TABLE 8: NOCTURNAL BIRD SONGS AND CALLS IN MARSHES, REEDBEDS AND AROUND LAKES

The birds listed here can be heard at dusk and at night from April to June. It is especially important to know and recognize them as the birds cannot be seen in the dark. Many also live hidden in the vegetation during the day. Depending on the habitat, Nightingale, Thrush Nightingale, European Nightjar, Cuckoo and Whinchat may also be heard. Several other species can be heard here during the day but are already listed in Table 4, for example Reed Bunting. All rail and crake species are listed together in Table 9 as they can be easily confused with each other but also with other nocturnal creatures.

British species

Rhythmic grumpy chortling from reedbeds, a sequence of harsh, medium-pitched, rasping notes, often repeated two to three times, *tiri tiri troo troo trett trett trett tseck tseck*, sometimes with mimicry; warning call *chrer*, softer than Sedge Warbler; reedbeds, also often reedy fringes: Reed Warbler, p.130

Similar to Reed Warbler, but more varied, faster and angrier with mimicry scattered throughout, often also whistling notes getting faster, also sings in flight; call *tseck* and rattling *kerr*; reedbeds, swamps and damp areas: Sedge Warbler, p.128

Call given from the water, cackling *kek-kek-kek*, ventriloquial *quorr*, rattling *arrr*; young birds beg a monotonous and high-pitched *billibillibillibilli*: Great Crested Grebe, p.46

High trill *bibibibibi*, also in duet; also high pitched *curree* and *si-lit-lit* calls; from the water or the vegetation at the water's edge: Little Grebe, p.46

Loud, low-pitched, dull, booming *uh-proomb*, can be heard from considerable distance, like the sound created when blowing over the top of an empty bottle. From far away it sounds like a cow's lowing; flight call hoarsely barking gull-like *kow*; larger reedbeds; rare in Britain: Bittern, p.52

Loud and hoarsely croaking *kraaak* and *khraa*: Grey Heron, p.54

Clockwork-like *tickeh tickeh tickeh tickeh…*, also produces a bleating or booming sound known as 'drumming' during display flight – this is created during a steep descent as the air in causes the fanned outer tail-feathers to vibrate (which sounds like a goat bleating); when flying up hoarse, squelching *etsh*: Common Snipe, p.76

Loud and full whistling, increasing in speed towards a bubbling trill; call a whistling *koorly* and *klooy*: Curlew, p.76

Partly brisk, partly woeful *kee-wit, kyoo-wit-wit-witt*: Northern Lapwing, p.72

Female gives familiar *quack-quack* call, male calls *piu* and *rhaab*: Mallard, p.36

Male gives bright *krick, kroock,* female a thin, nasal *aack*: Common Teal, p.36

In spring male gives wooden burping *krrrk, krrrk*, not rhythmically repeated: Garganey, p.36

Male gives high-pitched down-slurred whistling and loud, monosyllabic *wee-oo*: Eurasian Wigeon, p.36

Continental European species

Very loud and powerful, creaking, harsh song, at the beginning with frog-like croaking, then higher *korr korr karre karre keet kyek kyeh*; warning call loud *krek*; reedbeds, declining: Great Reed Warbler, p.130

More like Icterine Warbler than the other *Acrocephalus* warblers, full of masterly mimicry and with regular changes in speed, but also drier notes in between and a characteristic, nasal *tsabeeh*; call *tyeck* and rattling *tshirrr*; also sings in bushes away from water; very rare breeder in southern Britain: Marsh Warbler, p.130

Sounds like a sedate Sedge Warbler, with no momentum, change in speed or mimicry, mostly only *err didi* or *err pipipi tshrr didi*, also short song-flight; call smacking *tyeck* and dry *err*; wet meadows, swamps, breeds only locally in eastern Europe, very rare: Aquatic Warbler, p.128

Similar to Reed Warbler, but softer and characterized by scattered, ascending, melodic flute-like notes *loolooloo looh*, recalls Nightingale or distant Curlew; call harsh smacking *tsheck* and rattling *drr drr*; bulrushes within reedbeds in parts of continental Europe: Moustached Warbler, p.128

Similar song to Grasshopper Warbler, but slightly harder and faster, often started with Robin-like ticking *tik tik-tik surrrrrrr..*; call similar to Great Tit *tshing*; often sings at night, standing free on stems, in larger reedbeds; very rare breeder in southern Britain: Savi's Warbler, p.128

Monotonous, mechanical chafing song sounding like a sewing machine, but single notes are clearly separated, *dse dse dse dse dse dse* .... with quite high-pitched metallic undertone; call *dirr* and *tsick tsick*; sings especially at night in dense, moist bush thickets, mostly along water's edge, almost exclusively in the east: River Warbler, p.128

Continuous, pearly bright song, with scattered good imitations of other calls (can be confused with Marsh Warbler), characteristic light bell-like sounds getting faster, *tri tri tri ting-tingting* resembling a balalaika melody; call *track* and *heet tshakshak*; from end of March: Bluethroat, p.146

Every 2 seconds dull dripping *wro wro wro*...; alarm call *kekeke*; from May, also on smaller ponds with dense vegetation; mainly south Europe: Little Bittern, p.52

Utters a frog-like loud *kwack* in flight; only in the south: Night Heron, p.52

Trumpeting and very loud *krooh*; bogs and swamps in eastern and northern forests: Common Crane, p.68

TABLE 9: RAILS AND CRAKES

Special problems arise with the calls of rails and crakes. The species are often confused with each other, as several species have more than one call, and they are not well known by birdwatchers. Additionally, some of the calls are similar to calls of other bird species and even of some amphibians. Therefore we have presented them here in an overview.

British species

Wide range of calls; sudden, piglet-like squeaking sounds *grrrooeeh grrooit grree gree*, ventriloquial blowing and growling sounds *oookh, woorrg*, during display long, rhythmic, monotonous hammering sequences *kipp kipp kipp kipp* ...., also shorter *tik tik tiooorr*, or *tioorrrl* by the unpaired ♀ only; calls *kip kip kip* in winter, as well as squealing noises; reedbeds and densely vegetated banks: Water Rail, p.70

Explosive *koorrk* and *kioorrook*, harsh *keck keck*, during display also in flight *kreck kreck kreck…*; all types of wetlands: Moorhen, p.68

High-pitched, sharp and explosive *pix*, almost cackling *kock kock*, barking *kow* and *koov*, in night flights nasally trumpeting *peow*; young birds beg coarsly with ascending *frrreeh*; all types of wetlands: Coot, p.68

Loud, wooden and rhythmic in endless repetitive sequence *rrrp-rrrp rrrp-rrrp rrrp-rrrp* … , similar to rubbing a piece of wood across a comb; extensive meadows, often moist, occasionally also in grain fields, from middle of May; in Britain mainly in Outer Hebrides: Corncrake, p.70

Sharp, whip-like long sequences *quitt, quitt* …; reedbeds, sedges, flooded meadows, from April; silent outside breeding season; rare and local in Britain: Spotted Crake, p.70

Continental European species

♂ displays with sequence of quacking sounds, descending and getting faster at the end *quek quek quek-quek-quek-quaag-ooaagooaa-gooaagaagaag*, unmated ♀ calls with end trill *pock pock porrr* (often confused with less full trill of Water Rail); larger reedbeds, almost exclusively in east and south-east Europe, rare, from April: Little Crake, p.70

♂ sings with wooden rasping, not very loud, on same pitch or slightly wavering every 2-3 seconds for about 2-3 seconds *errrr errrrrr trrrrrr* … (can be confused with among others Garganey and Edible Frog), unpaired ♀ calls short and softly *shrrr*, similar to warning call of Reed Warbler; sedge fields, flooded meadows, very rare, only from end of May: Baillon's Crake, p.70

Several amphibians call at night and their voices can be confused with those of rails and other bird species, among them are the European Tree Frog (cackling *keckeckeckeckeck or rabrabrabrabrab*), European Green Toad (softly trilling *irrrrrrr*), Natterjack Toad (harsher *errr errr*), Edible Frog (quacking *quorrrr quorrrr)*, Marsh Frog (very loud *eh eh eh eh* …), Common Frog (softly *orrrrr*, very similar to Baillon's Crake), Midwife Toad (brightly ringing to whistling *oog oog oog*) as well as the Fire-bellied Toad and the Yellow-bellied Toad (harmonic low-pitched *ooh, oong*; the last three amphibians mentioned can also be confused with Scops Owl and Pygmy Owl). Most of these amphibians are rare or absent from Britain. The calls of Garganey, Common Snipe, Great Snipe, *Locustella* warblers, European Nightjar and Little Bittern, and even the Mole Cricket, can all sound very similar to rails and crakes.

TABLE 10: CALLS OF NOCTURNAL MIGRANTS

Many bird species migrate at night and their characteristic calls can then be heard as they pass overhead. They are usually identical to the calls described in the species accounts. Especially in autumn it is possible hear a varied chorus of mixed songs and calls, particularly along coasts when large-scale migrations are taking place. However, even inland, especially between September and November, conspicuous calls can be heard even over large brightly lit cities. Only a selection of the most common and most distinctive calls are listed in the following table.

Short and sharp *tsip*:	Song Thrush, p.142
High-pitched and drawn out *tzeee*:	Redwing, p.142
Soft, high-pitched *tsreeh*:	Blackbird, p.142
Fluid rolling *dioorrloo*:	Skylark, p.124
Mournful whistling *diooh*:	European Golden Plover, p.72
High-pitched and sharp *hididi*:	Common Sandpiper, p.82
Yodelling *huit-uit-uit*:	Green Sandpiper, p.78
Harshly whistling *tew tew tew*:	Greenshank, p.78
Fully whistling *koorloo, tlaooh*:	Curlew, p.76
Dry whirring *chreeep*:	Dunlin, p.84
Loud whistling *weeoo*:	Eurasian Wigeon, p.36
Domestic goose-like plain cackling *gahng gagaga*:	Greylag Goose, p.32
Musically cackling, bright *kiookioo* in between:	White-fronted Goose, p.32
Croaking *kraark, khrek*:	Grey Heron, p.54

FURTHER INFORMATION

For those who would like to delve deeper there is a huge range of information available on every aspect of birds and birdwatching via books, websites, CDs, specialist journals and magazines and bird conservation organizations. The following is just a selection:

BOOKS:

Cramp, S., Simmons, K.E.L., and Perrins, C.M. (eds). 1977-1994. *The Birds of the Western Palearctic*. Volumes 1-9. Oxford University Press, Oxford. The definitive reference work on the region's avifauna.

Jonsson, L. 1992. *Birds of Europe*. Christopher Helm, London. Excellent, lively, large colour illustrations and clear text.

Mitchell, D., and Young, S. 1997. *Photographic Handbook of the Rare Birds of Britain and Europe*. New Holland, London. The ideal companion to the *New Holland European Bird Guide* as it offers detailed coverage of all the vagrants (regular to extremely rare) to Britain and Europe.

Robson, C. 2005. *New Holland Field Guide to the Birds of South-East Asia*. New Holland, London. Covers the Siberian breeding species that are vagrants to Europe.

Sibley, D. 2000. *The North American Bird Guide*. Pica Press, East Sussex. Includes all the North American species that are vagrants to Europe.

Svensson, L., Grant, P.J., Mullarney, K., and Zetterström, D. 2000. *Collins Bird Guide*. HarperCollins, London. Complete overview of all species in the Western Palearctic, with extensive and very appealing accurate illustrations as well as detailed text.

Wernham, C.V., Toms, M.P., Marchant, J.H., Clark, J.A., Siriwardena, G.M., and Baillie, S.R. (eds). 2002. *The Migration Atlas: movements of the birds of Britain and Ireland*. Poyser, London.

SOUND GUIDES:

Constantine, M., and The Sound Approach. 2006. *The Sound Approach to Birding*. The Sound Approach, Poole. Book and two CDs.

Kettle, R. and Ranft, R. 2004. *British Bird Sounds on CD*. British Library and National Sound Archive, London. Two CDs covering 175 species.

Jännes, H. 2003. *Calls of Eastern Vagrants*. One CD of 68 Siberian vagrants.

Roché, J.C., and Chevereau, J. 2002 *Bird Sounds of Europe and North-west Africa*. WildSounds, Norfolk. 10 CD set covering songs and calls of 442 species.

INTERACTIVE GUIDES:

Doherty, P. 2004. *The Birds of Britain and Europe*. Bird Images, Yorkshire. Six DVD set running for more than 12 hours and covering 600 species.

Gosney, D. 2007. *DVD-ROM Guide to British Birds*. BirdGuides, Sheffield. Photographs, illustrations, video, maps, songs and calls of 347 species.

MAGAZINES AND JOURNALS:

Birding World (Stonerunner, Coast Road, Cley-next-the-Sea, Holt, Norfolk NR25 7RZ; www.birdingworld.co.uk). Monthly by subscription only. Many articles on recent reports, rarities and taxonomic advances.

Birdwatch (The Chocolate Factory, 5 Clarendon Road, London N22 6XJ; www.birdwatch.co.uk). Monthly in newsagents or by subscription. Many identification, where to watch, travel and other features, plus news and recent reports and rarity photos.

Bird Watching (Media House, Lynchwood, Peterborough PE2 6EA; www.birdwatching.co.uk). Monthly in newsagents or by subscription. Articles and news on all aspects of birdwatching.

British Birds (4 Harlequin Gardens, St Leonards on Sea, East Sussex TN37 7PF; www.britishbirds.co.uk). Monthly by subscription only – articles on behaviour, conservation, distribution, identification, status and taxonomy.

BIRD CONSERVATION ORGANIZATIONS:

BirdLife International (Wellbrook Court, Girton Road, Cambridge CB3 0NA; www.birdlife.org) is a global partnership of conservation organizations (the RSPB is the British representative) aiming to conserve birds, their habitats and global biodiversity. Publishes a quarterly magazine on world bird conservation issues entitled *World Birdwatch*.

British Ornithologists' Union (PO Box 417, Peterborough PE7 3FX; www.bou.org.uk) encourages the study of birds in Britain, Europe and throughout the world in order to understand their biology and to aid their conservation. The BOU keeps of the official British List and publishes a quarterly journal *Ibis*.

British Trust for Ornithology (BTO, The Nunnery, Thetford, Norfolk IP24 2PU; www.bto.org) aims to encourage greater the understanding and conservation of birds through field research based on a partnership between professionals and amateurs. Volunteers are welcome, whether it is to train as a ringer or count species for regular or one-off surveys – contact the BTO for further details.

Royal Society for the Protection of Birds (RSPB, The Lodge, Sandy, Bedfordshire SG19 2DL; www.rspb.org) has more than one million members, 200 nature reserves and a network of 175 local groups and more than 110 youth groups. It publishes a quarterly magazine entitled *Birds*.

BIRD OBSERVATORIES:

The Bird Observatories Council (www.birdobscouncil.org.uk) runs 19 bird observatories around Britain and Ireland and encourages volunteers to study of birds. Many of the observatories are open to visitors. They include such key migration sites as Fair Isle, Cape Clear, Portland Bill and Dungeness.

BIBLIOGRAPHY (ALSO USED DURING COMPILATION OF THIS BOOK):

Adolfsson, K., and Cherrug, S. 1995. Bird Identification: a reference guide. *Anser* Supplement 37, Lund.

Barthel, P.H., and Helbig, A.J. 2005. Artenliste der Vögel Deutschlands. *Limicola* 19:89-111

Forsman, D. 1998. *Raptors of Europe and the Middle East*. Poyser, London.

Harris, A., Tucker, L. and Vinicombe, K.E. 1991. *The Macmillan Field Guide to Bird Identification*. Macmillan, London.

del Hoyo, J., Elliott, A., and Sargatal, J. (eds). 1992-2007. *Handbook of Birds of the World*. Vols 1-12. Lynx Edicions, Barcelona.

Lewington, I., Alström, P, and Colston, P. 1991. *A Field Guide to the Rare Birds of Britain and Europe*. HarperCollins, London.

Madge, S., and Burn, H. 1988. *Wildfowl*. Christopher Helm, London.

Malling Olsen, K., and Larsson, H. 2004. *Gulls of Europe, Asia and North America*. Christopher Helm, London.

Hayman, P., Marchant, J., and Prater, T. 1986. *Shorebirds*. Croom Helm, London.

Mitchell, D., and Vinicombe, K.E. 2006. *Birds of Britain: the Complete Checklist*. Solo Publishing, London.

Peterson, R., Mountfort, G., and Hollom, P.A.D. 1993. *A Field Guide to the Bird of Britain and Europe*. 5th edition. HarperCollins, London.

INDEX TO BIRD NAMES:

The figures refer to the species accounts in the main text.
Scientific names are printed in *italics*.

PLUMAGE SEQUENCES FOR SELECTED SPECIES

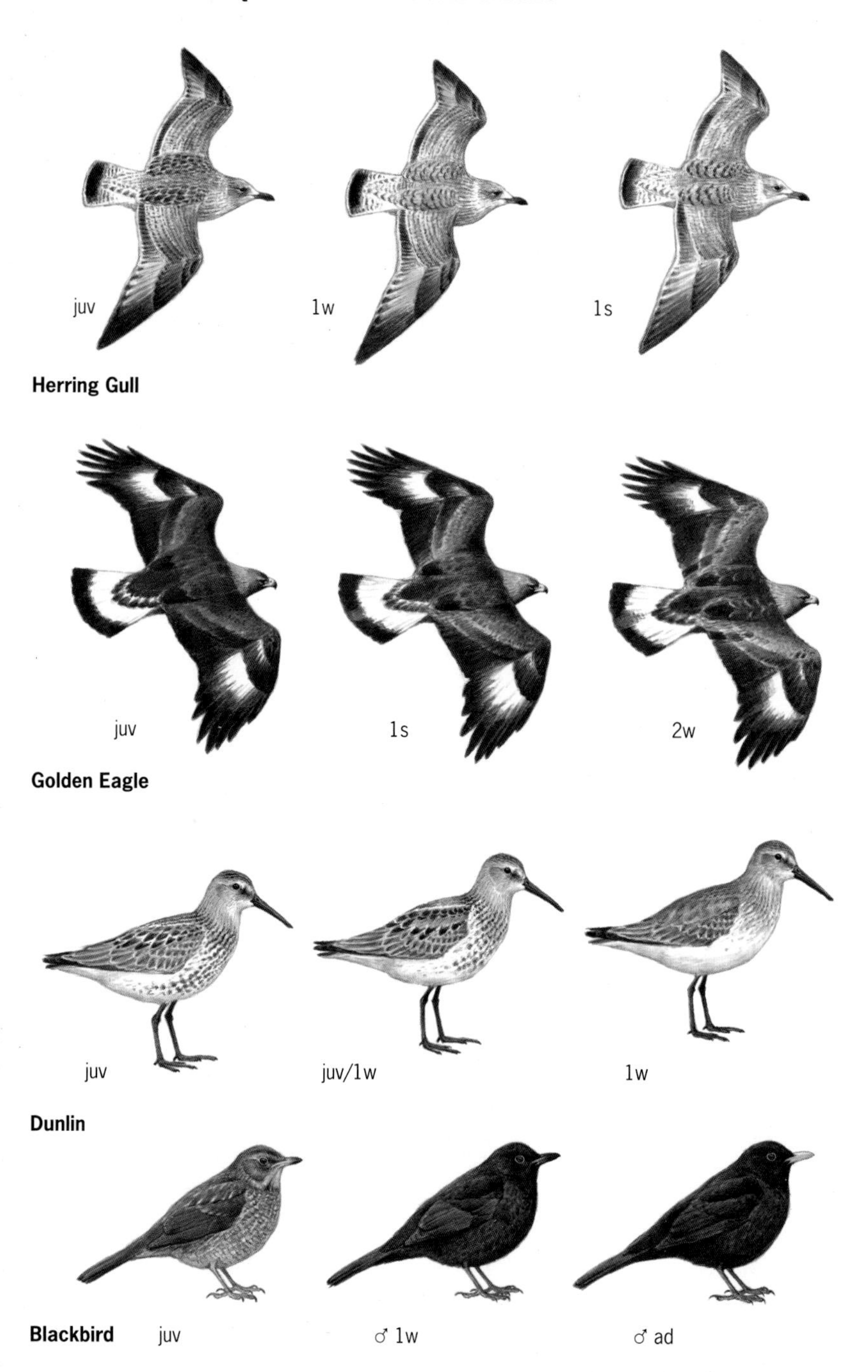